The Monteith College Library Experiment

by

Patricia B. Knapp

in collaboration with
Carol E. Ballingall and Gilbert E. Donahue,
and with the assistance of Grace E. Dawson

The Scarecrow Press, Inc.
New York   1966

The research reported herein was performed pursuant
to a contract with the United States Office of Education, Department
of Health, Education and Welfare as Cooperative Research Project 874.

Table of Contents

List of Tables

Acknowledgements

By definition the Monteith Library Project was a cooperative undertaking. We cannot, of course, name all of the administrators and faculty members and students who contributed work, suggestions, ideas, and criticism, who filled out forms and answered questionnaires and responded to interviews, who listened to proposals and read our memoranda, who, in short, lent themselves to the enterprise. We are most grateful to them all.

There were, however, special contributions which deserve special recognition.

Dr. Sally W. Cassidy, Chairman of the Division of the Science of Society, was deeply engaged with us in the project from start to finish. She helped us formulate our original plans and assisted in the designing of the study. She provided constant support and encouragement, devised ways of gathering and analyzing data and was responsible for some of our most fruitful ideas. Often she made us think better than we knew how.

Dr. Flint W. Purdy, Director of the Wayne State University Libraries, not only made the project possible by giving me the opportunity to work on "detached service" in Monteith while the project was being formulated, but he also saw to it that library resources and services were made available for every experiment we wanted to try. Furthermore, he contributed sound advice individually and as a member of the Wayne Advisory Committee.

This committee included, in addition to Dr. Purdy, Dr. William Wattenberg, Professor of Educational Psychology of the College of Education, and Dr. H. Warren Dunham, Professor of Sociology of the College of Liberal Arts. All three contributed generously of their time, their specialized knowledge and their wisdom.

Mr. Robert Grazier, Associate Director of the University Libraries, provided fullest cooperation from all the service divisions of the libraries. We are particularly grateful for his willingness to help in solving every problem--large or small--we laid before him. He served as a member of the Library Advisory Committee which met regularly with the project staff to help us make plans for student library assignments, to report their impressions on how such assignments had worked out, how the results might be analyzed and so on. We are most grateful for the always helpful consultation provided by this group, which included, in addition to Mr. Grazier, Mr. Paul Breed, Mr. Rowland Jones, Mrs. Joan Gilmore Pings, Mr. Donald Ewing, and Mr. Howard Sullivan.

We owe special thanks, also, for the special contributions of certain individuals within Monteith. Dean Woodburn O. Ross and Associate Dean Max Coral gave us wholehearted support and encouragement throughout the project and they were astonishingly kind and patient with us as we struggled to complete this report. Dr. Jerry Bails and Dr. Sara Leopold worked with us most productively as representatives of the Natural Sciences and the Humanistic Studies faculties, respectively, in the third semester of our operation. Mr. Paul Bluemle, Mr. Norman Cleary, Mr. Kenneth Feigenbaum, Dr. Paule Verdet, and Mr. Rolland Wright of the Science of Society Division gave particular assistance with interviewing and other activities carried on in connection with our small sample studies. During the course of our work, four secretaries served us--and served us well: Mrs. Ruth Hollingsworth, Mrs. Mary Witkowski, Mrs. Lila Kash Zorn, and my private secretary, Mrs. Queen Dooley.

I wish to express my personal gratitude and appreciation to my colleagues on the Library Project Staff. Although responsibility for the organization and style of this final report is mine, we worked so closely together that it is now almost impossible to identify the original source of the ideas and plans, indeed, even of the language contained in the report. But certain contributions can be specified. The analysis of social structure, reported in Chapter II, was the work of Miss Carol Ballingall, our Research Analyst. Together with Mrs. Grace Dawson, her assistant, she also produced the analyses of individual library assignments. As we began our work on the project, Gilbert E. Donahue, our Project Librarian, and I shared almost identical views about the nature of libraries and librarianship. Our thinking together as we worked together on the project provided the essential basis for the "model program" presented in Chapter V.

Patricia B. Knapp
August, 1964

Chapter I

Introduction

In April, 1960, Wayne State University entered into a contract with the Office of Education to conduct at Monteith College a research project concerned with exploring methods of developing a more vital relationship between the library and college teaching.[1]

The proposal for the study cited evidence in research literature to support the contention that:

> Traditional college instruction fails to exploit fully the library resources available for it and that the average college student's experiences with the library constitute a limited and fairly insignificant part of his education.

We felt that this was a problem of special concern at the present time because of the "current emphasis upon independent study, . . . since it is certainly reasonable to assume that capacity for independent study implies competence in the use of books and other library resources."

The objectives of the project were stated as follows:

> The ultimate purpose of the Monteith Library Program is to stimulate and guide students in developing sophisticated understanding of the library and increasing competence in its use. To achieve this end, it proposes to provide students with experiences which are functionally related to their course work. Planning such experiences will involve library instructional coordination on an unprecedented scale. The specific objectives of the first phase of the Program, the pilot project, therefore, are (1) an appraisal of a structure established for the purpose of attaining this coordination, (2) an exploration of new methods of relating the library to the instructional program, and (3) a preliminary assessment of the effectiveness of these methods.[2]

The contract for the pilot project, then, called for the establishment of a structure and machinery for a new kind of relationship between librarians and teaching faculty. In brief, it was proposed that librarians on the project staff participate with the teaching faculty in course-planning endeavors, that together they

11

attempt to devise course assignments which would involve extensive and meaningful student use of library resources, and that the operation of the structure thus established and the planning processes thus developed be subjected to analysis and preliminary appraisal.

This report presents the findings of the two-year investigation conducted in accordance with this contract. This introductory chapter provides background information. First, we describe Monteith College, the setting in which the investigation took place, commenting especially on the curriculum and objectives of the Monteith program. Second, we identify the personnel involved in the project and chronicle the main stages in its development. And, finally, we introduce the subsequent chapters of the report.

The Setting: Monteith College

Monteith is one of the eleven colleges which compose Wayne State University. It was established in 1959, with assistance from the Ford Foundation, to provide a program in general, liberal education planned to complement work in major fields of study, pre-professional programs, or advanced interdisciplinary work.

The College is administratively independent, with its own officers, its own budget, its own faculty. The faculty is organized into three divisions, each responsible for one of the three major areas of the curriculum. The chairmen of these three divisions make up the Administrative Council, which, under the chairmanship of the Dean, is the major decision-making body of the College.

Monteith is not a large college. During the period of the project, the total enrollment ranged from about 300 in the Spring semester of the academic year 1959-60 to about 700 in the Spring semester of 1961-62; the number of faculty ranged similarly from 15 to 30.

In the midst of a large university, the College attempts to maintain for its students the atmosphere of a small college. This atmosphere prevails in classes as well as in the college community as a whole. In the freshman year, the discussion sections have about twelve students. The sections are somewhat larger in later years. Each course meets twice a week in these small discussion groups and twice a week in large lecture sections. Except for office buildings and a small student center, however, Monteith has no separate physical facilities.   Classes are held in general-purpose classrooms on the University campus.   Monteith students use the University Libraries and all other general University facilities are also available to them.

The basic curriculum, required of all Monteith students, extends through the full four years of the student's undergraduate career, beginning with sequences in the social sciences and the natural sciences in the first two years, continuing with a humanities sequence in the second and third years, and culminating with a senior colloquium and a senior essay.   The program takes about half the student's time, the other half being devoted to his advanced or specialized work in Monteith or in the other schools and colleges of Wayne.

Monteith courses differ from many other general education courses in that they are truly interdisciplinary--staff planned and staff taught.   Every instructor in a division shares in the responsibility for the two lectures presented each week to all students in the course and is entirely responsible for the two discussion periods of his own sections.   The courses avoid both the superficiality of the usual survey course and the haphazardness of the series of "introduction-to's," attempting to find synthesis through integrating themes related to the important discoveries, the characteristic approaches, the significant concepts in each of the three large areas.

The Monteith program differs from other general education programs, also, in that it is organized to give the student increasing responsibility for directing his own efforts as he progresses through the four years.   The freshman discussion sections are very small, contacts between students and faculty are frequent, and the work is carefully directed and supervised.   As the student progresses through the College, his classes become larger, his contact with faculty less frequent, his learning less dependent on formal class instruction.   By the time he is a senior he is expected to have acquired the initiative, the knowledge, the habits, and the

skills which are essential equipment for mature independent study.
This stress upon independent study is characteristic of honors study
and other such programs for the superior student, but Monteith
admits any student who qualifies for admission to Wayne.

Thus, the advent of Monteith on the Wayne campus provided
a situation in which a new staff would be developing a new four-
year curriculum, one of whose principal objectives was the development in students, all students, the capacity for independent study.
Furthermore, as the Proposal states:

> Because it (Monteith College) is experimental, it is hospitable
> to specific experimental ideas and it provides the framework
> for testing them. Because it is concerned with general ed-
> ucation, it is receptive to ideas which are generally applica-
> ble in all subject fields, ideas which have to do with the
> desirable common foundation for all college education. 3

For all of these reasons, Monteith College offered a strategic setting for the pilot project.

Development of the Project

The planning stage. --In the period between April and
September 30, 1960, the library project staff was appointed and
began its work in preparation for the first semester of the operational phase which began in the academic year 1960-61. The principal members of the staff were Patricia B. Knapp, Project Director; Gilbert E. Donahue, Project Librarian; and Carol E.
Ballingall, Project Research Analyst. In addition, Grace E.
Dawson was appointed as Research Assistant, a secretary was employed, and fifteen students, most of them graduates, were assigned
to work to provide bibliographical assistance to members of the
faculty of the Science of Society Division.

The director was responsible for general administration, the
librarian was specifically responsible for training and supervising
the bibliographical assistants, and the research analyst was responsible for gathering and analyzing data on 1) the relationship
between project personnel and the faculty of the College, and 2) the
response of both students and faculty to the library program. The
three worked closely together in developing plans for the program

and they also met regularly with the social sciences staff as it
worked on the development of its course.

The first semester of operation. --In the Fall of 1960, the
project staff, cooperating with the social sciences faculty and its
planning committees, worked on four assignments which incorporated library experiences for students.   They gathered materials,
prepared exhibits, wrote briefing statements for distribution to
students, and presented library instruction in a few of the discussion sections.   In addition, the staff developed tentative plans for a
sequence of library experiences to extend through three years and
through the three areas of the Monteith curriculum.

The project librarian developed and presented an orientation
program for the bibliographic assistants and supervised the work
assigned them by the social sciences faculty.   The research analyst
gathered data on social structure through interviews and observation, on the work of the bibliographic assistants through regular
reports, and on the library assignments through logs, questionnaires, papers and other assignments prepared by Monteith students.

The second semester of operation. --In the Spring of 1961
the work was expanded to include the Natural Sciences and the
Humanistic Studies Divisions.   Project staff members continued to
work with the Science of Society Division, but they also attended as
regularly as possible the course planning meetings of these other two
faculties and they carried on the various activities involved in planning and conducting library assignments in all three subject areas.
Additional bibliographic assistants were also employed.   The humanities assistants were assigned to individual instructors as the
social science assistants had been; the natural sciences assistants
worked together as a team preparing a proposed natural sciences
library assignment.   The project librarian presented an orientation
program to the new assistants and continued his training and
supervisory program, extending it to cover all three subject areas.
The research analyst broadened her data-gathering and analysis
activities to cover the expanded program.

Summer, 1961. --At the end of the spring term a random

sample of twenty-one Monteith students was hired to spend two
days in the library in connection with an intensive examination of
library behavior and factors which might be related to it. The
students were given a series of specially prepared library performance tests and certain other mental and projective tests.
Questionnaires and interviews were used to provide information on
their backgrounds and their experiences with the library program.

Data from this small study contributed to revisions in the
program for the Fall semester, but most of these changes resulted
from the project staff's careful review of all aspects of the first
year's operation of the program.

The third semester of operation. --Three major changes
were made in the Fall of 1961. In curriculum planning, the project staff dropped the attempt to meet regularly with all three
divisional faculties, working instead with one representative from
each.   The bibliographical assistance program was reorganized by
the creation of a pool of assistants on call for specific tasks rather than
assigned individually to instructors.   The sequence of student
library experiences was revised by the development of new assignments and of new procedures for implementing them.   (The reasons
for these changes are revealed in the discussion of our findings in
the following chapters).

Spring and Summer, 1962. --Two assignments planned in
the previous semester were implemented in the second semester
of 1962, but all other operational activities terminated as the project staff turned its attention to analysis of the data which had been
gathered.   At the beginning of the summer term, however, another
small sample study was conducted to provide a check on the performance tests and other instruments used the previous summer.

The Organization of This Report

The exploratory nature of the pilot project should be underlined.   We began with the conviction that the key to library instructional coordination lay in the structure of the relationship
between librarians and teaching faculty.   But we recognized that we

had much to learn about what precise characteristics of that relationship would prove to be most crucial for our purpose. We
understood, also, that the structure with which we began would
change as we adapted to changes in the organization and curriculum
of the College, as we responded to what we learned about the effects of our work on students' experiences with the library, and as
our own behavior reflected our growing understanding of the nature
of librarian-faculty relationships.

Similarly, though we felt certain that the student could a-
chieve library competence if his experiences with the library were
both extensive and were functionally related to his "content" courses,
we were not at all sure about what kinds of experiences or what
types of course-relatedness would be most effective in fostering the
development of such competence.   Indeed, our notion of library
competence was not clearly defined.   Much of our exploration was
to be concerned with identifying the kinds of knowledge, understanding and skills involved in it, and in determining the kind and degree of library competence appropriate for college work.

The next three chapters are reports on these explorations
as they developed.   The first of these is concerned with social
structure, identifying certain features characteristic of the
Montieth community and showing their effect on our work at each
stage of the project.   The second deals with the library assignments presented to Monteith students.   In it we discuss some of
the ideas we acquired through the experience of presenting these
assignments, we summarize the sequence of assignments presented
to one Monteith entering class, [4] and we demonstrate possible ways
of examining the association between exposure to such assignments
and certain variables in the students' background and achievement.
Chapter IV presents the results of our efforts, through small ran-
dom-sample experiments, to define and measure library competence
and to identify factors associated with its achievement.

These three chapters together provide the basis for what
might be described as the product of our explorations, presented in
Chapter V.   This is a model program which takes into account
what the pilot project has taught us about social structure, about

student experiences with the library, and about the nature of library competence.

Chapter VI reports on what might be considered a by-product of our work. In order to increase our faculty's awareness of library resources and faculitate their use of these resources, the project provided them with bibliographical assistance; the chapter reports our analysis of faculty use of this service.

The final chapter summarizes our work by relating each aspect of it to the plans originally set forth in the Proposal for the investigation.

Notes

1. Project No. 874: An Experiment in Coordination Between Teaching and Library Staff for Changing Student Use of University Library Resources. Cooperative Research Branch, Office of Education, Department of Health, Education and Welfare.

2. Proposal (March, 1960), pp. 1-2.

3. Ibid., pp. 9-10.

4. Detailed analysis of all assignments presented during the operation of the pilot project are provided in the Appendix.

Chapter II

The Analysis of Social Structure*

Our report on the analysis of social structure in the Monteith Library Project begins with discussion of certain general characteristics of research of this type and with comments on the academic institution as a specific type of formal organization.[1] We turn next to a consideration of particular social science concepts found useful in bringing into focus significant features of the Monteith structure. Finally, we discuss the effect of these Monteith structural features upon the library project at each stage of its development.

The General Nature of Social Structure Research

In essence, social structure research involves the examination of a particular situation or institution in the light of certain potentially relevant models which may serve to highlight the many values and activities perceived.[2]

The models serve as convenient approximations which allow the researcher to grasp a given situation rapidly and to categorize it properly. Once the researcher has found the appropriate category, he knows what kinds of behavior he can expect to observe. After a remarkably short period of actual contact, he is able to frame questions which will bring pertinent answers about the characteristics of the particular situation he is analyzing.

This kind of research derives from both sociology and anthropology, or, more precisely, from an area of study in which there is considerable overlapping between the two. As sociology, the study falls into the category of institutional sociology and, more specifically, into that branch of institutional sociology which is concerned with the study of formal organizations;[3] as anthropology, the study falls in the area of social anthropology of the structural type.[4]

* Most of this chapter was first published in Library Trends, a publication of the University of Illinois Graduate School of Library Science. It is reprinted here by permission of Library Trends.

The primary discipline of the project's research analyst is
social anthropology. Her methods, therefore, were inevitably
shaped by certain characteristics of this field. Anthropology is
holistic; it strives to see a social unit as a whole.[5] Anthropologists
most often use non-quantitative methods. They look for "regularities," "configuration," and "pattern" in the whole.[6] Most of them
attempt to approach the social unit without preconceptions. Some
make a point of avoiding hypotheses to be tested.[7] They strive for
an "inside view," distorted as little as possible by personal and
cultural biases.

For these reasons, the anthropologist is inclusive in his
gathering of data. He attempts to encompass everything in his
notes on observation, in his recording of interviews, in his collection of artifacts and documents. However, his perception and,
consequently, his selection of data, is inevitably influenced by concepts which have theoretical weight, concepts which have proved
meaningful in anthropological studies. His analysis, moreover,
involves a great deal of systematic working and reworking of the
data collected.[8]

The academic institution as a formal organization. --The
study of formal organizations has been much influenced by the
classic statement of Max Weber on the nature of bureaucracy. The
features of bureaucracy as Weber enumerates them include a clear-
cut division of labor and a high degree of specialization, the organization of offices into a hierarchical structure, behavior governed in
accordance with formal rules and procedures, the expectation of an
impersonal relationship between officials and clients, and a career
orientation of staff.[9]

Like practically all modern large-scale organizations, colleges are bureaucratically administered, and a small college imbedded in a huge university faces not only its own bureaucracy but
also the bureaucratic demands of the giant institution of which it is
a part.

In the academic institution the tendency toward bureaucracy
is always tempered by the ancient tradition of the university as a
community of scholars. In Monteith, moreover, this tradition was

deliberately emphasized, so we find all the features characteristic of the bureaucracy considerably modified in this setting. For instance, while a division of labor and a degree of specialization is reflected in the organization of the teaching staff into three divisions, there is no departmentalization according to discipline, and interdivisional studies are fostered. The de-emphasis on hierarchy is apparent in the fact that the policy-making Administrative Council is made up of the chairmen of the three divisions, each of whom is in close contact with his respective teaching staff. Very little hierarchical structure has developed within the divisional staffs, partly because practically all instructors started at the same time and partly because the development of a staff-taught course fostered a sense of colleagueship. Bureaucratic rules and procedures do govern some Monteith activities, but such formalities are likely to have emanated from the bureaucracy of the University rather than from within the College, where flexibility and rule-by-consensus are cherished.

The impersonality of the official-client relationship is less likely to appear in the academic institution than in such bureaucracies as the employment service or the social service agency. It is particularly minimized at Monteith because the College has always been committed to creating a small-college atmosphere. The career orientation of a college instructor generally involves a strong identification with a specialized field. At Monteith the interdisciplinary staff group pulls in the opposite direction.

Thus, the Monteith situation has strong collegial aspects which might recall earlier patterns of the English common room where every member was a peer, where tolerance of eccentricity did not exclude vigorous debate of ideas, where each person acted when outside the common room as an independent, autonomous scholar, responsible only to the judgment of his peers and of history. Nevertheless, the College exists as a formal organization. This formal organization is the context within which the college teacher must function. Like a doctor, who needs a hospital, the academic intellectual needs the university to provide him with students, classrooms, laboratories, a library, an office, and a salary.

He must give up some of the freedom of action of the freelance artist or writer, though not as much as the civil servant or the technician.

He must find acceptance among his peers, who expect him to be independent and autonomous. He must regulate his activity to the extent that his students have a reasonable expectation of seeing him at class time, hearing his thoughts on roughly the areas he is scheduled to cover, receiving his criticism and evaluation of their performance. But how the man teaches, the standards he sets for the performance of his students, these are matters ordinarily thought of as entirely his own business. Only extraordinary infractions of expectations will be noticed by peers, who will, in any case, tend to defend his, and potentially their own, individuality and style as a matter of academic freedom.

At Monteith, however, the demands of the staff-taught course meant that these individualistic values had somehow to be reconciled with the traditional values of the common room, the shared values of colleagues engaged in a common pioneering effort.

In short, each of three models is partly reflected in the Monteith situation: (1) the model of the bureaucracy, (2) the model of the collegial organization, and (3) the model of the free and independent teacher. The library project faced the challenge of coming to terms with this hybrid creature. Our structural analysis reveals the lessons we learned through two years of trial and error before we finally achieved moderate acceptance.

Analysis of the Monteith Structure

The analysis of our experiences in the pilot project was based on three kinds of data: notes on observation, transcriptions of interviews, and transcriptions of tape-recorded reminiscences. The research analyst kept detailed notes on her observation of every formal and informal meeting which involved project staff members along with faculty individuals or groups. Three series of interviews[10] with the faculty were conducted, one at the beginning, one in the middle, and one at the end of the project. In addition, the research analyst and the project director each dictated a lengthy

reminiscence, about forty typewritten pages, covering the entire
period of the project.   We attempted to recall our own changing
views with regard to it as well as our estimate of our relationships
with each individual faculty member at every stage in the enterprise.

This voluminous body of data, filling approximately four
file-cabinet drawers, was systematically examined and re-examined
by the research analyst as she looked for regularities and deviations in the many patterns of relationship which appeared in the
Monteith structure.   This analysis resulted in the identification of
four characteristics which seem to have been particularly significant
for the development of the library project.   Each of these characteristics is related to concepts implied in the discussion, above,
of the academic institution as a formal organization, and of
Monteith as a particularly hybrid species.

1.   Many individuals in the Monteith structure carry responsibilities in two areas.   The dual role is accepted as
a normal pattern.

The concept of role is essential in the analysis of any social
system, but it has a particular flavor in the consideration of a
structure which is at all bureaucratic.   In the bureaucracy, role
is associated with office rather than with person.   The concept of
role implies the idea that people behave the way other people
expect them to behave.   An individual's behavior reflects not only
such general roles as those determined by his age, his sex, his
family, his social class, his occupation, etc., but also his membership in this, that, or another group, his "place" in that group
and the duties and responsibilities, the ideas and sentiments, in
short, the expectations attached to that place.   In this sense, an
individual's identity is conferred upon him by the social definition
of the behavior appropriate to a particular group, whether that
group is defined by an office held in a bureaucracy or by membership in a collegial organization.

The concept of role does not imply conscious play-acting,
however; it refers to a largely unreflective acceptance of the
socially conferred identity.   Furthermore, behavior in accordance
with a role not only expresses the ideas and feelings which are

consistent with the role, but produces them.   The individual iden-
tifies with his role. [11]

An individual who has a dual role acts in any given social
situation in accordance with his perception of the expectations
attaching to one or the other of his two roles.   The fact that the
dual role pattern was accepted in the Monteith structure meant that
usually the "others" expected the individual to be able to separate
his two roles in his thinking and behavior.

> 2.   The Monteith structure is marked by relatively little
> social distance between individuals at various levels in the
> hierarchy, but by considerable social distance between dif-
> ferent groups at the same level, especially between the
> three divisional teaching staffs.

The concept of "social distance" is related to the familiar
concept of "status" which is associated with the view of bureaucracy
as a system which prescribes and defines relationships in an organization which is hierarchical and in which functions are highly
specialized.   But social distance also implies distance on the hori-
zonal, the socially or organizationally defined separation which is
a factor in the ability of individuals and groups at the same status
level to communicate with one another.   Thus, it applies equally
well to the colleague-group relationships which characterized the
three divisions of the teaching staff.

> 3.   The organization of the teaching staff into three divisions
> has had a crucial significance upon the group organization of
> the College, since each staff has developed distinctive ways
> of organizing itself, of assigning responsibilities and pro-
> viding for internal communication and coordination.

The "group" we are concerned with here is a task-oriented
group, not a primary group like family or close friends.   But
neither is it simply an aggregate of individuals who fall into a particular classification.   The concept implies not only a common task
and real interaction in dealing with this task; it implies also a
more or less cohesive body which develops its own style of working,
sets its own boundaries and responsibilities, and defines the roles
of its members.   Like all groups in the sociological sense, it is
a mechanism for the control and coordination of behavior.

4. The Monteith instructor must deal with a degree of
ambivalence between his role as a member of a staff,
sharing the responsibility for a whole course, and his role
as an instructor, individually responsible for his own
discussion sections.

This characteristic of the Monteith structure is illuminated
by the concept of the "reference group." The "reference group"
does not mean necessarily an actual interacting group of people.[12]
It does mean those groups (or individuals) to whom one refers for
standards of value and behavior.[13] The concept is related to the
concepts of role and status; for the group to which one refers for
standards is likely to be determined by one's own role and status
in a given social situation, or more accurately, by one's perception
of that role and status. As indicated, each staff became a powerful reference group for every member in it. But it was not the
only reference group. A chronic problem of the service organization, of which the college is an example, is that of the professional's ambivalence between his own definition of his client's "best
interests," and the client's definition, or, in other words, the
client's wishes.[14] In the Monteith structure, as indicated, the
instructor is responsible with his colleagues for total course planning and for planning and presenting lectures, but he meets individually with each of his discussion sections and is solely responsible for what occurs in them. His ambivalence reflects the ten-
sions, discussed above, between the collegial model of the staff
and the model of the free and independent teacher. It also reflects
the instructor's reference group conflicts. In deciding what is in
the "best interests" of the students, he can refer to the definition
of the staff, the definition of the students themselves, or the
definition of his own internalized standards which have been set by
such "others" as former teachers, former colleagues, the "teaching profession," or the "scientific community."

Stages in the Development of the Library Project

The pre-project stage. --The four characteristics of the
Monteith structure which have been discussed--the dual role pattern,
social distance, the division of the teaching staff into three

divisions, and the instructor's staff-discussion section ambivalence
--were all of crucial importance for the library project at each
stage in its development. From the outset the project director-to-
be, had a dual role at Monteith. She was employed originally as
a half-time executive secretary for the College. Her second role
was that of emissary from the Wayne State University Library,
assigned half-time to the task of developing and gaining acceptance
for an integrated library program. As executive secretary her
role was clearly subordinate. She was responsible for implementing policies determined by the Administrative Council. Because
of the lack of social distance in the vertical structure of Monteith,
however, she had no hesitance about campaigning for her ideas to
her superiors and experienced no difficulty in getting a hearing and
support for the proposed program.

As soon as the faculty of the Science of Society Division
arrived on the campus and began to meet in course-planning sessions, the Chairman of the division invited her to meet with them.
Because of the pressure of other duties, however, it was impossible
for her to do so regularly. It was soon found that when she was
there her presence was accepted with grace and friendliness, but
she was not part of the cohesive interacting group which they
quickly became. In short, she was not accepted into full membership.

During the first year of the College, the year in which the
library project was being planned and the proposal to the Office of
Education formulated, two library assignments were presented.
For a number of reasons, students found one of these assignments
both difficult and burdensome. They expressed their dissatisfaction
forcibly in their discussion sections, thus bringing to the surface
the instructor's reference group ambivalence. As a member of
the staff the instructor had, along with his colleagues, agreed to
the assignment. As an individual, responsible for a discussion
section, he faced a number of rebellious students. To some of
the instructors the rebellion seemed justified; the assignment was
interpreted as meaningless "busywork, " and the students became

the effective reference group. The lack of social distance within
the divisional staff, moreover, made it possible for student dissatisfaction and the instructor's acceptance of the validity of this
dissatisfaction to be quickly and effectively communicated to the
divisional chairman. The chairman had no power to override the
objections of the staff colleague-group. [15]

The first stage. --Thus, by the spring of 1960, when this
became an official project, it had already felt the effect of the
four structural factors, though, of course, we were not consciously
aware of these characteristics at the time. Mr. Gilbert Donahue
was appointed Project Librarian, and was expected to serve the
project full time. But he also had dual roles; he joined the director in participating with the teaching faculty in course planning; at
the same time, he was assigned responsibility for supervising the
work of the bibliographical assistants. These two roles were complementary in the sense that each was concerned with furthering
the aims of the faculty, rather than with shaping them. As super-
visor of bibliographical services, he supplied skilled assistance;
as participant in course planning, he presented the library as a
means of achieving objectives determined by the faculty. Similarly,
the director's two roles were parallel, if not complementary.
Both as Executive Secretary and as a librarian on the project
staff, she aimed at implementing rather than determining faculty
goals.

There was the possibility of conflict, however, in the two
roles carried by the research analyst. As a member of the teaching staff in the social sciences division, she carried her full share
of responsibility for course planning, for lectures, and for leading
her own discussion sections. As a research analyst on the project,
on the other hand, she was expected to stand a bit apart to observe
and analyze the relationship between the faculty and the project.
Probably her experience as an anthropologist led her to accept this
dual role without hesitation. [16]

The expectation that the Monteith faculty would recognize
the distinction between the two roles each of the project staff

carried--admitting their separability--seems to have been justified
only in the case of the social scientists.

The dual role pattern involved even the bibliographical
assistants. Initially these students were assigned individually to
work for individual members of the social sciences staff. They
were expressly given the responsibility of interpreting the individual
needs and demands of the instructor to the library on the one
hand, and the necessarily bureaucratic regulations and procedures
of the library to the faculty, on the other. They were expected to
work under the close supervision of the project librarian, not
only in order that what they produced would profit from his professional knowledge and skills, but also in order that they might
demonstrate the value of library competence. In this role we expected them to be "good-will ambassadors," as it were, for the
project; in their role assisting the faculty, we expected them to
adopt the values and style of the academic researcher.

Here, however, the dual role pattern failed. Almost every
assistant formed a fairly firm one-to-one attachment with his
faculty principal. Most of them avoided the supervision and guidance of the project librarian. They were reluctant to report to
the research analyst on the nature of the tasks the faculty asked
them to perform or on their own relationships with the faculty.
Actually, some instructors used the assistants merely as messengers, some treated them as apprentices, and some gave them a
sort of junior colleague role. But, however they were treated,
they saw themselves not as representatives of the library project,
but as research assistants for the faculty. Perhaps this was the
only model of behavior with which they were familiar.

There was no notable difference in the operation of the
social distance factor on the project during the first semester.
But there was a new development in the effect of the factor of the
group organization. During the period before the project started,
the social sciences staff worked together as a total group. In the
Fall of 1960, however, having grown from 10 or 11 to 13 or 14 in
number, the staff decided to break into small committees for

preliminary planning of various segments of the course. The three principal library project staff members, therefore, spread themselves
among these committees. Meeting with groups of two or three or four,
they were able to get more library assignments accepted than
either before or after this period. But the assignments were not
very successful. One difficulty had to do with the fact that three
or four people can meet informally rather than calling a formal
meeting. Since their offices were not close to faculty offices,
the project librarian and the project director were often simply
not around when informal gatherings took place. They were
frequently not fully aware of all the considerations involved
in the committees' plans. Consequently, some of the assignments proposed, though accepted, were not really in tune
with the units to which they were expected to contribute.

Another difficulty which stemmed from the changed organization of the social sciences faculty arose from the fact that the
total faculty did not feel fully committed to the plans developed in
committees since these plans did not reflect the thinking of the
faculty as a whole. As a result, individual instructors worked
quite autonomously in their discussion sections, emphasizing those
aspects of a given unit with which they felt sympathy, de-emphasiz-
ing other aspects. The aspect most often de-emphasized was the
library assignment. The chain of relationships might be summarized as follows: With the increasing cohesiveness of the committees, the solidarity of the total faculty decreased. As the solidarity of the faculty decreased, its power as a reference group
diminished, and students or "generalized others" gained reference
group power proportionately.

The second stage. --During the second semester of operation, which was from February to June, 1961, all four of the
structural factors had a negative influence on the development of
the project. It was at this time that the operation was extended
to include the natural sciences and the humanities division as
well as the social science division. Bibliographical assistants
were provided for the instructors in these other divisions and the

project staff began to meet with them in their course-planning
sessions.

At this time lack of acceptance of the dual role pattern
began to appear. As Executive Secretary, the project director had
by this time become an ex-officio non-voting member of the Administrative Council of the College, which is made up of the
chairmen of the three instructional divisions. Evidence later appeared that some instructors saw her primarily as a member of
the reputedly powerful Council. Her role as a librarian,
attempting to serve the instructional goals of the faculty, or, at
most trying to gain acceptance for her own library goals, was
quite overshadowed. Similarly, as they began to work with the
faculty in the two additional divisions, all three project staff
members were seen not so much as representatives of the library
project but rather as social scientists or quasi-social scientists
meddling in the business of natural scientists and humanists.

In a sense this view was justified. The research analyst
is, indeed, a social scientist and the project librarian and project
director by training and inclination, probably merited the label
"quasi-social scientist. " Nevertheless, in their library project
roles they did not see themselves as representing the social
scientists. They were, in fact, painfully conscious of the fact
that the librarians among them had never won full acceptance as
members in the social sciences faculty. It was surprising to
discover, therefore, that the library project had come to be
identified not as a general educational effort but as a social
science enterprise.

These comments on relationship with the humanities and
natural sciences divisions should not convey the impression of
general hostility toward the library project or toward its staff as
individuals. The natural sciences staff and the humanities staff,
no less than the social sciences staff, were gracious and friendly
in inviting the project staff to participate in their deliberations.
Certain individuals on each staff were most sympathetic to both
the aims and the methods of the project, and, in fact, acted as

sponsors for the project.   Other instructors were always willing to give the project staff a chance to try out their ideas, whether or not they found these ideas persuasive to begin with.

There was, nevertheless, a pervasive, perhaps largely unconscious, attitude of rejection on the part of the "ideal-typical" instructor.   Experience during these months indicated a breakdown of acceptance of the dual role pattern.   It reflected, furthermore, the considerable horizontal social distance among the three staffs.

The group organization factor created additional difficulties for the project in the second semester.   Just as the project staff continued to have trouble relating themselves to the subgroup organization of the social sciences staff, they were now faced with a similar subgroup organization in the other two divisions.   The natural sciences staff had, from the very beginning, tended to organize itself into subgroups based upon disciplinary specialization. The humanities staff, consisting of only four members, had no need of such subdivision.   On the other hand, the three rank-and-file members often gathered informally.   The chairman of this division was also Director of the College and was frequently occupied with general administrative duties.   Formal meetings of the humanities staff, therefore, tended merely to serve the purpose of crystallizing the results of informal discussion.   The formal meetings of the natural sciences staff served, similarly, to crystallize the plans developed in the specialist committees.   When library project personnel participated in these meetings, therefore, they found that they could contribute little.   The library assignments suggested were likely to be out of tune with prior discussion.   Acceptance of one assignment in the humanities course and one in the natural sciences course was achieved, but neither of these was successfully carried out.

By the end of the second semester of the project, the morale of the project staff was, understandably, at low ebb.   They felt ineffectual and rejected.   Naturally enough, they began to turn to one another for comfort and support.   Eventually, as they became increasingly aware of their own solidarity as a group, they found themselves able to take a more constructive approach to their work.

The third stage. --During the summer of 1961, major attention was devoted to analyzing and discussing past experiences and
to developing plans for what was to be the last semester of the
project's operation. By the end of the summer three important
changes in   organizational structure were developed. The attempt
to meet regularly with the three divisional staffs was discontinued.
Instead one member of the natural sciences faculty and one member
of the humanities faculty was asked to serve as library project
representative for his colleagues. (The research analyst continued
her dual role in relationship to the social sciences staff). These
two faculty representatives met with the three project staff members to consider the objectives and methods of the library program
in general. We worked with them individually in making detailed
plans for assignments in their respective areas. The new structure
preserved the dual role pattern--in fact, it extended it--but it also
recognized the importance of full membership in the interacting
faculty group responsible for course planning. We felt that giving the dual role responsibility to the instructor would make it
possible for library assignments to be in tune with the objectives
and pedagogical style of the faculty to be proposed at crucial
decision-making moments in the course-planning process.

The second change in organizational structure was discon-
tinuance of assignment of individual bibliographical assistants to
instructors. The number of assistants was decreased and those
remaining were pooled into a group who would work directly under
the project librarian. Requests for bibliographical service were
channeled through him to whichever assistant he thought best qualified for the particular job; for a long-term or highly specialized
project an assistant might be sent to work directly with an instructor.

All of the assistants were given a carefully developed training program which included a series of bibliographical problem
tasks. As a result of these changes the bibliographical assistants

became a highly cohesive group, a group which clearly identified itself with the library project.

In general, this new organization of our bibliographical services departed from the dual role pattern, but it created a loyal, cohesive group, capable of producing work of high quality. [17]

The third major change in structure was in the presentation of assignments to students. [18]   This change was that of having librarians take an active part in the presentation of assignments.

It was originally assumed that librarians should remain in the background as much as possible and the implementation of library assignments had been left to the faculty.   Beginning in the Fall of 1961, every assignment, once it had been accepted by the teaching staff, was presented by and discussed under the leadership of one or another of the members of the library project staff. Every effort was made to see to it that each instructor demonstrate his support by participating fully in discussion of the assignment and by showing that he considered the assignment an essential part of the student's experience.   This change in procedure reinforced the power of the divisional staff as reference group because the very presence of the project staff member in the discussion section represented a staff decision.   At the same time, the new procedure gave the project staff an opportunity to contribute to students' thinking about the assignment and thus to influence the standards that they, as a reference group, presented.

Conclusion

As the final semester of the operational phase of the pilot project ended in February, 1962,   we   felt that a workable social structure for our purposes had been achieved. [19]   A review of this structure may serve to summarize the findings presented in this chapter.

The organization calls for the dual role pattern which is accepted in the Monteith structure, but by shifting the dual role assignment to a representative of each of the three faculties, it attempts to ensure that each role is fully accepted.   The instructor who serves as a library project representative will have already

been accepted to full membership in his faculty colleague group.
He will have no difficulty attaining full membership in the smaller
and intensively interacting library project staff group. It appears
reasonably certain that, in this group, he will acquire a more
sophisticated view of what real knowledge and skill in the use of
library resources involves.

The new arrangement also recognizes the impossibility of
having two or three librarians participate effectively in the dis-
persed subgroups organization that existed in each of the three
divisions. The faculty representative has a much better opportunity
to do so. He should find it possible to play the role of library
project sponsor at those crucial points of interaction when pre-
suppositions are being expressed, when ideas are taking shape,
when plans have not yet crystallized.

The participation of an instructor from each division, together with the library project staff, in discussions pertaining to elements common to all three course sequences may help to bridge
the social distance among the three faculties. It should, in any case,
lessen the significance of this factor in the development of the library project, since no one identified with one divisional staff will
be in the position of having to concern himself directly with the
teaching plans and procedures of the others. And finally, the new
procedures for presenting assignments to students helps to overcome the problem of the instructor's reference group ambivalence.

Notes

1. Because this sort of inquiry is not common in library investiga-
    tions, we have quoted liberally in footnotes from methodological
    statements to be found in the writings of sociologists and
    anthropologists.

2. 'The term 'social structure' has nothing to do with empirical
    reality but with models which are built up after it. This
    should help one clarify the difference between two concepts
    which are so closely related to each other that they have often
    been confused, namely, those of social structure and of social
    relations. It will be enough to state at this time that social
    relations consist of the raw materials out of which the models
    making up the social structure are built, while social structure
    can, by no means, be reduced to the ensemble of social rela-
    tions to be described in a given society. " Claude Levi-Strauss,

"Social Structure, " in <u>Anthropology Today</u> (Chicago: University of Chicago Press, 1953), p. 525.

3. A survey of research in this area is presented in: Peter N. Blau, <u>Formal Organizations: a Comparative Approach</u> (San Francisco: Chandler Publishing Co., 1962).

4. The article by Levi-Strauss, <u>op. cit.</u>, pp. 504-533, discusses a number of studies of social structure.

5. "The purpose that defines the position I have suggested that my reader assume requires that we remain attendant to the configuration. But it requires also that we strive to make explicit the arrangement of parts within the configuration. We seek to know the whole through identifying the parts of the whole and describing the interconnections among these and their relations to the whole." Robert Redfield, <u>The Little Community</u> and <u>Peasant Society and Culture</u> ("Phoenix Books"; Chicago: University of Chicago Press, 1960), pp. 159-160.

6. "For instance, sociologists and social psychologists have on occasion taken for granted that the 'informants' of the anthropologists could be equated with their 'respondents' and 'subjects.' Actually, the anthropologist often thinks of an informant much more as an historian thinks of a document in a period whose main outlines are already familiar, or as an art historian will treat a new specimen that fits into a series of recognized style. That is, the question is not that of incidence or distribution, but rather those of: what point in what pattern? or: in what slightly variant ways is a known pattern manifested? But in questions of pattern analysis, the relevant point may be that of configuration or of abrupt alternation from one configuration to another. Figures may not only be beside the point; they may obscure the issue.
. . . .
"It has sometimes been asserted that when anthropologists analyze their material they do so by 'feel' or 'apperception' or 'artistic insight.' Instead of these epithets, certain critics might as well have said flatly: Anthropologists are 'unscientific' or at any rate 'very sloppy workmen.' Less unfriendly critics, however, use these terms, I believe, because they sense that anthropologists are carrying out--or trying to carry out--a type of analysis which has little place in the repertory of some of the other varieties of behavioral science. This is the approach which anthropologists have variously referred to as that of 'pattern,' 'configuration,' or 'contextualism.'" Clyde Kluckhohn, "Common Humanity and Diverse Cultures," in <u>The Human Meaning of the Social Sciences</u>, ed. by Daniel Lerner (New York: Meridian Books, Inc., 1959), pp. 259-261.

7. "Good training in theory and acquaintance with its latest results is not identical with being burdened with 'preconceived ideas.' If a man sets out on an expedition determined to prove certain hypotheses, if he is incapable of changing his

views constantly and casting them off ungrudgingly under the pressure of evidence, needless to say his work will be worthless. " Bronislaw Malinowski, Argonauts of the Western Pacific ("Dutton Everyman Paperback"; New York: E. P. Dutton Company, Inc. , 1961), p. 9.

8.   Malinowski refers to his use of detailed and elaborate chronologies, charts of economic transactions, genealogical and other synoptic tables. Malinowski, op. cit. , pp. 11-25.

9.   Weber's discussion of the characteristics of the bureaucracy may be found in N. N. Gerth and C. Wright Mills (trans. and eds.), From Max Weber: Essays in Sociology (New York: Oxford University Press, 1946), pp. 196-204.

10. The first series of interviews, limited to members of the social sciences staff, was conducted by Mr. Rolland Wright, a sociologist on that staff, during the summer before the project began. His interview was completely unstructured, since we were concerned with learning about the attitudes and preconceptions about the library and its place in the educational process with which we would be faced. The second series, conducted by the writer at the close of the first semester of operation, was also limited to the social sciences staff. It was somewhat concerned with the general reactions to the project thus far, but it focused primarily on the faculty member's experience with the bibliographical services he had received and on his plans for future use of them. The third series, conducted by the research analyst after the operational phase of the project was terminated, attempted to arrive at the instructor's evaluation of the enterprise as a whole and his view of its potential for the future.

11. "The reader will recall Thomas' understanding of the social situation as a sort of reality agreed upon ad hoc by those who participate in it, or, more exactly, those who do the defining of the situation. From the viewpoint of the individual participant this means that each situation he enters confronts him with specific expectations and demands of him specific responses to these expectations. . . The role provides the pattern according to which the individual is to act in the particular situation. . .It would, however, be missing an essential aspect of the role if one regarded it merely as a regulatory pattern for externally visible actions. One feels more ardent by kissing, more humble by kneeling and more angry by shaking one's fist. That is, the kiss not only expresses ardor but manufactures it. Roles carry with them both certain actions and the emotions and attitudes that belong to these actions. . . . . Every role in society has attached to it a certain identity. . . This significance of role theory could be summarized by saying that, in a sociological perspective, identity is socially bestowed, socially sustained and socially transformed. . .In

other words, identity is not something 'given' but is bestowed
in acts of social recognition. " Peter L. Berger, Invitation
to Sociology: a Humanistic Perspective ("Anchor Books";
Garden City: Doubleday and Company, Inc., 1963), pp. 94-96.

12. "The now established term 'reference group' is something of a
    misnomer for the term is applied not only to groups, but to
    individuals and to social categories as well. " Robert K.
    Merton, Social Theory and Social Structure (Rev. and enl. ed.;
    Glencoe: the Free Press, 1957), p. 284. For a review of
    studies in this area, see also Tamotsu Shibutani, "Reference
    Groups and Social Control, " in Human Behavior and Social
    Processes, ed. by Arnold M. Rose (Boston: Houghton Mifflin
    Co., 1962), pp. 128-147.

13. Merton, op. cit., pp. 283-284, refers to "two major types of
    reference groups: . . . the first is the 'normative type' which
    sets and maintains standards for the individual and the second
    is the 'comparative type' which provides a framework of com-
    parison relative to which the individual evaluates himself and
    others. The first is a source of values assimilated by des-
    ignated individuals (who may or may not be members of the
    group). . . The second is instead a context for evaluating the
    relative position of oneself and others. "

14. Blau, op. cit., pp. 42-45, classifies formal organizations on
    the basis of their "prime beneficiary. " He distinguishes
    among: (1) mutual benefit associations, unions, for example,
    which are designed to serve the interests of the rank-and-file
    members; (2) business concerns, which exist to benefit the
    owners or managers; (3) service organizations, such as schools,
    hospitals, libraries, and the professions, which are designed
    to serve the interests of clients; and (4) commonweal organiza-
    tions, e. g., prisons and other such general welfare institu-
    tions, which serve the interests of the general public.

    Also of interest in this connection is the discussion by Merton,
    op. cit., pp. 207-224, of the contrast between the "bureau-
    cratic intellectual, " who has an advisory or staff role in the
    bureaucracy and the "unattached intellectual, " (a category
    which includes teachers) who work independently.

15. Note, in contrast, that although a few individuals on the staff
    of the University Library expressed doubts about the wisdom
    of expending library resources on the Monteith experiment in-
    stead of improving "normal" services, the project, neverthe-
    less, received the fullest cooperation from the library. This
    cooperation was assured by the fact that Dr. Purdy, the Direc-
    tor, and Mr. Robert Grazier, the Associate Director, fully
    supported our efforts.

16. "Ideally, the anthropologist's attitude toward his informants is
    that of 'attached-detachment. ' That is to say, he studies his

fellow men not solely as a dispassionate observer but also as
a participant observer. . . As an anthropologist, he recognizes
that no adult can--or should want to--shed his own culture
completely.   While remaining firmly a detached outsider in his
total role, he nevertheless behaves with warmth and sympathy
in immediate personal relations.   Anthropological research
demands that we not only observe our fellow men but also live
with them.   In short, the anthropologist must behave and see
and feel from within the foreign cultural context and, at the
same time, withdraw and analyze. " Kluckhohn, op. cit. , pp.
251-253.

17. By the end of the semester, as their employment by the
    project was about to terminate, some of them felt so competent
    that they took tentative and, as it turned out, inconclusive
    steps toward setting themselves up as a bibliographical search
    service.   Five of the fifteen, incidentally, decided to become
    librarians.   At least two of these went on to library school.

18. The assignments, themselves, were considerably different
    from those we had tried previously.   Our new assignments,
    discussed in Chapter V, appealed to the faculty as appropriate
    and sufficiently challenging for college work.   This change, of
    course, was the most important factor in the acceptance we
    managed to achieve in the last semester of the project.   But
    it is not structural change, so it is not pertinent to the present
    discussion.

19. This is the structure proposed for implementation in the
    model program presented in Chapter V.

Chapter III

Library Assignments in the Pilot Project

By the time the pilot project ended its operation in the Spring
of 1961, fourteen library assignments related to the basic courses
in the Monteith curriculum had been carried through. These
assignments are described and analyzed individually and in some
detail in Appendix I. This chapter deals first with some general
ideas about course-related library work which were acquired as a
result of experiences with these assignments. Next, in order to
illustrate ways in which a library program might be studied as
one element in the students' total college experience, the sequence
of library assignments presented to one Monteith class are summarized and certain characteristics of students exposed to this
sequence are examined.

What Was Learned about Course-Related Library Assignments

Course-relatedness is not enough. --One assumption on which
this study was based was that students attain library competence,
however it is defined, only when they actually use the library and
only when their use of it is significantly related to what they consider the real business of college, that is, to substantive content
of courses. Concerned primarily that every library experience be
directly and immediately related to regular course work, it was
assumed, in essence, that what was important was the student's
motivation, that if he really needed to use the library for his work,
he would manage somehow to find what he needed in the library and
thus indirectly become acquainted with its organization.

But it was soon found that the problem was not so simple. In
the first place, the student's "need" to use the library derives
from the value placed upon such work by his instructor. The instructor is, generally, less concerned with the student's experience in locating materials in the library than he is with what the

student makes of such materials when he has located them. At
the end of the first semester of the program in action we reported:

> We are reasonably well satisfied with the plans which have
> been made, but there is disturbing evidence of their lack of
> implementation in actual teaching. Some instructors have
> omitted one of the library assignments. Others apparently
> give no weight to bibliography in their grading of papers.

> Such omissions make it hard for us to arrive at general anal-
> yses of the effect of the students' experiences. But, more
> important, they suggest that these library experiences are not
> really valued by some instructors. We suspect that their
> students are aware of this and therefore slight the library as-
> signments.

> Our own diagnosis of the problem at this point is that our con-
> cept of "sophisticated understanding of the library and increas-
> ing competence in its use" as a goal of general education is
> not accepted, perhaps not understood, by most of the faculty...
> We conceive of the library as a highly complicated system, or
> better, a network of interrelated systems, which organizes and
> controls all kinds of communication. A few instructors under-
> stand the conception, but we believe that more conceive of
> sophisticated library understanding and competence as "command
> of the literature of a field of study. " This is what they,
> themselves, have acquired in their years of training and ex-
> perience, and this is what they hope to stimulate their students
> to acquire. [1]

The sink-or-swim approach is hazardous. --In the Spring of
1960, each student enrolled in the Science of Society course was
required to carry out an elementary research project. The first
step in this project required him to find out what the library had
to offer on the topic he had chosen for this research. He was
asked to keep a record of his library work, a log of where and
how he looked for references, what led him from one tool to
another, what he found and what he failed to find. It was hoped
that these reports would provide useful information about what
students experience when they know little or nothing about the topic
on which they seek information. But, more important, it was
hoped that the reports would heighten the student's own awareness
of the thinking processes involved in his search.

In preparation for the assignment, the students were introduced to the major reference tools which might be useful for work

in the social sciences. They were urged to seek assistance from
members of the library staff, who had done some preliminary
searching on the total list of topics available. But in the main,
the students were exposed to a sink-or-swim approach, and most
of them floundered. They had difficulty in finding relevant materials; they considered keeping the log an annoying waste of time;
many of them emerged from the experience with not a little hostility toward the library project.

What was more surprising--and more disturbing--however,
was the fact that the faculty were dismayed at the quality of the
references cited in the students' reports. This indicated that the
student may not have learned to swim even when he thinks he has
and that his conception of "finding what he needs in the library"
may not be that of his instructor.

Students tend to be uncritical in their choice of sources of
information. --Having found what they called "pure garbage" among
the sources cited by students for the first research project assignment, some of the faculty were inclined to conclude that students could not be trusted to find appropriate sources on their
own, and that, therefore, they must be told what to read. Later
experience with the book evaluation task in the small sample experiment[2] supported the diagnosis but not the remedy. Students
are not skilled in the use of surface clues as to the quality of
books they find on the open shelves; they tend to be content with
"something on" the subject, regardless of its validity. Experience
with the "Book Evaluation Assignment"[3] indicates, however, that
students can profit from training in the appraisal of sources of
information and that they need not be limited to pre-selected,
prescribed reading.

The "system" of scholarly reporting and the "system" of
the library are not identical and the difference is relevant. --The
first experience with the research project assignment indicated
also that students' difficulties in locating what the faculty considered appropriate sources resulted partly from the fact that the
common organizing tools of the library, the classification system,

the card catalog, and the periodical indexes, did not perform adequately in bringing such sources to light.   Attempting to overcome these inadequacies and abandoning the sink-or-swim approach, subsequent classes were introduced to such specialized tools as the "guide to the literature, " the annual review, the abstracting services, and the bibliographical review.

    Through discussion with faculty and students and through our own reflections, it gradually became evident that substituting these specialized tools for those normally introduced to freshmen was not merely providing information useful for a particular subject. It was making explicit a distinction which had been implicit in the behavior of the scholar working in the literature of his own field-- a distinction between a framework that stresses subject, form, source, date, place as against a framework stressing discipline, "school, " concept, method. [4] As soon as such distinctions were discussed in connection with the Bibliographical Review Assignment and with the Joyce Assignment, [5] many instructors seemed to see a new dimension in the efforts to teach students how to use the library.   We were now dealing with matters which they recognized as relevant in their own academic experience.

    The organization from simple-to-complex is not simple. -- Tentative plans for a sequence of student library experiences, "designed to present the student with increasingly challenging problems of library use, " were developed in the Fall of 1960.   One assignment in this sequence was in connection with a segment of the Science of Society course dealing with "socialization. " The proposed assignment was described as follows:

> The assignment: an analysis of the process of ego-identification (in accordance with a framework provided by one of the readings in the course syllabus) of an individual, using as data that individual's autobiography plus other materials about him or his environment.

> Library experience: Identification and location of information about the autobiographee and his milieu.

> Rationale: As the first assignment involving a subject approach to the library, the assignment has the merit of being concerned with a person.   A person has a name; he exists at a particular time in a particular place.   The student is

exposed to the importance of name, time and place as keys
to classification, to the catalog, to indexes, and to biographical and historical reference tools. [6]

This rationale is persuasive.   It is usually easier to find
information about topics which are safely and unvaryingly named
and placed in time and space than about topics not so fixed.   The
idea of introducing the student to the subject approach to the library
by way of a biographical assignment can be defended, but our experience indicates that a course-related library experience takes
on the complexion of the host assignment of which it is a part.
Many, perhaps most, of the students were unable to handle the
extremely difficult concept of "ego-identification. " They felt be-
trayed, because they had somehow come to believe that the library
would help them "answer the question. " What was intended as a
relatively simple problem of locating information was confused with
an extremely difficult problem of using the information found.

Conclusion. --The notions discussed above are sufficient to
illustrate the kind of general understanding acquired through these
first naive and fumbling efforts in planning library assignments
during the pre-grant period and the first year of the project's
operation.   This understanding began to take a positive turn as a
result of the first small sample study[7] and our reflections and
discussions in the summer of 1961.   The assignments presented in
1961-62 represented, at last, an approach that promised to cope
with the problems and difficulties uncovered in the first two years.
All of these later assignments are incorporated in the "model program" presented in Chapter V, so they need no further comment
here.

Appraisal of Student Learning from Library Assignments

The Proposal for the pilot project stated:

Data on the students' library experiences will be analyzed
in terms of the library personnel, organization, and facilities required for library assignments and in terms of the
kinds of briefing and guidance which are associated with
successes and difficulties students encounter in carrying out
library assignments.   The exploratory evaluation of student
response to library instruction will be directed toward the

development of valid instruments for appraisal of student attainment of library competence and for examination of the importance of such competence for general academic achievement.

In the analyses of individual assignments in Appendix I, each of the assignments presented is considered as a unit and is appraised on the basis of subjective criteria such as the reaction of students, faculty, and project staff and on the basis of whatever objective measures were feasible and seemed individually appropriate in the circumstances.   Chapter IV presents that part of the exploratory--and the word should be underlined--evaluation concerned with development of valid instruments for appraisal of student attainment of library competence.   Chapter V, in connection with plans for appraisal of the proposed model program[8] discusses some of the difficulties involved in any attempt to assess the contribution of library competence to educational achievement.

Thus, much of what might be discussed under the heading of "appraisal of student learning from library assignments" is dealt with elsewhere in this report.   But the students did experience actual assignments during the course of the pilot project, and they experienced them not individually, as they are reported in the Appendix, but as a sequence.   There were three sequences in the pilot project:

> Sequence A, experienced by the students who entered in the Fall of 1959 and the Spring of 1960.   All of the library assignments experienced by these students were carried out before the revisions we made in the program in the summer of 1961.   All were implemented exclusively by the faculty.

> Sequence B, experienced by the students who entered in the Fall of 1960.   This was a mixed sequence, including, in the freshman year, assignments developed before the summer, 1961 revision, and, in the sophomore year, two assignments developed after the revision.

> Sequence C, experienced by students who entered in the Spring and Fall of 1961.   This sequence included only two assignments, both developed after the revised program was put into effect.

There appeared to be some value in trying out possible ways of examining the association between exposure to a sequence of library assignments and objective indexes of such other factors as general educational achievement, home and school background, scholastic aptitude, etc. Data on these other factors were available for the 1959 class through the Monteith Program Study, [9] so this class was studied. What follows, then, is a summary of Sequence A and an analysis of the association between exposure to this sequence and certain other identifiable variables among students to whom the sequence was presented. The primary aim of this analysis, let us repeat, was not to arrive at the "findings"-- such as they are--but to demonstrate methods, the rationale behind the choice of indicators, the assumptions involved in the use of certain statistical measures and so on.

Table I presents the summary of Sequence A. For only three of the six assignments, numbers 2, 5, and 6, was there an attempt to get a report of some sort from every student enrolled. For a group of 37 students in the class, such reports were obtained on at least two of the three assignments. Thus, it can be said with certainty, that these 37 students did, in fact, carry out at least two of the six assignments; they almost certainly carried out others as well; some probably carried out all six. Because of difficulties in gathering reports through the faculty, it cannot be said that the rest of the class did not carry out any or all of the assignments. But there is at least a shade of presumption that many either a) did not do the library work involved in the three assignments, or b) did not do it as thoroughly or conscientiously as did those in the group of 37, or c) worked under an instructor who placed so little value on the task that he neglected to hand in the report.

Admitting, then, that the evidence is completely inferential, the 37 students may be considered a sample which represents those more thoroughly exposed to experiences requiring extensive exploration of library resources than the rest of the class. It should be emphasized that in comparing them with their classmates there is no intention to imply that library experiences led to or caused the differences found. Indeed, as some of the evidence suggests, the relationship may be the other way around. Differences in

Table 1
Sequence A

Assignment Number	Library Experience	Purpose of the Library Experience	Aids Designed to Help Student in the Library	Point of Coordination with the Host Course
1 (1st semester)	Location of items listed in one of six short bibliographies selected by the faculty and printed in the required book of readings for the course. Call numbers were not supplied.	To introduce the entering freshman to the topography and organization of the university library and to some procedures to use in locating references.	"Library Notes," printed in the required textbook, were designed to help the student locate the required items, and to find others if he wished.	The items to be located were to be the basis for a class report related to the general topic under consideration in the Science of Society course.
2 (2nd semester)	Location of information on one of 113 topics posed by the faculty. Preparation of a report of the library search process in 3 parts: 1) a log of the search process, 2) a summary of its results, 3) an essay on the subjective experience.	To make the student aware of his own search pattern, to bring him to see for himself that the library is an organization and that various bibliographic tools are keys which lay open various parts of it, to introduce the "literature search" as part of the research process.	1) A briefing session led by a university librarian. 2) The WSU Library Handbook distributed at this time.	The bibliographic work was the first step in a semester-long research project to be designed and executed by the student.

Table 1 - continued

Assignment Number	Library Experience	Purpose of the Library Experience	Aids Designed to Help Student in the Library	Point of Coordination with the Host Course
3 (3rd semester)	Locating of references on a revolutionary social, political, religious, or artistic "movement."	To demonstrate a search process which begins with a concrete event, one which can be located in space and time, to introduce some of the bibliographical tools which organize the whole range of library resources, i.e., newspapers, letters, documents, as well as books.	A list, on cards, of little known revolutionary social changes and a bibliography on them, compiled by project bibliographic assistants (available to the student on request).	The references were to be used in a paper on a social movement.
4 (3rd semester)	(optional) Location of references on one of several suggested themes—social mobility and its dilemmas, the relationship between communication systems and social organization, for example.	To demonstrate the search process involved in locating sources on a fairly abstract theme.	No special aid provided though, as always, the project librarian and the faculty were available for help on request.	Students were required to write a paper on "the nature of civilized society" or "what it means to be a human being in a civilized society." Citations beyond the assigned readings were not required.

Table 1 - continued

Assignment Number	Library Experience	Purpose of the Library Experience	Aids Designed to Help Student in the Library	Point of Coordination with the Host Course
5 (4th semester)	Location of information on the social and intellectual milieu of an artist studied during the first Humanistic Studies term.	To demonstrate a search process which begins with an individual person (who can be located in space and time).	"Notes on the Use of the Library" which directed the student's attention particularly to the organization of biographical sources.	The information located was expected to lend depth and richness to the student's understanding of the artists dealt with in the course.
6 (4th semester)	The identification, through browsing in the literature of one of fifteen broad areas in the philosophy of science, such as cybernetics, probability, the relationship between technology and culture, of sources to be used in selecting a manageable topic for a paper, assigned in the last semester of Natural Sciences.	1) To demonstrate the use of a) the bibliography in a standard textbook, b) an article in a standard encyclopedia which always includes a selected bibliography, and c) the card catalog as a starting place for beginning the study of a large and unfamiliar field. 2) To introduce the popular and the academically respectable literature and certain non-technical bibliographic aids in the natural sciences.	A leaflet, "Suggested Library Procedures for Your Term Paper" which was based on a dry-run of the assignment carried out by project bibliographical assistants. Bibliographies resulting from the dry-run were put at the disposal of the faculty, to be used in advising students.	The sources located were to be used in the selection of a topic for and writing of a required paper.

capacity, in background, in prior experience with libraries, may account for the differing degrees to which the students permitted themselves to be exposed to the library assignments.

Outcomes. --The first question is how well our "exposed sample" fared in their total academic career in comparison with their fellows.   Table 2 shows status with respect to keeping up with the normal four-year schedule for obtaining a degree. The "exposed sample" is over-represented among those who graduated on time, and under-represented in every other category.   (The difference is significant at $p<.001$, on the basis of x^2 calculations, with "Spring, 1960 Entrants" and "Transfers" dropped from the population).[10] The evidence suggests an association between completing library assignments and fulfilling other requirements and fulfilling them on time.

Table 2
Status of Fall, 1959 and Spring, 1960
Entrants in Winter, 1963

Status	Total Class		"Exposed Sample"	
	No.	Percent	No.	Percent
Graduatables * who graduated in June, 1963	52	16. 1	20	54. 1
Other graduatables	28	8. 6	2	5. 4
Slow-downs	31	9. 6	3	8. 1
Drop-outs who subsequently returned	15	4. 6	0	0
Spring, 1960 entrants, on schedule	21	6. 5	2	5. 4
Transfers to professional schools	16	4. 9	4	10. 8
Drop-outs	160	49. 5	6	16. 2
Total	323		37	

*We use the term "graduatable" to refer to students who were "on schedule, " i.e., needing to carry only a normal load in order to graduate in June, 1963.   Some of these subsequently had an "incomplete" or in some other way failed to meet the degree requirement on time.

Notes:

1. x^2 = 24. 2 (significant $p<.001$) with "Spring Entrants" and "Transfers" omitted from the population and with all other

categories collapsed as "Graduatables" and "Others. "

2.   The Kolmogorov-Smirnov One-Sample Test, used in the same
     way, confirms the significance of order in the categories, i. e.,
     ranging from the graduates who are completely "on schedule"
     through three levels of being "behind schedule" to the drop-
     outs, who are completely "off schedule. "

Table 3 which, in effect, removes the drop-outs from the
comparison, shows the "exposed sample" as faring slightly better
than the rest of the class as to grades.   The difference is not
significant ($p < .10$) at the levels usually applied for statistical tests,
but it is high enough to justify further investigation under conditions
of better control. [11]

Table 3
Cumulated Honor Point Average
Winter, 1963[1]

Honor Point Average	Total Group		"Exposed Sample"	
	No.	Percent	No.	Percent
3.5 and above	9	6.5	4	12.9
3.0 - 3.4	36	25.9	11	35.5
2.5 - 2.9	42	30.2	11	35.5
2.0 - 2.4	42	30.2	5	16.1
1.5 - 1.9	10	7.2	0	0
Total	139		31	
No information[2]	184		6	
Grand Total	323		37	

[1]The scores for four students in the "exposed sample" who trans-
ferred out of Monteith to another college at Wayne are for Spring
or Summer, 1962.

[2]Information is lacking on drop-outs and some but not all transfer
students.

Note: The differences are not significant.   The Kolmogorov-
        Smirnov Two-Sample Test results in a D of .213. x^2 =
        4.54; significant at $p < .10$)

Table 4, comparing the two groups as to scores on the Graduate Record Examination, shows a higher average score for the "exposed sample" on each of the five tests. But the samples are too small to allow for adequate measurement of the statistical significance of the difference. Tables 5 and 6, comparing scores on the Test of Critical Thinking and the College Characteristics Index, also show slight differences.

The findings with regard to association between "outcomes" and "exposure" to library assignments may be summarized as follows:

1. There is an association between the two when "outcomes" refers to long-range performance, i. e.,

    a. a clear, and statistically significant association between "exposure" and "staying on schedule, " or meeting degree requirements on time,

    b. a possible, but not statistically significant association between "exposure" and maintaining a good honor point average.

2. There is an association, which might prove to be significant if the sample were large enough for an adequate measure, between "exposure" and a one-shot traditional measure of educational achievement, the Graduate Record Examination.

3. There is no significant association between "exposure" and "outcomes" when the latter is understood to refer to:

    a. A change in intellectual capacity, such as is measured by the Test of Critical Thinking,

    b. perception of the college, as measured by the College Characteristics Index.

Table 4

Scores on the Graduate Record Examinations

Test	Fall, 1959 and Spring, 1960 Entrants[1]		"Exposed Sample"[2]	
	Group Average (Raw score)	Group Average (Percentile)	Group Average (Raw score)	Group Average (Percentile)
Aptitude				
Verbal	540	69	554	72
Quantitative	516	68	527	72
Area				
Social Science	552	71	563	75
Humanities	559	74	574	77
Natural Science	538	69	557	74

[1]Fifty-nine members of the class took the two aptitude tests; 63 took the social science and humanities area tests; and 62 took the natural science test.

[2]Scores on the aptitude tests were available for 17 members of the exposed sample; those on the area tests were available for 20 of the sample.

Table 5
Average Scores on Test of Critical Thinking

Group	1959	1963	Change*
"Exposed Sample"	35.36	39.10	3.74
Entering Class, 1959-60	33.68		
Graduatables	33.52	40.29	6.77

*The Wilcoxen Matched-pairs Signed-ranks Test indicates that there is no statistical significance in the change for individuals in the "exposed sample."

Table 6
College Characteristics Index
Average Scores on Intellectual Climate

Group

| "Exposed Sample" | 83.8 |
| Graduatables | 84.2 |

Intellectual capacity and personality. --Intellectual and personal traits were investigated--in addition to those reflected in the Test of Critical Thinking and the College Characteristics Index--to determine which might be associated with the fact that the sample group exposed itself to the library assignments.

Table 7, presenting a summary of performance on tests given by the Admissions Office of Wayne State University, shows that, in comparison with the 1959 entering class as a whole the "exposed sample" had a slightly higher proportion of students who scored above average on all three tests, a considerably lower proportion who scored below average on all three. But there is a reversal in the two middle positions, which would indicate that the differences are not significant.

Two factors, Theoretical Orientation and Impulse Expression, were chosen from the Omnibus Personality Inventory as measures of possibly relevant personal traits. The reason for these choices can be illustrated by the following items from the Inventory:

The main object of scientific research should be the discovery of truth rather than its practical application. (High scorer on Theoretical Orientation would tend to agree.)

I dislike assignments requiring original research work. (Low scorer on Theoretical Orientation would tend to agree.)

I have always hated regulations. (High scorer on Impulse Expression would tend to agree.)

I have never done anything dangerous for the thrill of it. (Low scorer on Impulse Expression would tend to agree.)

Table 7
Summary of Scores on WSU Entrance Tests

Students Scoring	Total Class Entering in Fall, 1959		"Exposed Sample"	
	No.	Percent	No.	Percent
Above average on 3 tests	88	30	13	35
Above average on 2 tests	78	26	8	22
Above average on 1 test	64	21	12	32
Below average on 3 tests	55	18	3	8
Not ascertained	11		1	
Total	296		37	

Table 8 shows average scores on these two factors of various groups of students tested. The "exposed sample" scored lower than any other group on Impulse Expression, both in 1959 and in 1963. Note also that its change in average score between 1959 and 1963 was considerably higher than that for the graduates. Since scores were not available for every individual at both times, the Wilcoxen Matched-pairs Signed-ranks Test was used to study the change in individual graduates in the "exposed sample" for whom "before" and "after" scores were, in fact, available. (The change for each individual was "signed" in accordance with whether it was greater or less than the average change for graduates.) This test produces a score, $T = 28.0$, which is significant at $p < .02$.

Table 8
Omnibus Personality Inventory: Average Scores for
Theoretical Orientation and Impulse Expression

Group	Theoretical Orientation		Impulse Expression	
	1959	1963	1959	1963
"Exposed sample"	20.20	21.89	25.23	32.29
Total group tested	19.33	21.00	31.87	36.54
Graduates	20.95	22.34	29.95	35.07
Slow-downs	20.11	20.17	34.89	41.98
Drop-outs	18.60		32.78	

The change on Theoretical Orientation for the "exposed sample," though slight, was also greater than that for the graduates. The same test applied here produced a score, $T = 27.5$, also significant at $p < .02$.

Interpretation of these tests is difficult. On Impulse Expression it might well be that the students in the sample scored so low to begin with that they had farther to go. But on Theoretical Orientation they began with scores higher than any group except the graduates and they changed more than the graduates. It may be that the measure reveals a trait which is associated with willingness to expose oneself to experiences like the library assignments and which is at the same time associated with a tendency to grow in the capacity tested.

Background factors. --Two factors were used to analyze the possible relevance of background factors: a rating of the high school attended and the amount of education of parents. From Table 9 which shows high school rating, it is apparent that the "exposed sample" does not differ from the total class on this factor. And, as shown in Table 10, although the parents of the sample had more education than those of the total class, the difference is not statistically significant. ($p = .15$, Kolmogorov-Smirnov Two-Sample Test.)

Table 9
Rating of High School Attended

High School	Total Entering Class (Fall, 1959)		"Exposed Sample"	
	No.	Percent	No.	Percent
Superior	77	26.0	11	29.7
Good	121	40.9	15	40.5
Medium	74	25.0	10	27.0
Detrimental	19	6.4	1	2.7
Not ascertained	5	1.7	0	0
Total	296		37	

Table 10
Parents' Education

Education of Parents	Total Entering Class (Fall, 1959)		"Exposed Sample"	
	No.	Percent	No.	Percent
Both parents attended college	44	14.9	9	24.3
One parent attended college	63	21.3	7	18.9
Both parents finished high school	20	6.8	4	10.8
One parent finished high school	68	23.0	8	21.6
One parent went beyond grammar school	53	17.9	1	2.7
Neither parent went beyond grammar school	18	18.2	1	2.7
Not ascertained	30	10.1	7	18.9
Total	296		37	

College associations. --And, finally, asking if those who
exposed themselves to the library assignments were dutiful drudges
for whom college was merely a matter of going to class and doing
one's homework, their membership in the campus cliques was
examined. Table 11 shows which cliques they belonged to. The
distribution is particularly interesting in two categories: first, the
absence of representation in the "Intellectual Fringe, " and second,
the over-representation in the group of women who entered Wayne's
Teacher Educational Experimental Project, supported by the Ford
Foundation. The Intellectual Fringe group is composed of the students interested in creative activities, some are protesters, some
are seen as "beatniks. " The group includes embryo poets, artists,
dramatists, cartoonists, etc. They are described as students who
are looking for a "life-style" rather than a profession. TEEP students are not just would-be teachers, but students who are seriously
concerned with innovation in education. Unfortunately, the sample
is not large enough to permit a test of the statistical significance
of the overall distribution.

Table 12, however, gives an ordered progression of roles
within cliques. The "exposed sample" appears disproportionately
at the leadership end of the scale. (The association is statistically significant at the $p < .05$, on the basis of the Kolmogorov-
Smirnov Two-Sample Test, $x^2 = 6.59$).

Table 11
Clique Membership

Cliques	Total Class		"Exposed Sample"	
	No.	Percent	No.	Percent
1. Monteith "core" (active in Center or on Student Board)	39	24.4	5	16.1
2. "Intellectual fringe"	13	8.1	0	0.0
3. Students who share a common background or traits	41	25.6	9	29.0
4. Professional and fraternity	23	14.4	6	19.4
5. Women's world (Assn. of Women Students, etc.)	34	21.2	6	19.4
6. Students in the Teacher Experimental Project (TEEP)	10	6.2	5	16.1
7. TEEP students also in clique no. 4 (women's world)	(5)	(3.1)	(3)	(9.7)
8. TEEP students also in clique no. 1 (Monteith "core")	(5)	(3.1)	(2)	(6.4)
Total	160	99.9	31	100.0
No information	15		6	

Table 12
Role in Cliques

Role	Total Class		"Exposed Sample"	
	No.	Percent	No.	Percent
1. Full membership in more than two cliques	7	4.2	5	16.1
2. Full membership in two cliques	20	12.0	5	16.1
3. Full membership in one clique, marginal reciprocal contacts in others	41	24.7	11	35.5
4. Firm attachment solely in one clique	34	20.5	6	19.4
5. Marginal attachment (i.e., with one-half of clique) and friends outside	17	10.2	1	3.2
6. Marginal attachment in clique, no friends outside	24	14.5	3	9.7
7. Tenuous relationship with one clique	18	10.8	0	0
8. Isolates	5	3.0	0	0
Total	166	99.9	31	100.0
No information	6		6	

Conclusion. --The group of students examined here represents the class which was exposed to the library project at its earliest and most fumbling stage. The class moved out of our range at precisely the time when the morale of the project staff was at its lowest ebb, when students were expressing hostility at what they felt as "busy-work" assignments, when some of the instructors were on the verge of rebelling against the obligations implicit in the mere existence of the project.

This analysis was, therefore, approached with some trepedation. The studies noted above indicate that those students in the class who are known to have been most heavily exposed to the project's efforts -- or to have been most willing to expose themselves--were at least none the worse for the experience. Nor were they merely peculiarly "conditioned" by factors in their background to accept "requirements" as inevitable. Their staying power was remarkable. Their grades and their scores on the Graduate Record Examination were better than the grades of their classmates. They scored about the same as their classmates on measures of growth in intellectual capacity and of perception of college climate. They participated at least as actively in the group life of the campus, carrying more than their share of leadership roles.

The most interesting finding, unquestionably, was that the graduating seniors among them changed significantly more than their fellows on the Theoretical Orientation score on the Omnibus Personality Inventory. We should like to interpret this as indicating that our "exposed sample" represents students who are willing to lend themselves wholeheartedly to the academic enterprise and that when they do, their respect for that enterprise, their willingness to continue to engage in it, is enhanced.

Notes

1.   Progress Report, no. 2, p. 19-20.

2.   See Chapter IV, p. 62-79.

3.   See Appendix I, p. 173-176, Appendix III, p. 242-256.

4. See Chapter V, p. 82-83, for further discussion of this distinction.

5. See Appendix I, p. 176-178, 182-189; Appendix III, p. 257-260, 271-273.

6. Second Progress Report, p. 3-4.

7. See Chapter IV.

8. See p. 107-111.

9. Monteith Program Study, Project No. 1455, Cooperative Research Branch, Office of Education, Department of Health, Education and Welfare. The Impact of a High-Demand College in a Large University on Working-Class Youth.

10. The statistical measures used are derived from Sidney Siegel, Nonparametric Statistics for the Behavioral Sciences (New York: McGraw-Hill, 1956).

    A comment about some of the assumptions involved in these statistics may be in order here. The group of 37 students can be considered as a "sample" of the total "population" which constitutes the 1959-60 entering class. (Nonparametric statistics were used to avoid making the assumption of a "normal" distribution in that population). If the sample were random, i.e. not selected in accordance with the variable of "exposure" to the library assignments, we would expect members of the sample to reflect within the limits of statistical probability, the distribution of the total population. The significance tests measure the extent to which this sample differs from this expected distribution.

11. Note, also, that the fact that the entire class is treated as the total population from which the "exposed" sample is drawn means that the slightly higher scores of students in the sample are included in the base making up the average of the whole class. If we had omitted them, thus, in effect, comparing the "exposed" students with the rest, the difference might have been great enough to be statistically significant. But we wished to avoid the assumption that students not in our sample were, in fact, not exposed to the assignments.

Chapter IV
Analysis of Library Competence
Introduction

Librarians have long been dissatisfied with the standard pencil-and-paper tests of library knowledge and skill. Certainly such tests seemed inadequate as instruments to measure the subtle and complex qualities involved in the high-level library competence we hoped ultimately to develop in Monteith students. Our proposal stated that the pilot project would attempt to produce a series of instruments, such as observation schedules and tests, for evaluating student attainment of library understanding and competence,[1] and we knew that estimation of the success of any instructional program the project produced would, in the last analysis, rest upon the validity and persuasiveness of its measures of student achievement. We decided that a reasonable way to begin experimenting with measuring instruments was with a small sample of our students.

A small sample study appealed to us from another point of view as well. We were interested in studying the relationship between the library program and the student's total educational experience at Monteith, the impact of the program on his experience as well as the impact of his experience on his attainment of library competence. And yet, the difficulty of studying this two-way relationship suggested that we might try to get at a large number of variables by limiting ourselves to intensive scrutiny of a small number of students. Our plan for this scrutiny--it would be pretentious to call it a "research design"--involved three aspects:

Background	Monteith library experiences:	Library competence:
capacity or aptitude	courses,	
family characteristics	faculty,	
library experiences,	library assignments	
school and public	(other college experiences)	
attitudes		

Library competence, in the right hand column, we understood as being still in process of definition. Monteith library experiences, in the middle column, we thought of as including whatever variables we might uncover relating to exposure to particular project assignments--administration of assignments, perception of instructors' attitudes toward assignments, nature and quality of experience in the library, etc.--which could be considered as influencing the impact of the library project on any individual student. Background, in the left-hand column, we thought of as including those variables in the student's aptitude and pre-college experience which might be associated with more or less susceptibility to the library experiences of the program. In other words, we thought we might consider the student as individually sensitized by his background to respond in a particular way to the program he experiences, and the program itself as varying from student to student, because of differences among instructors and through time. The plan was frankly exploratory, seeking to identify three sets of variables at the same time that it studied the relationships among them. We hoped this weakness might be offset by the intensiveness of our study and by the strict randomness of our sample. [2]

For quantitative analysis of the data from the sample studies we used nonparametric statistics. [3] Such measures are suitable for use with small samples. They make few assumptions about the population from which the samples are drawn and they may be applied to attributes which are merely classified or ranked rather than exactly measured. We did not expect to produce conclusive evidence on the association among the many variables we were interested in, but we did hope to find clues suggesting fruitful lines of future analysis.

Two small sample studies. --In June, 1961, between the Spring and Summer terms, we hired twenty-one Monteith students to perform various library tests, to provide information on their background, and to take certain written tests. We paid the students so that they would not feel exploited, and set the rate high enough

(25 dollars for two six-hour days) to be appealing to all students,
the cooperative and the uncooperative alike, the well-off as well
as the poor. (We were refused by only one of the students in the
original sample drawn on the basis of a table of random numbers.)
The experiment was carried on in the Wayne State University
Library where we could supervise the various library performance
tests, the written tests, and the interviews, all carefully scheduled
to avoid congestion and to provide for individual interviewing by a
limited number of interviewers.

The second study, conducted between Spring and Summer
terms, 1962, we handled in cooperation with the Monteith Program
Study,[4] using the same sample of students and some of the same
intelligence and projective tests. The experimental group consisted
of a randomly selected sample of thirty. To these we added another
ten students selected randomly from three rosters representing
students who had completed every library assignment in their appropriate class sequence and on whom our assignment data were
complete.[5]

Defining and Measuring Library Competence

Rationale for the Library Performance Tasks. --The standard
paper-and-pencil tests of library knowledge measure only such
elementary processes as those involved in interpreting the information on a catalog card, selecting a fairly obvious subject heading
to fit a fairly commonplace topic, interpreting the information in the
entry in a periodical index, selecting an appropriate reference book
for an elementary factual reference question, and translating common
bibliographical abbreviations. We were convinced that really skill-
ful use of the library involved much more than this, but, at the
same time, we were aware that we were a long way from being
able to identify the elements in a more advanced level of library
use and to perceive or describe the relationship among these elements which might constitute a search strategy. The performance
tests designed were the result of careful reflection on our own experience as librarians and on our understanding of the nature of the
bibliographical apparatus of the library. We were aware of the

limitations of our experience and of the fact that the bibliographical apparatus of the library is not entirely rational, complete, or unified. We felt justified, nevertheless, in beginning with the assumption that tasks emerging from such reflection--and, of course, from many hours of discussion--were valid. The standard of performance on each test was set by having "experts" do the same tasks. These experts were professional librarians, faculty members, and graduate students. The total group was not used for each test, but the raters for any one test included more than one category. Standards of performance, then, became a composite of the performance of the expert raters. Where there was serious disagreement among the raters, the item was dropped from the test.

Finding entries in the card catalog and in the periodical index.-- In one test, students were required to find specific entries in the card catalog, recording the steps they took in moving from one entry to another by indicating the number of the drawer in which they found each. In each case the object of the search was stated differently from the "proper" catalog entry. The "distance" between the stated object of the search and the correct answer varied to provide a range of difficulty from, for example, the simple problem of following a cross-reference or finding one's way from a non-hyphenated word to a hyphenated word to the quite difficult task of following a logical organization of ideas from the general to the specific. The whole set of questions was designed to call for various kinds of thinking involved in the catalog search, such as:

1. alertness to cross references

    e. g. Tchaikovsky to Chaikovskii

2. flexibility or ingenuity in the use of clues

    e. g. De Tocqueville (entered under Tocqueville), bee-keeping, entered under BEEKEEPING

3. ability to translate from one framework to another

    e. g. A novel about the "forty-niners," entered under CALIFORNIA - GOLD DISCOVERIES

4. sense of order and organization

e. g. a study of Shakespeare's use of national characteristics, entered under SHAKESPEARE - CHARACTERS,
where this heading is to be found within a fairly complex
organization (first drawer: the Works: second drawer:
SHAKESPEARE (ABOUT); within the second drawer, sub-
headings alphabetically arranged, with guide cards)

5. sense of rank (level of generality)

e. g. information on the physiology of rage, entered under
EMOTIONS with a "see also" reference from PHYSIOLOGY
to perhaps twenty-odd terms, including EMOTIONS.

We imposed a time limit on the test to put a premium on
rapid decision-making.   The efficient user of the catalog does not
plow doggedly through hundreds of cards; rather, he constantly
estimates and reestimates the probability of success in each search
tactic, basing his estimates on the kinds of books he finds listed
under any given heading, on the organization of sub-headings, etc.
--and moves, in accordance with these odds, quickly from one
tactic to another.

A set of questions directed toward a volume of the Education
Index involved a similar range of difficulty and called upon similar
kinds of thinking.

Selecting entries in the card catalog. --Too often it is assumed
that the user's difficulties with the card catalog are over as soon
as he finds the "proper" entry for the topic he wants, and yet we
all know that in any large catalog, the titles entered under a given
subject heading can number into the hundreds.   The efficient catalog user, we believe, is alert to clues which help him select likely
prospects for his purpose.   To measure the student's alertness and
discrimination in the use of such clues as publisher, date, and
bibliographical notes for estimating the probable worth of particular
titles, we designed a test which directed him to select, for a
hypothetical term paper topic, a specified number of titles entered
under two "voluminous" headings.   He was asked, further, to
designate his reasons for making each selection.

Using surface clues to evaluate books. --Our first library

assignment, the so-called "pretest" assignment (See Appendix I, p. 147-153) had left students to rely largely on their own resources to find materials for the freshman research project. As a result, we had received many complaints from the faculty about the quality of the references in the students' bibliographies. The instructors were convinced that students were incapable of judging sources of information, that they must be told what to read. This conviction was, of course, a serious obstacle to our program. We designed a task, therefore, which we hoped would measure students' sensitivity to surface criteria and thus help us understand how students select books from the open shelves. Each student in the sample was given one hour and a half to rate twenty books as good, fairly good, fairly bad, or bad, and to state in each case his reasons for the rating. The books, all in the general area of psychology, ranged from rather sensational self-help to highly technical reports on research.

A skilled library user, or a practiced reader, for that matter, has learned to pay attention to date, publisher, qualifications of the author, footnotes, bibliography, and other such surface criteria whenever he "sizes up" a book. He certainly does not let any final evaluation of a book rest upon such dubious criteria of real worth, but his choice from the open shelves of books deserving more thorough examination usually stems from rapid, automatic application of these criteria. The student's efficiency in the use of open shelves particularly in a large university library, is, in large measure, dependent upon his awareness of these surface criteria and upon his ability to use them with speed and judgment.

Using the annotated bibliography. --One of the tests required the student to identify books which might be expected to provide specified kinds of information about a particular discipline, in this case, architecture. For this purpose he used, primarily, Winchell's Guide to Reference Books, and its supplements, although a few questions directed him to Ulrich's Guide to Periodical Literature, the Standard Catalog for Public Libraries, and Hoffman's Bookman's Manual. We wanted to see the extent to which the student

perceived the relationship between one discipline and another--ar-
chitecture as a part of art, for example--and applied this understanding in using a bibliography whose organization reflects this
relationship. We also wanted to find out how effectively he could
use annotations--noting, for example, whether a given biographical
directory was limited to living persons or whether a given bibliography included American publications.

The skilled library user is alert to the scope and organization of a reference book; he is quick to relate the information given
in annotations to his own purposes and needs. The reference tools
used in this task, however, are usually not familiar to the library
patron, no matter how skilled he may be; they are, on the other
hand, the tools most relied upon by librarians. The magic in the
librarian's trade, if there is any, lies not in his ability to find the
answer but in his ability to suggest a likely place to look for it.
For this purpose, there is scarcely a better source than Winchell.
Using the four tools offered for this test, one can assemble a fairly
creditable "guide to the literature" of almost any subject field. The
questions we gave our students were, in fact, so structured that
the books listed for the answers comprised, in effect, a rough and
very brief guide to the literature of architecture. The student's
perception of this total product of his work was to be measured
not in this task but in the next one, described below.

Developing a "search strategy". --When the student had finished all the other tasks, we asked him to prepare a bibliography
of not more than twelve items, "the most important discussions...
in the sense that they provide what a non-specialist would need to
read in order to acquire a reasonably adequate grasp of the topic"
on the subject, "cooperative cataloging." The topic was one which
we could be reasonably certain was not familiar to the student; we
knew that the entries in the card catalog would not provide the
answer; and we found that entries in Library Literature were not
selective enough to provide a good current bibliography. We wanted
to see what kinds of procedures each student would employ when
the habitual approaches, through the card catalog and a periodical

index, were not fruitful. We hoped that some students might
generalize from their experience with Winchell[6] or, at least, that
we would be able to discern a logical pattern in their procedures.

The results of the work of our first experimental sample
taught us that such expectations were not justified, and we dropped
this test from the battery we gave to the second sample.[7] We
persist in the belief, however, that the skilled library user should
have grasped the concept of the "structure of the literature" of a
subject. He should understand that every field is provided, to a
greater or lesser degree, with sources of organized information
about terms and concepts, ideas and methods, about people, places,
and times, with indexes and abstracts, and with bibliographies,
comprehensive and selective, annotated and unannotated, classified
and unclassified. And he should be capable of using this knowledge
to find his way about in the literature of a subject, even though he
is unfamiliar with the field. In other words, we are still convinced
that our expectations for this test were disappointed not because the
test itself provided an invalid measure, but because the level of
library competence it attempted to measure was so high. This
level of competence is not just "picked up" by the bright student.
It must be taught. If we really mean what we say when we expect
college to "provide the student with the capacity for continuing self-
education," moreover, library skills should be taught at the undergraduate level. [8]

Analysis of the data on library performance. --From our first
sample we learned that the performance tests were operationally
feasible and that, of the six tests given, five had produced a distribution of scores which followed a fairly normal curve. As expected, the scores of the second sample were similarly distributed. [9]

We used the Kendall Coefficient of Concordance to learn the
extent to which the tests as a group seemed to measure the same or
related qualities. The coefficient was .401 for the first sample
and .339 for the second sample, both significant at the $p < 01$ level.
The coefficient we judged high enough to justify the use of an average rank on all five tests as a composite score for computation of

rank order correlations with the "background" factors discussed
in the next section.

Since the inter-test relationship was not extremely high, however, we used the Friedman Two-Way Analysis of Variance as a
further check.   The result was a x_r2 of 7.48, which, with 4df shows
a p between the .20 and .10 levels (p = .10 with x^2 7.78, p = .20
with x^2 5.59).   Clearly the significance level is too low to justify
rejection of the null hypothesis that the difference in individual
tests produces a difference in performance.   On the other hand, it
is high enough to justify further investigation.

As a step in this direction we compared our performance tests
with the Library Orientation Test for College Freshmen.[10]   Rankings on this test correlated with those on the average ranks for the
five performance tests with a coefficient of .333, significant at the
p $<$.0055 level.   Using the Kendall partial rank correlation coefficient T_{xyz} we next measured the association between these rankings, holding constant the student's rank on reading comprehension,
our best measure of scholastic aptitude.   The coefficient was .305,
only slightly less, which suggests that the association is little influenced by general scholastic aptitude.

We fully expected to find a degree of association between our
performance tests and a standard paper-and-pencil test of library
knowledge and skills.   But since the association seemed to be far
from perfect and since the performance tests were deliberately
planned to measure skills quite distinct from those measured by
the usual standard tests, we computed the correlation between the
Library Orientation Test and each of our five performance tests
separately.   The results were as follows:

Book evaluation test	(see p. p. 66-67): = T. 02
Catalog selection test	(see p. 66): = T. 26
	significant (p = .0228)
Catalog finding test	(see p. 65-66): = T. 15
	not significant (p = .15)
Periodical Index test	(see p. 66): = T .29
	significant (p = .0113)
Annotated bibliography test	(see p. 67-68): = T .43
	highly significant (p = .0005)

The fact that the <u>Library Orientation Test</u> showed a lower correlation with all but one of the five performance tests than it did with the composite scores on all five is probably the effect of regression. Note, further, that of the five performance tests, only the book evaluation test shows no correlation whatsoever and that this test alone was directly related to a particular assignment. [11]

The book evaluation test scores of the 19 freshmen and juniors, who had not been exposed to the assignment, were spread fairly evenly over the whole range.   Of the 11 sophomores in the sample 6 had actually done the assignment, 5 had not.   Of the 6 who had done the assignment:

>4 scored high
>2 scored in the medium range
>0 scored low

Of the 5 who had not done the assignment:

>1 scored high
>2 scored in the medium range
>2 scored low

The one high scorer in this second group was in a sample of students interviewed as part of the analysis of this assignment. (See Appendix I, p. 175).   The other four may or may not have been present when the assignment was discussed in class. This evidence suggests that not all college students have acquired the knowledge and skill involved in rapid evaluation of books, <u>and</u> that those who have not do, in fact, profit from direct training.

<u>Conclusions from the performance tests</u>. --Our exploratory analysis of the library performance tests supported our initial contention that a complex array of knowledge and skills is involved in library competence and that this complexity would profit from more intensive analysis than it has had heretofore. The correlation between the composite scores on these tests and the <u>Library Orientation Test</u> indicates that use of such a standard paper-and-pencil test is justified, because it is inexpensive and easy to administer, wherever a gross measure of fairly elementary library knowledge and skill is all that is required. It is not adequate as a measure of the elements in high-level competence; it is likely to be of little use as a measure of the effectiveness of specific learning

experiences designed to produce such competence.

Performance tests of the sort we used are feasible. They show considerable promise as tools to be used in further investigation of the nature of library competence, in the development of learning experiences designed to foster it, and in the study of the factors involved in its attainment.

Library Performance and Background Factors

The performance tests and student "capacity." --In addition to scores on the usual entrance examinations, we had for most of the students scores on a battery of intelligence and personality tests given by the Monteith Program Study. One additional instrument, the Terman Concept Mastery Test was given to the first sample. This test was recommended to us by Mr. Gabriel Breton, psychologist member of the Monteith Science of Society Division, when we asked for a test which would provide some measure of the student's ability to make a quick decision about the probable fruitfulness of a particular line of inquiry and his flexibility in moving to another line when the odds seemed to be against the one he had been pursuing. (Unfortunately we do not have scores on this test for the second sample.) Table 13 presents Kendall rank order coefficients for the association between all of these tests and the library performance tests.

Note that the Terman Test shows the highest correlation, thus supporting our hunch that this particular kind of mental ability might be especially relevant to efficient library use. This test should be used in future investigations of this sort.

Where we have scores for both samples, they are consistent-- with one notable exception. The high coefficient for the first sample on the Originality Score of the Omnibus Personality Inventory is at odds with the very low coefficient for the second sample. Perhaps the looser administration of the first panel gave students with higher "originality" scores greater scope to use this quality of mind. Or perhaps these students were particularly susceptible to the "halo" effect, mentioned above,[12] resulting from the briefing sessions provided for the first group but not for the second. Such speculations, too, deserve further investigation.

Table 13

Correlation Between Library Performance
Tests and Student "Capacity"

TEST	KENDALL τ	SIGNIFICANT AT p
Terman Concept Mastery Test		
First panel	.515	.0008
Second panel (test not given)		
Reading Comprehension		
First panel	.353	.0132
Second panel	.355	.0034
Grade Point Average		
First panel	.358	.0104
Second panel	.247	.0281
Omnibus Personality Inventory		
(Originality Score)		
First panel	.442	.0107
Second panel	.193	.1401
Omnibus Personality Inventory		
(Thinking Introversion Score)		
First panel	.377	.0250
Second panel	.339	.0262
Test of Critical Thinking		
First panel	.345	.0314
Second panel	.381	.0139
Reading speed		
First panel	.210	.0968
Second panel	.204	.0571

The discrepancy between the sample groups on the coefficients
for grade point average is probably also large enough to justify
comment. The probable explanation is that grades tend to level
out with the passage of time. The spread is likely to be more for
a sample of freshmen and sophomores than for a sample which includes juniors as well. At any rate, grade point average is rather
a measure of achievement than "capacity," and is, therefore, less
relevant to our present concern than the tests listed.

The correlation between reading speed, and the performance
tests was unexpectedly low. Quite possibly a higher coefficient

would result from computation of the association between reading
speed and certain individual performance tests, particularly that
calling for rapid evaluation of books.

The performance tests and other "background" measures. --
To provide data on his pre-college educational and library experiences, his educational interests and goals, and his family background, each student in the two samples filled out a lengthy questionnaire.   From the responses we developed for each student a
"home bookishness" score and a "pre-college library experience"
score.   The former was intended to reflect the quality and quantity
of books and reading in the student's home.   The latter attempted
to reflect the extent and depth of his experiences with school and
public libraries before college.   We found no correlation between
the rankings on these scores and the composite ranking on the library performance tests or on our measure of the student response
to library experiences in college, discussed below.   A correlation
of τ = 1.47, significant at the level, p = .708, indicated a possible
association between rank on "home bookishness" and rank on the
book evaluation test.   This possibility should be pursued probably
through a more carefully designed questionnaire.   Although we found
no similar correlations to encourage further exploration of the possible association between the student's pre-college library experience
and his response to library work in college, we are still convinced
that an improved questionnaire, supplemented by information from
other sources, might be fruitful.   We should like to know, for instance, if the student's response and performance varies with the
quality of the library program in the high school attended.[13]

We used a word-association projective test in an attempt to get
data on the student's perception of the library -- e.g. as a source of
information or as a source of enjoyment, as a complex organization
or as a warehouse, as related to educational processes or as a
place of busy-work drudgery.   This test, at least in the form we
had devised, proved to be too subtle for our purposes.   Probably
there is too little emotional weight carried in the terms used to describe aspects of the library to justify use of this sort of instrument.

Another projective test was designed to find out how the student perceived his instructors' aims and standards. This was a cartoon completion projective which showed an instructor saying to a student: "To do a good job on this assignment you should. . ." Our respondents were asked to complete the sentence for each instructor they had had in any course segment in which there was a library assignment. Results from this projective were interesting. Out of 177 responses, only 30 mentioned the library, sources of information or data, or books or reading - other than the course syllabi. Matters of form, spelling, etc. were more frequently mentioned. Out of 29 instructors, 23 were perceived by at least one student as likely to refer to such mechanical factors. Although the number of cartoons for any one instructor was too small for statistical analysis, we concluded that the instrument might be useful with a larger number of respondents.

Student response to the Monteith Library Program. --The middle column of the chart on p. 62 lists, under the heading "Monteith Library Experiences, " a number of variables we planned to examine in the sample studies. The data were gathered for the first group through interviews and for the second group through questionnaires. Each student was queried about his experiences with those sections of his Monteith courses in which he had had library assignments. He was asked about what he remembered of what he actually did for each assignment, about his impressions of his instructor's evaluation of the library component of various assignments, about his own estimate of the value of his library experiences, and about his view of the impact of the library program in general on his own work. From the questionnaires we developed a very crude score reflecting the percentage of assignments on which the student had a high "response" to assignments in comparison to his classmates. The student's rank on this score showed no association with his rank on the "background" rankings described above nor with his average rank on the performance tests. (A computation based on grouped data, i. e. high, middle, and low groups for each measure, resulted in a x^2 of 6.56, which with 2df indicates a p between .10 and .20.) From this we have conluded, first, that we were mistaken in our attempt

to develop a single "response" score out of several variables such
as "understanding the assignment, " "seeing value in the assignment, " "enjoying the assignment, " etc. Such reactions must be
considered individually. Second, we concluded, data of this sort are
much more likely to emerge from interviews than from questionnaires. The interviewer need not let a question remain unanswered
or an ambiguous answer stand. And third, the sheer number of
variables in this category of our analysis simply overwhelmed the
small number of students in the samples.

The last point deserves further comment. The second sample
consisted of 30 students. These students were divided among the
three sequence-of-assignment groups, [14] and, similarly, they were
subject to the influence of the three stages of development in the
social structure of the library project, described in Chapter II.
Their library assignments were presented in discussion sections
scattered among 23 different instructors. These three variables are
the most easily identifiable of the factors which probably influenced
student response to the library program and, among them, there
was certainly a degree of interaction. [15] It is no wonder that we
were unable to find statistical evidence of their association with the
other categories of our analysis.

Nevertheless, we expect future panel studies to yield data on
these matters worthy of statistical analysis. Our chief reason for
this expectation lies in the fact that the program we propose for the
future provides for greater uniformity in the assignment sequence
each student will have and for closer control over administration of
assignments. In essence, we expect the variables to be fewer and
certain of them to be less powerful as our program moves from a
stage of pioneering to a stage of frontier settlement.

Conclusions From the Sample Studies

The sample studies served admirably their primary purpose
of providing the opportunity to experiment with measures of library
competence. Indeed, the tests used with both samples produced
consistent results indicating a satisfactory degree of reliability.
Even the tests which were not successful in this sense were

productive because they revealed levels of library competence which are so far beyond the student's normal experience that we can expect no measurable performance unless previous training is provided. And, finally, the evidence from the one test which closely paralleled an assignment indicates that performance reflects the impact of specific learning experiences.

Our attempt to study the effect of "background" factors and "response" to assignments through the sample studies was less successful. Yet there were values here too. We learned something of the advantages and limitations of various kinds of instruments and procedures for the kind of research we were attempting. We are more certain about what kinds of information can be gathered from questionnaires, what kinds only from interviews, and what kinds have doubtful relevance in any case. The evidence on the association between the performance tests and measures of student "capacity" supports our hunches that high-level library competence calls upon a wide range of knowledge and skills and that it probably involves a particular kind of mental quality. Further testing of such hunches should be facilitated by small sample studies in the context of a less fluid situation.

Notes

1. Proposal, p. 8.

2. Another obvious weakness of the plan is that it suggests a commonly made, but nonetheless dubious, inference from "effect" to "cause."

3. Discussion of the measures used can be found in Sidney Siegel, Nonparametric Statistics for the Behavioral Sciences (New York: McGraw Hill, 1956).

4. Project No. 1455, Cooperative Research Branch, Office of Education, Department of Health, Education, and Welfare.

5. For each Monteith class, the sequence of library assignments differed; some students failed to complete every assignment; some faculty members failed to transmit questionnaires or reports for every student. We were concerned that at least some of the students scrutinized carefully in the experiment be those who we could be sure had experienced the full sequence provided for their respective classes. Our statistical analyses were applied almost exclusively to data pertaining to the

random sample of thirty.

6. Winchell, in fact, provides the clue to the "ideal" procedure in
    this case. The second supplement lists the <u>American Library
    Annual</u>, the most recent of which, in turn, listed "outstanding
    books of the year, " among them a volume on cataloging in the
    "State of the Art" series, which, again in turn, has a chapter
    which provides a bibliographical review on cooperative cata-
    loging.

7. In the second experiment, we used the ten students on whom
    our assignment data were complete to try another approach to
    this problem. We were not able to analyze the results of this
    approach in time for reporting here, but the design may be of
    sufficient merit to justify a brief description: We assembled
    two collections of books, mostly bibliographies and indexes, one
    in the field of education, the other in English literature. First,
    five students were assigned to each collection and told to pre-
    pare a brief annotation on each book in it. Second, they were
    sent to another room and were told to use their own annotations
    as the basis for indicating the most likely source for the an-
    swers to certain hypothetical questions. Third, each group pre-
    pared annotations on the other collection, and, again, used these
    annotations to answer questions posed. We proposed to analyze
    the four sets of annotations to see if the differences reflected
    the experience of answering the hypothetical questions or if they
    merely reflected the differences in the organization of the two
    fields, as reflected in the two sets of books. Finally both sets
    of students prepared annotations on a collection of books in
    library science, ranked these annotations in order of their an-
    ticipated usefulness for the preparation of a bibliography on an
    unidentified topic in that field, and then, using the books rather
    than their annotations, prepared a bibliography on the topic now
    identified as "cooperative cataloging. " We proposed to analyze
    the students' performance on these last steps in terms of the
    skill and learning revealed in the earlier steps.

8. Note that the model program presented in Chapter V includes
    assignments designed to produce this level of competence.

9. Since essentially the same set of performance tests was given
    to the two samples we expected their scores to be parallel. We
    found, however, that the first group achieved higher average
    scores than the second, though the range was the same for
    both. Two of the tests had been revised to remove ambiguities
    we had discovered or to provide more specific directions. But
    the lower scores appeared not so much in the revised tests as
    in those which had not been revised at all. Two factors seem
    to account for the difference. First, we were able to maintain
    stricter control of time limits on individual tests with the
    second group, because our experience had taught us how to
    avoid certain administrative problems. Second, we did not
    provide the second sample with any briefing. We had divided

the first sample into three groups in order to study the effect of different kinds of briefing upon their performance. One group was instructed only as to the "rules of the game," how they had been chosen, when they would be paid, where they were to be when, who would be supervising each test, etc. The second group was given, also, a short, fairly theoretical talk on the library as a complex organization of bibliographical resources. The third group was given a longer talk in which the theoretical presentation was illustrated with a very few concrete examples of problems paralleling those posed by the tests. Because there was no significant difference in the performance of the three groups of the first sample, we simply dropped the briefing session with the second. We are now convinced that, regardless of the content of the briefing, the briefing itself produced a "halo" effect on the performance of the first sample. This conviction is supported not only by the scores they achieved but also by our impression of an esprit de corps which seemed to be lacking in the second sample.

In spite of the difference in average score between the two, however, we found that the rankings were similarly correlated with other attributes of the students. We computed these correlations for both samples where our data were complete for both, though we feel more certain of the performance scores of the second sample.

10. Lorene T. Feagley, A Library Orientation Test for College Freshmen (New York: Columbia University Press, 1955).

11. See Appendix I, p. 173-176, for a discussion of this assignment.

12. See note 9 above.

13. The rating of Detroit high schools used in the analysis in Chapter III (p. 55-56) was developed by the Monteith Program Study after the analysis reported in this chapter had been completed.

14. See Chapter III, p. 44.

15. It is interesting to note, in this connection, the lack of significant differentation among the three classes in performance on the library tests. The Friedman Two-Way Analysis of Variance result was $x^2 = 3.70$, significant at a level between $p = .10$ and $p = .20$ ($x^2 = 3.22$, with $p = .20$, 4.60, with $p = .10$, with 2 df). Did the freshmen do as well as the juniors because their assignments, though fewer, were better, more carefully planned and more uniformly executed?

Chapter V

Teaching the College Student to Find His "Way"
in the Library

We are now prepared to present a model program of instruction in the use of the library.   The program consists of a sequence of ten assignments coordinated with a four-year curriculum   in general, liberal education.   Although the sequence is designed specifically for the Monteith curriculum it presents a view of the library which is appropriate for any undergraduate liberal education program.   The assignments are planned to accommodate classes of up to 500 and a college population of 1200, but they can be adapted for use with even larger enrollments and, of course, with smaller ones.   Furthermore the program illustrates what we have learned from our experience with the pilot project about library-faculty relationships in the social structure of the college, about the nature of library competence appropriate for college work, and about methods of planning, preparing, conducting, and evaluating library instruction.   All of this, we are convinced, is relevant wherever there is concern for the role of the library in higher education.

This chapter presents, first, a discussion of the theoretical framework for our program; second, a review of the sequence as a whole and of the criteria it is intended to meet; third, an examination of the objectives and implementation of each assignment in the sequence, and   finally, plans for administration and appraisal of the program.

The Idea of the "Way"

Perhaps the most gratifying outcome of our work with the Monteith pilot project was an idea for a theoretical framework for college instruction in the use of the library.   Our work had begun with the assumption that the obvious ineffectiveness of traditional library instruction was due to its isolation in orientation courses, in the freshman English course, and in the occasional bibliography

course for the subject major.   We saw our fundamental problem as
that of designing library experiences which would be functionally related to "content" courses.   We were naturally concerned that these
library experiences have a unity and coherence of their own, but
we did not at first see this as a major problem.   We assumed that
the customary organization of the library unit in freshmen English,
for instance, could be applied to a series of library assignments
spread over a number of courses and over a considerable period
of time and that the unity and coherence in such organization would
be self-evident.   In recognition of the growing knowledge and maturity of the student, we thought that the assignments might well
be graded as to difficulty, but, for the rest, we were content to
place particular assignments wherever they might fit with reasonable comfort in any part of any course.

As we planned the program, however, and especially, as we
tried to convince the faculty of the existence of something we called
"sophisticated library competence,' we became painfully conscious
of the lack of conceptual unity in an organization which consists of
an introduction to the classification, to the card catalog, and to
certain "important" reference books of certain types, such as
bibliographies, indexes, encyclopedias, and dictionaries, these
types brought together, at best, within larger classifications of
"general" and "special" or "direct" and "indirect."   As we developed assignments in response to students' evident needs, we became
aware, furthermore, that these basic reference sources constitute
just one facet of the bibliographic organization which the library
encompasses.   Another facet, and one of crucial importance in the
academic world, is the organization of scholarly communication.

We have concluded, therefore, that library instruction at the
college level must stem from a unifying theoretical concept of the
library and from one which embraces the bibliographic organization
of scholarship.

The unifying concept we propose is one which centers on the
intellectual processes involved in retrieval of information and ideas
from the highly complex system our society uses to organize its

stored records. But this is the language of the documentalists,
the information theorists. To express the idea in English, we have
settled on a simple metaphor: our program is designed to teach the
student the library as a system of "ways. " We use the term "way"
because it implies both "path" and "method. " Anyone who uses the
library must select a "path-way. " The "path-way, " if it is to be
appropriate, depends, first, on where he is, i. e., what information
he brings to his search. The scholar has the information which
makes it possible for him to use an exhaustive bibliography effectively; the beginner is bewildered by it. The "path-way" depends,
second, on where the library user wants to go, i. e., what is the
object of his search. Neither the scholar nor the beginner should
select the same "way" to find "a good book on... " that he would
select to find "the latest report on... "

   The term "way" in the sense of "method" implies knowledge
and understanding of the interlocking organization of the library
and scholarly communication. Whoever would use the system must
know the "way" to use the system. Knowing the way means understanding the nature of the total system, knowing where to plug into
it, knowing how to make it work.

   The system of the library embraces both library organization,
i. e., what we think of as library tools (typically the tools developed
by libraries, by librarians and by library service organizations),
and the networks of scholarly communication. The two are not
identical, and yet they are so intertwined in the library itself and
in professional library training that it is hard to see the difference
unless one points to extremes. In an ideal-typical sense, then, the
library is organized primarily on the basis of subject; scholarship
is organized on the basis of discipline. (The librarian is likely to
classify Weber's The Protestant Ethic and the Spirit of Capitalism
as a book about religion rather than as a work of sociology.) Library organization is a relatively closed system into which each new
item must be fitted; the organization of scholarship is an open
system, growing out of functional needs as they develop. The library stresses permanent relationships; scholarship, particularly

modern scholarship, can shift and change on an ad hoc basis to
accommodate new specializations, interdisciplinary collaboration,
discussions which cut across several subjects or several disciplines to focus on method, or concept, or place, or time. (The
librarian is left to puzzle over the proper classification for a book
on biomathematics, the number of analytics needed in the card catalog for a symposium on motivation, the entry in a bibliography for
a phonorecord of "Great Moments from the Living Stage. ") Library
organization rests upon a few types of tools to which every user
must adapt; the literature of scholarship produces any number of
tools to suit various levels of scholarship and various functions of
scholarly communication. (Contrast the classification, the card
catalog, the periodical index, the union list, on the one side, with
the "guide to the literature, " the "state of the art" bibliographical
review, the abstract service, the professional news bulletin, on the
other.)

Knowing the way to use the library, at least at the college
level, means being able to comprehend such distinctions. It means,
on the one hand, understanding that the nature and degree of bibliographic control characteristic of any discipline is likely to depend
on the maturity of the discipline, the extent to which its work is
cumulative, the economic support society is willing to give it, the
social structure in which its practitioners work. It means appreci-
ating, on the other hand, that there are communication needs and
purposes common to all disciplines. It means knowing and being
able to use the tools of scholarly communication, the tools of library organization, and the tools which connect the two.

The proposed Monteith Library Sequence is designed to teach
the college student to find and use his "way" in the library. The
idea of the "way" can be summed up in the following diagram:

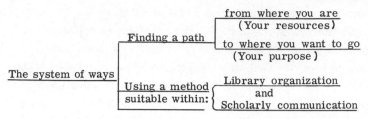

The Sequence of Assignments

Table 14 lists a proposed four-year sequence of library assignments along with the sequence of basic courses in the Monteith
curriculum.   Note that the plan calls for one assignment each quarter through the second quarter of the junior year and an additional
one for the Senior Essay.   In order to reach all Monteith students
and to reach them early, we place most of the assignments in the
Science of Society course sequence.[1]   The learning experiences involved in these assignments, however, and the concepts with which
they deal are relevant to all three fields of the curriculum.   Furthermore, at least one assignment is placed directly in each of the
other basic course sequences, and two assignments vary in accordance with the field of the student's particular ability or interest.

Four of the ten proposed assignments have already been used
in the pilot project, a fifth was used in our bibliographic assistant
training program, and a sixth was tried out in our small sample
studies.   (These six assignments are described more fully in the
chapters dealing with these aspects of our project.)   The other four
have been discussed with members of our faculty, but they have not
been planned in detail.   The stated theme of the assignment is intended merely as a brief indication of what each assignment contributes to the sequence.

In planning the program we set up four criteria:

1.   The sequence must have intrinsic unity and coherence

2.   The total program must be functionally related to the
     curriculum.

3.   Every assignment must have genuine intellectual content.

4.   Every assignment must be practical, that is, it must not
     require extraordinary library services or resources.

Unity and coherence. --The metaphor of the "way" serves as a thread of continuity through the entire sequence. In his first assignment the student learns something of the limitations of the card catalog and the Readers' Guide, two "ways" already familiar to him, and he is introduced to new "ways." The emphasis here is on finding a "way" which will take you where you want to go, perhaps deciding against a familiar way which is inappropriate. In the second assignment he again experiences the limitations of a way with which he is already familiar, but this time the stress is on finding the way from where you are, i.e., the knowledge and judgment you need to bring when you use the open shelves.

The third assignment introduces an alternative way. The student is exposed to the literature of research through the experience of using one of the most valuable of the bibliographical tools of scholarship. In the fourth assignment he uses the various reference, as distinguished from bibliographical, tools of scholarship.

Up to this point the student's experiences have been with specific path-ways and specific method-ways. The fifth assignment gives him the opportunity to stand back and view the overall bibliographic apparatus, to see how it works in one discipline. This experience provides the basis for his first assignment (No. 6) as an independent student; he now discovers the way to map out the literature of one discipline in the area he has elected to study independently.

With the seventh assignment common to all students, he again uses sources of data, but this time the sources are in the natural sciences. The eighth assignment introduces him to bibliographic control of scholarship, particularly current scholarship, in the humanities; in the ninth he draws upon the whole heritage of this area.

In the final assignment he can bring everything he has learned in the whole sequence to bear upon a topic of his own choosing. His grasp of the systematic organization of the library will be reflected in his command of "the literature" on this topic.

In short, the sequence as a whole is unified around a view of the library as a system of "ways." It is coherent in that it moves

Table 14
Sequence of Library Assignments for
the Monteith Curriculum

Title of the Assignment	Product of Assignment	Theme of Assignment	Subject of the Host Assignment	Basic Courses in the Curriculum*	Year & Quarter
1. Independence	Answers to questions on "Great Ideas," from card cat., OED, Int. Index, Readers' Guide, Syntopicon	The pluralism of "ways"	Foundations of Society	Sci. of Soc. 131 (Nat. Sci. 131)	Fresh. I
2. Book Evaluation	Preliminary and rapid appraisal of 10 books	The "way" of the open shelf	Case study	Sci. of Soc. 132 (Nat. Sci. 132)	Fresh. II
3. Review of the Literature	Hypothetical research problem and references for it	The org. of the lit. of research	Research Project	Sci. of Soc. 133 (Nat. Sci. 133)	Fresh. III
4. Economic Index	Paper predicting economic growth of one country	Using sources of data in social science	Underdeveloped Areas	Sci. of Soc. 231 (Nat. Sci. 231)	Soph. I
5. Winchell Exercise	List of references on discipline selected from Winchell, Ulrich, etc.	Basic organization of a discipline	Social Movement	Sci. of Soc. 232 (Nat. Sci. 232)	Soph. II
6. Guide to the Literature	Annotated bibliography of standard sources of information on a discipline	A bridge between library org. and org. of discipline	(Independent Study)	Sci. of Soc. 232** Nat. Sci. 233** Hum. Stud. 431**	Soph. II Soph. III Senior I

Table 14 (Continued)

Title of the Assignment	Product of Assignment	Theme of Assignment	Subject of the Host Assignment	Basic Courses in the Curriculum*	Year & Quarter
7. Popular Science	Paper on limitations & distortions of popular presentation of a scientific subject	Sources of data in natural science		Nat. Sci. 233 (Hum. Stud. 231)	Soph. III
8. Bibliog. in the Humanities	Paper evaluating three bibliographic tools in the humanities	Org. of scholarly lit. in humanities	Joyce (or another artist)	Hum. Stud. 331	Junior I
9. Plan of Reading	Proposed reading list for two terms in course	Sources of criticism		Hum. Stud. 332, Hum. Stud. 333, Hum. Stud. 431	Junior II, Junior III, Senior I
10. Bibliographic Review	Bibliographic Review of the literature for two terms in course	Exploration of scholarship in depth		(Senior Colloq.) Senior Essay, (Senior Colloq.) (Senior Essay)	Senior II, Senior III

* No library assignment is scheduled for courses indicated in parentheses.

** Every student is required to take the final segment of at least one of the three courses independently, i.e., without attending classes. We propose a "guide to the literature" assignment for the first term in which he does this.

from one level of organization to another, from one subject field
to another, each assignment contributing to the student's growing
capacity for independent study.

Relationship to the curriculum. --Our original notion that the
ineffectiveness of traditional library instruction is due to its isolation from "content" courses was reinforced by our experience with
the pilot project.   But we are no longer content with the simple
goal of getting the library somehow or other built into such courses.   The relationship is more complicated than we thought.   If it
is to be effective, the library program must be not merely presented in the context of "content" courses, but truly consistent in
goals and methods, in tone and style, with the overall educational
program in which it occurs. An individual assignment may be related to a specific course in either of two ways: a) it can deal
with the content-the ideas or topics under consideration, or b) it
can deal with processes which contribute to the student's ability
to achieve the objectives of the particular assignment with which it
is connected.   In either case, the relationship to that part of the
course in which it occurs must be recognized by both faculty and
students.

More important, the entire sequence must be directed toward
the kind and quality of behavior which the educational program in
whole and in part is designed to produce.   Its style of presentation
must be attuned to theories of learning implicit in the organization
and methods of the curriculum.   Where the emphasis is upon intellectual processes, the library program must not call for the mere
acquisition of facts and skills.   Where the student is encouraged to
question authority, to be able to tolerate ambiguity, the library
must not be presented as the place to find the "right" answer or the
"definitive" source.   Where the empirical approach to learning is
stressed, the student should not be merely told about the library
but should be given the opportunity to experience it.   Where the
method of small group discussion is valued, the library program
must not rely solely on lectures, readings, and audio-visual aids.

Our sequence as a whole and every assignment in it is intended to contribute to Monteith's stated objective of developing the

student's capacity to pursue learning independently. [2]   In addition,
each individual assignment deals with either the content of the
course unit in which it occurs or with processes involved in performance of the host-assignment.   The processes involved in using
the card catalog, the Syntopicon, etc., for the Independence Assignment are not particularly relevant to the Foundations of Society unit.
But the "great ideas" which the student looks up in these tools are
the ideas discussed in class; what he finds in the tools contributes
to the sense of history the unit is intended to convey.   On the other
hand, the bibliographical review assigned the student in the third
quarter of the social sciences course may or may not deal with the
topic or the concept of the research project he plans to work on.
But in doing the assignment, he employs precisely those processes
he should use in preparing for his research project.   Both assignments are justified by their contribution to the student's capacity to
find and use his way in the library, and both assignments are consistent in tone and style with the Monteith program as a whole and
with the specific course segments in which they occur.

     College level instruction. --Most college faculty members see
library instruction as dealing with bits of information, undeniably
useful, but fragmented, not related to any single, coherent framework, not calling for problem-solving behavior, for critical thinking, for imagination.   Most college students see it as sheer high
school busy-work.   Our program is intended to overcome such
objections by, first, presenting a view of the library as a highly
complex system of "ways" to find and use resources, rather than
a storehouse for the conglomerate records of history.   Our unifying
metaphor is designed to convey the sense of a theoretical structure
of communication, a structure in which elements are related to one
another systematically and in accordance with general principles.
Secondly, the program stresses in every individual assignment the
intellectual processes involved.   We have tried in various ways to
present each assignment as a problem to be solved, as an exercise
in judgment, as an illustration of principles, as an opportunity for
creative thinking.

<u>Practicality</u>. --The program we propose presents concepts
and materials which are unprecedented in undergraduate instruction
in the use of the library. It involves exposing a large number of
students to actual experiences with a wide range of library resources. It calls for considerable individual guidance in the early
stages and for small group discussion almost all the way through.
It demands a variety of different approaches so that students may
pursue special interests or make use of special abilities. In spite
of all this, however, our experience with the pilot project has
convinced us that it is entirely manageable.

The descriptions of individual assignments, below, include
discussion of the specific practical problems posed by each and of
the methods we have used or propose to use to cope with them. In
general, however, we can say here that we found that we could
avoid congestion in the library by limiting the time for completion
of an assignment and by spacing the presentation of assignments
among discussion sections over a period of a few weeks. This
scheduling also made it possible for us to provide sufficient individual guidance and to meet with every discussion section. We
avoided strain on library resources by preparing several variations
of each assignment. For the Independence Assignment, for example,
we prepared fifteen sets of about thirty questions to be answered
through five library tools. Each student in a discussion section
had a different set, relating to a different "great idea, " and not
more than five students in a section were referred to any one
volume of, for example, the <u>International Index to Periodicals</u>.
These materials and others, prepared for the pilot project, are
ready for use in our model program. But the more important contribution of the pilot project lies in the fact that it convinced us of
the feasibility of illustrating the same key concepts and processes
with a variety of experiences and materials. This is the <u>practical</u>
virtue of a program which stresses concepts and processes rather
than specific library tools.

The Assignments

<u>The Independence Assignment</u>[3]--This assignment was developed

for the introductory section of the Science of Society course, a section
which included readings from Plato, Rousseau, Thoreau, and
Jefferson and which was intended to focus the student's attention
on the tension between man as a unique individual and man as a
subject and citizen of government. Discussion centered on such
large, abstract ideas as "justice," "liberty," "duty," "independence," and "the state."

Here, it seemed, was an opportunity to complement the
necessary abstraction and generality of the ideas being discussed
with an assignment requiring the use of specific library tools to
locate specific information. For each of fifteen such abstract ideas,
therefore, we prepared, with the help of our bibliographical assistants, a set of questions to be answered through consultation of
the Oxford English Dictionary, the Syntopicon, the card catalog,
the Readers' Guide, and the International Index. For each word-
concept there were about five questions per tool or thirty questions
in all. To serve as a model of the assignment, an essay based on
the word "independence" was printed in the students' book of readings. 4

Besides finding answers to one set of questions, each student
was required to write a page presenting and explaining a metaphor
for his assigned "idea." We hoped, through this device, to keep
the student from focussing too narrowly on the "word." Copying
answers was minimized since each student in a discussion section
worked with a different set of questions. In order to spread the
use of reference tools, we gave the assignment to only six or seven
sections per week, for a series of four weeks, allowing only one
week for completion of the task.

One of the three members of the project staff attended each
discussion section to explain the assignment and to set a two-hour
period, one for each section, when we would be available in the
library to help with the work. When the assignment was completed
we again attended the class, this time to lead a full-hour discussion.
The discussion highlighted two points: one, that there are many
"ways" to get at the resources of the library; and two, that the
choice of a "way" depends upon what resources you want.

The freshman is familiar with two of the tools involved in this assignment, the card catalog and the Readers' Guide, but he is not likely to be aware of their limitations and complexity. In this assignment he experiences the inefficiency of these tools and of the International Index in dealing with abstract ideas and, in contrast, the comparative efficiency of the Oxford English Dictionary and the Syntopicon for the same purpose.

The instructors were pleased with the assignment. The theoretical, systematic view of the library was new to some of them. Most were not accustomed to the view that use of the library calls for problem-solving behavior and inductive reasoning rather than for memory and sheer persistence. The metaphor part of the assignment, in particular, demonstrated the need for original thinking in college work. And, of course, all appreciated the fact that it dealt with the "great ideas" under discussion.

Even with more than 250 students, we found the assignment to be eminently manageable. It was planned so that it required no reference resources beyond those already in the library, and its scheduling provided sufficient time for individual guidance of small group discussion.

The Book Evaluation Assignment. --The open shelves provide the most familiar "way" of getting at the resources of the library. From his pre-college experience with small, selected collections, the freshman is likely to assume that the easiest and pleasantest way to get what he wants in the library is to find out where books in the general field of his topic are shelved and then to browse until he finds something on his specific topic. [5] Sooner or later, however, he discovers that his instructor is not satisfied with references which are simply "something on" the topic. He must learn to discriminate among sources of information, to distinguish between what is merely relevant and what is also valid. Usually he learns to ask his instructor for recommended sources. If he is a serious student, he gradually becomes acquainted with authors and publishers, and he begins to pick up the clues which guide him in the preliminary appraisal of books.

The book evaluation assignment[6] is designed to speed up this

process for the serious student and to make the student who is not
so serious less dependent upon his instructors. After a briefing on
the clues useful for quick evaluation of books, the students are
presented with a simulated open-shelf situation. The experience
demonstrates the hazards of the open shelf "way" to the resources
of the library. It introduces the student to the kinds of information
which can help him to use this way effectively.

In the class discussions following the assignment in the pilot
project, we neither repeated nor supplemented the information provided in the preassignment briefing statement. Instead we led the
students to discuss the kinds of inferences to be made from such
clues as date of publication, qualifications of author, type of publisher, footnotes, and bibliography. We did not expect the student
to acquire specific information about authors, publishers, and the
like, but were content that he should become alert to the significance
of such factors, that he should understand the importance of being
critical in one's use of the open shelf.

Our instructors were astonished at the naivete students revealed in the discussions. The need for training was underlined.
Once again, the faculty respected an approach which stressed critical
thinking rather than knowledge of specific facts and once again, they
appreciated the fact that the books examined dealt with the topic of
the host-assignment.

The assignment passed the feasibility test with ease. Members
of the pilot project staff assembled five sets of ten books. Each set
related to one aspect of the case study being dealt with in the host-
assignment and included examples of old and recent imprints, popular and scholarly publishers, and so on. Using student assistants
as proctors, we gave each student 90 minutes to evaluate one set of
books, again spacing the assignment among discussion sections over
a few weeks to avoid traffic jams and to make it possible for us to
discuss the experience with every class section.

Review of the Literature Assignment.[7] -- The third assignment
takes the freshman from his accustomed "ways" of the card catalog,
the index, and the open shelf and introduces him to the "ways" of
the scholarly world. For a number of reasons, the bibliographic

review serves this purpose admirably. It is the (temporarily) culminating point in the whole network of the communication of scholarly work. Out of the welter of reports and articles and monographs, lists and indexes, abstracts and reviews, it presents a summary which gives some measure of order to the whole. It shows the student that the world of scholarship need be neither overwhelming nor chaotic, that he can, indeed, find his way about in it. It illustrates, furthermore, some of the contrasts between library organization and the organization of scholarship. The bibliographic review may center on a method, a conceptual approach, an interdisciplinary specialization. Usually it brings together and shows the relationship among works which are not brought together in the classification system, the card catalog, or the periodical index. At the same time, it lacks the impersonal objectivity of these library tools. It is selective. It reflects the biases of its author, of his "school," or, perhaps, of the views currently in fashion in his field.

The proposed assignment is a revision of one given in the pilot project. The revised version was used in the second sample study. 8 The student is referred to a particular bibliographical review, as before, but the questions he is asked require him to use it as a take-off for the formulation of a hypothetical research problem and as a source of references pertaining to that problem. The products of the assignment would be harder to evaluate because they would not be uniform, but the experience would be more useful for the student's research project, his principal assignment of the term, and, ultimately, for all of his subsequent work with scholarly literature.

Class discussions should again stress the place of the bibliographic review in the network of scholarship and the differences between scholarly and library organization. But these discussions should consider also the nature of research problems in the social sciences, kinds of evidence, kinds of methods and instruments, and the relevant references supplied by the bibliographic review.

Instructors participated vigorously in discussion of the assignment when it was given. They should be even more interested in

the revised version we propose because it sets precisely the kind
of problem the student faces in developing his own research project
and because it calls for original thinking, thus reiterating the point
made by the metaphor part of the first quarter's assignment. The
discussion should emphasize the inadequacy of any bibliographical
tool as a substitute for hard thinking, the idea that, especially in
research, what has been done is not necessarily what ought to be
done. The change in the assignment would not alter its feasibility.
For the pilot project the library obtained duplicate copies of certain
volumes which contained several reviews. We used xerox copies of
journal articles. All the reviews were placed on short-term loan.
And again we spaced the assignment over several weeks to avoid
congestion and to enable us to meet with every discussion section.

The Economic Index Assignment. --The first sophomore quarter of the social sciences course begins with a unit on "The Economics of Underdeveloped Areas. " Several of the readings are concerned with the various indexes of economic status and growth. The
assignment we propose in connection with this unit requires the student to gather from various sources of national and international
statistics, information pertaining to a country, commonly defined as
underdeveloped. He then plays these figures against his understanding of their limitations, as derived from his readings, and ar-
rives at a prediction of the country's economic development for the
next ten years. The assignment is designed to teach the student
the "way" to use sources of data upon which scholarship draws.

The plan has yet to be worked out in detail and pretested, but
as of now we would recommend that the sources be gathered ahead
of time, so that, in this instance, the student's attention would be
directed solely toward the ways to use such sources. Class discussion could deal with problems of the bibliographical control
through indexes, documents, catalogs, etc.

It should not be difficult to assemble enough sources of data
to give the student a reasonably comprehensive experience of using
sources of this type. We are concerned with the student's having
this experience rather than with the validity of his prediction.

The Winchell Assignment. --Constance Winchell's Guide to Reference Books is without peer as a link between the organization of the library and the organization of scholarship. It is the magic wand the skilled librarian uses to get his bearings in unfamiliar territory. It reflects remarkably well the state of bibliographic organization which specific fields of study have attained.

Library handbooks almost always refer to Winchell and cours- es of instruction in the use of the library always recommend it, but students rarely use it and most faculty members are unaware of its existence. Probably the greater one's mastery of one's own field, the less one is likely to have occasion to use such a primary tool. And yet it is precisely in the process of acquiring mastery of a field that one finds Winchell most useful.

The assignment we propose is the fairly simple one we used in our sample studies. [9] The student is presented with a series of questions which call upon him to identify and select items listed in Winchell, the Bibliographic Index, Ulrich, and perhaps the Standard Catalog for Public Libraries or the new Shaw list, when it becomes available. The list of items thus compiled constitutes the standard, recognized sources of various types of information about a particular discipline.

We think that placement of the assignment in the fifth and final quarter of the social sciences sequence is suitable and we are confident that it would have faculty acceptance, though we have not settled on a way of relating it to the larger concerns of the course. The assignment was originally suggested by instructors who inter- viewed participants in the sample studies. These students had reported their delight with the discovery of Winchell and their re- gret that they had not been introduced to it earlier.

If students are scheduled to use the reference tools, the as- signment can be managed with seven or eight copies of Winchell and three or four copies of the other titles. Use of the Biblio- graphic Index can be spread through several different volumes.

Guide to the Literature Assignment. --Every Monteith student is required to take the final segment of one of the three basic courses on an independent basis. He is not ordinarily permitted to attend classes, though he may attend lectures or listen to tape recordings of them if he wishes. Once he has successfully met this requirement, he is permitted to take any of the following portions of the basic courses independently. In connection with this first required experience in independent study, therefore, we propose an assignment requiring each student to compile an annotated "Guide to the Literature" of one discipline within the area he plans to study independently. The Winchell assignment described above would prepare him for this task. (Students who have elected to meet this independent study requirement during the quarter in which the Winchell assignment is given would be asked to do both.) He is required to perform the assignment in a discipline which is not already equipped with a guide to the literature, but one in which there is at least enough organization to provide the rudimentary beginnings of one. In other words, we want the student to face neither a situation in which his job is done for him, nor a situation in which the job is not doable. When the student is about to embark on his first experience in independent study we think it particularly appropriate that he should begin by getting an overview of the communication needs of one whole subject field whether or not an apparatus for meeting them has yet been developed. He should understand that every discipline has need for tools which define its terms, which identify its past and present practitioners and their associations, which outline its history and development, which report on its current interests, which list, abstract, review, and periodically summarize its publications, which tell its news. He should, in short, see the guide to the literature as a highway map for a field of learning.

Since our bibliographic assistants reported this assignment both challenging and enlightening, we are fairly certain that the faculty would find it acceptable. There should be no difficulty in having sufficient materials in the library because the students are distributed among all three areas of our curriculum. In order to prepare for it, however, we would have to survey the literature of as many disciplines, both traditional and new, as possible in order

to identify those suitable for assignments and in order to set standards for evaluation of student work.

  Popular Science Assignment. --General education in the sciences aims to produce not scientists but men who understand science. Unless he is a scientist, the educated man is not likely to
continue his interest in science by working in a laboratory or even
by reading technical scientific treatises. After he is through college
his contact with science is likely to be through books and articles
written for a lay audience. The generally educated man, the man
who understands science, should understand the distortions and limitations inherent in translation of science for popular consumption.
C. P. Snow is witness that such translation is a key problem link
in the network of communication in science.

  The assignment we propose for the last quarter of the Natural
Sciences sequence addresses itself directly to this problem. The
student is asked to trace the information presented in a popularly
written scientific article back to its sources in technical and scientific publications and to report on the changes that have occurred
in the translation process. The assignment should increase his
critical skill as he becomes aware of these translation difficulties,
and, at the same time, give him a meaningful experience in tracking down scientific information through the bibliographic apparatus
by which it is organized.

  The idea for the assignment came from the member of the
Natural Sciences staff who worked with us during the last term in
which the pilot project was in operation. We have reason to expect
that his colleagues would, in general, support it.

  In planning for this assignment, more than for any of the
rest, we move into new bibliographical territory. We travelled a
short way into that territory in preparing the one assignment we
used with the Natural Sciences sequence in the pilot project.[10] Our
work on the three approaches, 1) through the card catalog, 2)
through periodical indexes, and 3) through references in the student's text, provides a fairly good starting place but considerable
pretesting of topics discussed in specific articles from popular
journals is still needed.

Assignment in the Bibliography of Literature and Art. --As the
student begins his work in the Humanistic Studies sequence, we
direct his attention to the organization of scholarship in literature
and the arts. The course opens with intensive examination of one
work of art. The work is viewed as a reflection of the social
milieu in which it appeared, of the life history of an individual person, of a philosophical point of view, and of a set of aesthetic values.

In the pilot project the library assignment was related to the
consideration of   James Joyce's Portrait of the Artist as a Young
Man. [11] (At another time the work under consideration might be
different, but the library assignment should be essentially the same.)
As an introduction to sources of information and references, we
prepared six sets of three items each, exemplifying:

1.   a comprehensive, unannotated, non-selective bibliography,
     e. g. the card catalog, the Annual Bibliography of English
     Language and Literature.

2.   a source which provides direct information and selective
     but limited bibliography, e. g. an article in a biographical
     directory, or in a bibliographical review such as The
     Dictionary of National Biography, The Years' Work in
     English Studies.

3.   a trade or textbook on the specific subject.

Each student was asked to examine and write a short paper
evaluating one set of three items, comparing them as to comprehensiveness, informativeness, usability, selectivity, potential contribution to such bibliographical purposes as a) exhaustive coverage,
b) general introduction or orientation, and c) sources of information on relatively obscure aspects of the subject.

This assignment can be used to demonstrate interesting contrasts between the organization of the sciences and the organization
of the humanities. In the humanities, more than in the other two
areas, the   resources, the "data, " so to speak, as well as the
results of scholarship are organized in the library. The library
supports the scholarship of the humanities by supplying it with the
novels and plays and poems, the scores and recordings, the prints
and perhaps the slides, to be studied. The bibliographic apparatus

for getting at these resources falls into the category which we have
called library organization, as distinct from the apparatus used to
organize scholarship. Students need to know the way to use both,
but they are more likely to be aware of the former than of the latter.

Scholarship in the humanities contrasts with scholarship in the
sciences, also, in that it is not in the same sense cumulative. The
scholar needs to be in control of the works which are landmarks
in his field, not only for their historical or methodological significance but also for their intrinsic validity and relevance whenever
they may have appeared. Because a work of art is a product of a
person, however, it is an event to be located in time and place.
Time and place are, therefore, more crucial factors in use of the
bibliographic organization in this area. In addition the assignment
provides a particularly vivid demonstration of the notion of the
"way" as a path-way from where you are to where you want to go.
The student is likely to find the individual book or article, with its
selected bibliography, more useful than the comprehensive bibliography. Having examined both, he can see that he might find the
latter more useful if he were a scholar, thoroughly in command of
the literature on the topic and, at the same time, likely to be interested in questions more esoteric than are dealt with in a standard
introductory book or article.

Our experience with the assignment using Joyce as a subject
was easily manageable because the Wayne State University Library
has an excellent collection of Joyceana with multiple copies of many
titles. If another artist were chosen for the subject, the library
might have to acquire duplicate copies of a few titles, but, for the
most part, the assignment relies on bibliographies published in
many volumes so that they can be used by several students at a
time. What is important is that each student have the opportunity
to find out for himself what kind of information the bibliography
presents.

The Reading Plan Assignment. --This assignment, occurring
in the second quarter of the student's junior year, could be something of a milestone marking his progress toward independence.

From the two previous quarters in the Humanities sequence he
would have derived an understanding of the objectives and methods
of the sequence as a whole. At this point he would be provided,
also, with an outline and a schedule of lectures for the rest of the
sequence. Thus prepared, he would be asked to develop his own
list of readings for the remainder of the course and to be prepared
to defend it in consultation with his instructor. He would find it
necessary to draw upon scholarly history and criticism in order to
identify and select outstanding works in literature, art and music
which relate to the ideas to be presented in the course.

The student's previous experience in examining the bibliographic organization of scholarship in the humanities should have prepared
him reasonably well for the assignment. He should at least be
aware of the necessity of selecting a path-way which leads from
what he knows to what he needs to know about the topics which
appear in the course outline. The challenge would be new in that
he would not be referred to particular bibliographies, indexes, etc.
and in that the approach would be from a series of ideas or concepts rather than from particular artists or works of art.

The scheme should provide for some diversity among the students, thus enlivening discussion, but we assume that the instructors
would see that enough of the same titles are selected so that class
discussions would still be fruitful and examinations would not be too
difficult to prepare.

This assignment was proposed by two members of the Humanities staff. It should be hard for their colleagues to resist an assignment which is so precisely related to the course's stated objective of developing the student's interest in and capacity for continued
exploration of his cultural heritage.

Existing library resources should be adequate for the assignment, since the students would use more or less standard historical
and critical works to select the titles on their proposed reading
plans. We expect that most of the titles selected would be available
for purchase as paperbacks, as are most of the readings now
assigned.

    The Bibliographic Review Assignment. --The Monteith

curriculum culminates with the Senior Essay, which has been described as follows:

> The essay is meant for the student to express himself, his
> wisdom, his talent and taste, his intellectual acumen, his
> acquired know-how:
>
> a) in choosing a topic which he deems worthy of prolonged and
>   thorough application;
>
> b) in organizing his approach to it, including background read-
>   ing, conversation with other scholars, experimentation,
>   field work, creative effort, etc.;
>
> c) in expressing his successive intellectual steps, choices, and
>   discoveries, in written form, for examination, reflections
>   and criticism by himself and others;
>
> d) in presenting a final product as polished, honest, and sig-
>   nificant as possible -- something which will be a contribu-
>   tion to the idea and the wealth of Monteith.[12]

With the Senior Essay the student reaches a climax in his
progress toward independence. The library assignment we propose,
therefore, is designed to give him the opportunity to demonstrate
his achievement of one prerequisite of independent study, that is,
his command of the literature on the topic he chooses to pursue.
He would write a review of the literature on this topic. This review would accompany his plans for his own work, and the two together would serve as the basis on which his advisor appraises his
competence to proceed with the essay.

In preparing the bibliographic review the student should find
it necessary to use much of the bibliographic apparatus pertaining
to his topic: the general and special indexes, the abstracts, the
periodic reviews, the summaries of research completed and in
progress. He would need to be acquainted with the classic studies,
the work of the key thinkers in the field. He would have to know
something about pertinent concepts and appropriate methods. His
review should organize all of this in a fashion relevant to his own
plans. It should indicate not only what has been done, but what has
not been done. The assignment thus becomes a culmination of the
whole sequence of library experiences at the same time and in the
same way as it is the culmination of the Monteith curriculum.

The assignment has been heartily endorsed by the chairmen

of the three Monteith divisions. We expect that the faculty would welcome it as an opportunity to review the student's capacity for work at this level before he has invested an inordinate amount of time on the enterprise. The student's comments on the state of the literature on his topic should provide a good indication of his critical abilities and of his grasp of the problems he is likely to face in his own work.

The assignment makes no greater demands on the library than should be made by the Senior Essay itself. In asking the student to write a bibliographic review we are simply asking him to report systematically on the results of his use of materials which he should have used in any case.

Administration of the Program

A six-year period would be necessary for implementation and appraisal of the proposed program at Monteith College. We would devote one year to planning, preparing, and pretesting assignments and instruments for gathering data on the operation and effectiveness of the program. The students enrolled in the College during that year would serve as the population for one trial run of the sequence. The next four years would be needed to enable one entering class to experience the entire sequence, as developed in the pretest year. The sixth year would be devoted to analysis and reporting. Using the Monteith program in effect in 1962 and projected enrollments, Table 15 presents a schedule for administration of the first five years, indicating the quarter segment of each divisional course sequence in which a library assignment occurs, and the estimated enrollment in the class to which it is given. (The table does not show summer quarters, in which Monteith College offers a minimal program. We would use this time primarily for experimental studies, for preliminary analysis of data, and for other such research activities.)

Planning. --Our plan for administration of the proposed sequence reflects certain changes in our thinking which have resulted from our experience with the pilot project. We are now convinced that the librarians cannot, merely by participating in staff

Table 15

Schedule for Administration of Program

Class entering in:	Pre Testing			Quarters of Program											
	9-63	1-64	4-64	9-64	1-65	4-65	9-65	1-66	4-66	9-66	1-67	4-67	9-67	1-68	4-68
1960		E* 100	HIII* 30												
1961	HI 100	HII* 80	NVI 150 (NVI)* 50	HI 135	HII 125	(HIII) 45									
1962	SIV* 190	SV* 170 (SV)* 60	SIII 350	SIV 300	SV 270 (SV) 90	NVI 250 (NVI) 60	HI 225	E 120							
1963	SI 480	SII 390	SIII 350	SI 480	SII 390	SIII 350	SIV 300	HII 210	(HIII) 70		E 200				
1964							SIV 300	SV 270 (SV) 90	NVI 250 (NVI) 60	HI 225	HII 210	HIII 70		E 200	
1965							SI 480	SII 390	SIII 350	SIV 300	SV 270 (SV) 90	NVI 250 (NVI) 60	HI 225	HII 210	(HIII) 70

Table 15 (Continued)

Class entering in:	Pre Testing				Quarters of Program										
	9-63	1-64	4-64	9-64	1-65	4-65	9-65	1-66	4-66	9-66	1-67	4-67	9-67	1-68	4-68
1966										SI 480	SII 390	SIII 350	SIV 300	SV 270 (SV) 90	NVI 250 (NVI) 60
1967													SI 480	SII 390	SIII 350

SI-SV=quarters in Science of Society
NVI=sixth quarter in Natural Science
HI-HIII=quarters in Humanistic Studies
E=Senior Essay

() Guide to the Literature
*=new preparation

meetings, achieve the degree of involvement necessary for effective planning. [13] Each division of the College, therefore, would assign one staff member to serve part-time as a member of the library program staff. He would participate actively in the general over-all planning of the program, and would thus be in a position to understand the goals and methods of the sequence and to convey this understanding to his teaching colleagues. As a full-fledged member of the divisional staff, he would be in a position to see to it that the library program was consistent with the objectives and style, that it fitted the schedule and teaching plans of the divisional course sequence.

The crucial matter of faculty-library coordination should not rest solely on this one link with each divisional staff. Our experience in the pilot project has reinforced our conviction that the success of an integrated program of library instruction depends ultimately on the degree to which it shares the values, the goals, the academic world-view of the curriculum in which it occurs and of the faculty primarily responsible for that curriculum. Though the pretest year would be one of particularly intensive collaboration between the library program staff and the faculty, as assignments are perfected, and instruments for evaluation are developed, we would continue throughout the program to cultivate every opportunity for regular face-to-face contacts with both students and faculty. In short, we would see to it that the library program remained congruent with the social environment in which it occurred.

Preparing assignments. --Under this heading we include preparation of briefing statements, design of exercises, pretesting, scoring, etc. The project librarian and the project director would carry the major responsibility for this work. Their work would stem from the plans developed by the program staff as a whole and would benefit from frequent individual consultation with the staff representatives and other instructors and from occasional participation in committee and staff meetings. Graduate student assistants might help with the work.

Presentation and discussion of assignments. --Although we no longer think that the librarian can remain in the background, we have not reverted to the traditional procedure of turning the class over to the librarian for a lecture or two. The procedure we have found most successful is one in which the librarian presents and leads discussion of the assignment while the instructor demonstrates his support of it by participating fully in the discussion and by indicating that he values its contribution to the course. The active participation of librarians is necessary, at least in the introduction of such a program, because most faculty members simply do not have a systematic view of the library. Once they have acquired this, it might be preferable to leave the presentation and discussion of the assignments entirely to them.

As the sequence is planned, however, three or four assignments are presented every quarter, one assignment calls for scheduled consultation hours in the library, and seven out of ten require attendance at dozens of discussion sections. Clearly the librarians would need assistance. Each staff representative, therefore, would carry a major share of the load for assignments in his own course and would assist with those in the other divisions. We would use graduate student assistants, whenever possible, for library consultation service and for presentation of assignments.

Appraisal of the Program

Our general plan for appraisal of the proposed program is designed to produce evidence on two primary questions:

> 1. How effective is each assignment and how effective is the sequence as a whole for the attainment of library competence?
>
> 2. To what extent does library competence contribute to the achievement of educational objectives?

Appraising the individual assignment. --Uniform precoded instruments would be used to evaluate each assignment as to:

> 1. Its effectiveness in involving students. Data on the student's involvement would be gathered from the products of the assignments, from systematic reports on discussion sections and, from questionnaires or interviews with instructors and perhaps, with random samples of students. The reports should show whether or not each student did the assignment, completed it, attended its discussion, participated in the discussion.

2. Its effectiveness for learning. Products of the assignments themselves could be one source of evidence on student learning. Other natural opportunities for evaluation occur
in regular course examinations and in work on subsequent assignments. Developing criteria, rating scales and the like
would require careful coordination between the library program
staff and the faculty. As we see it now, each assignment is
followed in the sequence by at least one opportunity for ar-
riving at an appropriate measure. (See Table 16)

3. Its feasibility. Reports would also include information on
the procedures used in preparing the assignment, on methods
and materials used to guide students in carrying it out, on
the traffic volume and pattern and the materials used in the
library, on the discussion themes and style, and on the time
and materials cost of all activities. Our own records should
be supplemented with questionnaires and/or interviews with
members of the Wayne State University library staff.

The information on the feasibility of each assignment would
have obvious practical value not only for us but also for others who
might be interested in developing a similar program elsewhere.
From data on the other two factors, we would hope to be able to
estimate the contribution of each assignment to the sequence as a
whole.

Assessing library competence. --We propose two measures of
the student's attainment of library competence. The first is the
final assignment in the sequence, the bibliographical review written
in preparation for the Senior Essay. An assessment, made by the
essay advisor, would be considered as evidence of the student's
familiarity with the literature pertaining to the topic of his essay
and thus, inferentially, of his ability to use the bibliographic apparatus through which the literature is organized. As a further
check, we would collect the bibliographic reviews produced through
the full four years of the program and present them, unidentified
by name of the student or by year of writing, for separate assessment by subject specialists (other faculty members and librarians).[14]

As a second measure we would ask instructors from other
colleges at Wayne to evaluate the work of Monteith and non-Monteith
students enrolled in senior courses outside Monteith College. We
would select from one to four courses in which a term paper
calling for fairly extensive use of library resources is a customary

Table 16

Evaluation of Individual Assignments

Assignment	Locus of Measure	Criteria	Primary Evaluator
Independence	Quarterly Exam.	Skill in selecting the appropriate "ways" (multiple-choice questions)	Librarian
Book Evaluation	Term paper	Quality of sources cited	Instructor
Review of the Literature	Research paper	Awareness of literature on topic, from sources cited	Instructor
Economic Index	Prediction paper	Data cited	Instructor
Winchell Exercise	Guide to the Literature Assignment*	Accuracy and comprehensiveness of the guide	Librarian
Popular Science	Paper on "translation effect"	Scientific sources cited	Instructor
Bibliography in the Humanities	The assigned paper	Comprehension of nature and function of bibliographic tools	Librarian
Reading Plan	Defense of reading plan	Sources cited	Instructor

* This assignment occurs later in the same quarter or in a subsequent quarter of the library program.

requirement and ask the instructors in these courses to rate all
the students enrolled as to their acquaintance with the literature on
the subject of the course, the extensiveness and quality of the
sources used for their term papers, and as to the degree to which
they seemed to be prepared for independent study. We would ask
that the term papers be submitted in duplicate, one copy being re-
tained by us for separate anonymous scoring of the bibliography by
members of our own faculty and library program staff.

Appraising the effectiveness of the sequence. --In order to
study the relationship between the attainment of library competence,
measured in the fashion indicated above, and the sequence of library
assignments, we propose that measures of the student's experiences
with the library program be developed. As indicated in Table 15,
the student's exposure to the sequence would vary depending on the
year he entered Monteith. From our analysis of individual assignments we would have in our records information on each student's
participation and success in the planned learning experiences to
which he was exposed. From the same analysis we would have
arrived at an estimate of the contribution of each assignment to the
sequence as a whole. In broad outline, our plan for appraisal of
effectiveness of the sequence rests upon analysis of the inter-
relationships among three major factors:

1. The effectiveness of individual assignments.

2. Student attainment of library competence (as revealed in
bibliographic reviews and non-Monteith senior courses).

3. Student experience (exposure, involvement, and learning)
with the sequence.

Estimating the contribution of library competence to the
achievement of educational objectives. --The very existence of a
program of instruction in the use of the library implies acceptance
of library competence as an educational objective. Similarly, the
institution of a program such as we propose implies at least some
degree of acceptance of the particular kind of library competence
the program is designed to produce. We frankly admit our own
conviction that the kind of library competence we envision is a
necessary component in the capacity for continued purposive learning

which should be a goal of all liberal, general education. We admit
further, that we believe that this capacity should be a goal for all
college students, not only for the elite ten or fifteen percent.
Furthermore, our experience tends to show that even those instructors who do not at the outset accept our views may, through experience with the program, be ultimately persuaded. In short, the
faculty may define educational objectives as including library competence and measure achievement of these objectives accordingly. If,
then, we used faculty judgment as our measure of student achievement of educational objectives and, at the same time, attempted to
estimate the contribution of library competence to that achievement,
we might simply confound our data. We feel, nevertheless, that of
all measures of educational achievement, faculty judgment is the one
most likely to be accepted as valid - by faculty members.

   With these observations as a caveat, we propose, therefore, an
analysis of the association between our measures of library competence and our students' performance on the host-assignments to
which our measures are attached, i. e., the correlation between
scores on the bibliographical reviews and grades on the senior essays subsequently written and similarly, that between the library
competence ratings and the students' grades on the term papers
written in the non-Monteith courses.(We would, of course, use suitable statistical methods to partial out the effect of intelligence and
aptitude factors.) The association we found, if any, should indicate,
at least, the contribution of library competence to student work
which would have been assigned had there been no library program,
and to work which is normally used as evidence of the student's
achievement of educational objectives.

Conclusion

   The program presented in this chapter illustrates an approach
to instruction in the use of the library which is quite unprecedented.
While the elements which it knits together are not essentially new
in themselves, they are joined in a new way, some of them are
applied in a new setting.

   The unifying idea of the library as a system of "ways" is

merely a teachable version of the conception of the library as a
system of bibliographic organization.[15] What is new in our proposal is the suggestion that this view of the library serve as a
theoretical framework for instruction.

Librarians are well-acquainted with the tools which organize
the literature of scholarship; instructors are thoroughly in command
of it in their own fields. What is new here is the proposal that
the general pattern of the organization of scholarship be presented
in an undergraduate program.

Research in higher education is increasingly directed toward
examination of the social structure of the academic world.[16] As
college librarians grow more consciously aware of the influence of
the social milieu on the functioning of the library in the college,
they take it into account as one factor to be considered in planning.
Our program has been developed out of experience which is not un-
common. What is new is that this experience has been analyzed
systematically and in searching detail by a trained social scientist.

Countless imaginative library assignments have resulted from
collaboration between librarians and teaching faculty. What is new
here is a program which consists of an entire sequence of such in-
novating assignments, a sequence which cuts across three subject
areas, which extends through a full four-year curriculum, and
which is feasible with a large number of students.

Notes

1. The Monteith curriculum begins in the freshman year with sequences in the Science of Society and the Natural Sciences. Engineering students do not take the Natural Sciences sequence.
   The Humanistic Studies sequence begins in the third quarter of
   the sophomore year.

2. We believe that this objective, whether stated or not, is inherent in the idea of liberal education in the modern world. It
   follows, therefore, that a program such as ours would be
   equally justified in any college or university which aims to provide a genuinely liberal education.

3. See Appendix I, p. 179-182, Appendix III, p. 261-270.

4. The complexities of the card catalog might well be underlined
   by the addition of a few questions addressed to the List of

Subject Headings Used in the Dictionary Catalog of the Library of Congress.

5. We do not intend to belittle the delights nor, indeed, the educational value of browsing. It is an experience which the natural reader will enjoy in any case. A student with sufficient imagination can use almost any book as a stimulus to creative thought. Perhaps we will one day find ways to help the average student develop such imagination, but, for now, we are concerned with lesser tasks of helping all students learn to browse not haphazardly but with discrimination and judgment.

6. See Appendix I, p. 173-176; Appendix III, p. 242-256.

7. See Appendix I, p. 182-184; Appendix III, p. 271-273.

8. See p. 64.

9. See p. 67-68.

10. See Appendix I, p. 160-164.

11. See Appendix I, p. 176-178; Appendix III, p. 257-260.

12. Monteith College Faculty, Committee D. "Recommendation Concerning Senior Essay" Topic No. 3, 1960.

13. Chapter II discusses, in some detail, factors other than participation which affect librarian-faculty relationships.

14. As indicated in Table 2, each set of seniors would have had another year of the program in preparation for this assignment. Only those students who enter in the pretest year and the following year would have had the entire sequence.

15. The librarians who served on the pilot project were once students of Pierce Butler, Margaret Egan, and Jesse Shera. They are happy to acknowledge the profound influence of these eminent librarians and gifted teachers.

16. Note, especially, Daniel P. Bergen, "Socio-Psychological Research on College Environments, " College and Research Libraries, XXIII (November, 1962), 473-481.

Chapter VI

Faculty Use of Bibliographic Service[1]

In offering bibliographic service to the Monteith faculty we were breaking new ground. There is considerable justification for the notion that teachers, as the most expensive employees of colleges and universities, ought to be provided with the kind of library service which is presumed normal for the engineers and scientists served by the special libraries of business and industry. But if any college or university provides such service in any systematic way, it has not so reported. We wanted to know, then, what faculty members would do with this kind of service if it were given to them.

We were breaking new ground, too, in the sense that we were addressing ourselves to faculty use of library resources for teaching.[2] There has been some investigation, through citation analysis, for example, of scholars' use of library resources for research, but none specifically concerned with teaching. Lacking guidelines from previous research, therefore, we felt free to experiment with various methods of organizing the service and gathering data on its use. We were concerned, furthermore, that whatever methods we used interfere as little as possible with achievement of our primary aim, that of building a relationship between the project and the faculty which would enhance the library's role in basic course work.

The analysis which follows, then, should be regarded as, indeed, tentative and exploratory. It is based primarily on reports prepared by the assistants, themselves. In the first semester of our program we asked the assistants to keep detailed diaries, reporting on every contact with the instructors to whom they were assigned and on every step of their procedures in the library. But we did not insist that they probe for more information than the faculty offered voluntarily. And though we constantly stressed our

dependence on reports as data for our research, we never felt
justified in interrupting a good relationship between an assistant and
his faculty principal merely because the assistant failed to report
fully and regularly. In the second semester, moreover, we sub-
stituted a brief form for the detailed diary, in spite of the fact
that we were quite aware that we were sacrificing comparability of
data in order to make reporting less burdensome.

Several of the assistants, however, did report fully, accurate
ly, and conscientiously. They were sensitive to nuances of relationship, interested in attempting to discern patterns in scholarly
work, intrigued by their own adventures in searching. (The quotations in the discussion below are from reports submitted by this
group.) Furthermore, we were ourselves close enough to the interests and work of the faculty to be able, usually, to supplement
or interpret on the basis of our own knowledge the information contained in the sketchier of the reports we received. In short, while
we would warn that the quantitative aspect of our analysis must be
viewed with considerable caution, we are satisfied that our data
reflect valid categories and indicate gross proportions.

Data. --The analysis covers the first two semesters of the
bibliographic service program, the period during which the assistants were assigned to individual faculty members. It covers the
tasks performed by 24 assistants for 24 faculty members. Of the
24 faculty, 16 were in the Science of Society Division, which was
provided with the service for two semesters. Four each were in
the divisions of Humanistic Studies and of Natural Sciences, which
were provided with the service for only one semester. This means
that twice as many social scientists were serviced twice as long as
the people in the other fields. Thus, here again, we must warn
against generalizing too far on the basis of our quantitative analysis.

The fields of the faculty were as follows: 5 each in anthropology and sociology, 3 in psychology, 2 each in philosophy, math-
logic, and English literature, and 1 each in economics, history,
biology, art, and music. The spread of the tasks among these
many fields was such that we were unable to discern any measurable pattern.

The fields of the assistants largely matched those of their
faculty principals, though there were some exceptions. Their academic class levels were: 1 Ph. D candidate, 3 Master's candidates,
8 Bachelors beginning graduate work, 5 seniors, 2 juniors, 4
sophomores (all Monteith students), and 1 freshman--with experience in a bookstore specializing in anthropology.

We found that the assistants had three kinds of relationships
with the faculty. They were treated as students or student apprentices, as bibliographical experts, or as quasi-colleagues. Almost
all of the assistants were occasionally used as messengers. Only
those at the top academic levels achieved a quasi-colleague relationship with their respective faculty principals, while the undergraduates were most likely to be treated as students. The beginning graduate students were usually given a more distant role. The
faculty seemed to expect them to behave as bibliographical experts
--or, perhaps as people whose access to the project librarian
meant access to bibliographical expertise. These assistants were
not invited to enter as colleagues might, into discussion of the research or teaching problem for which library resources were required, nor were they expected to need, as students might, background information about the nature of the problem, promising
sources of information on it, types of approaches which might be
fruitful, etc.

In spite of these variations, however, we found little difference in the nature of the tasks assigned to the various relationship
types. We do know that the assistants who were treated, rather
distantly, as bibliographical experts were often dissatisfied with
their work and we suspect that in general, the work they did was
much poorer in quality than that done by either the "quasi-colleagues"
or the "students. "

The tasks themselves we classified, first, in terms of their
purpose--research, teaching, other--and second, in terms of their
nature--bibliography, information, other. There were 180 tasks reported as separate items, but we base our calculations on 131,
having eliminated the categories we designated as "pick-up" and
"non-library. "[3] (We attempted to analyze the tasks in quantitative

terms, also, with respect to the assistant's interaction with the faculty principal--instruction, background, feedback--and with respect to the assistant's procedures in carrying it out--starting place, tools used, people consulted, etc. But the reports were too incomplete and uneven to provide comparable data.)

The tables presented on the next few pages show--in gross terms, as we have warned--what our faculty used bibliographical services for, and the types of activities involved in the tasks they assigned. We feel more secure about the categories we have established, which we discuss later, than we do about the quantities involved. But figures do provide some basis for tentative conclusions about what kind of training would seem to be appropriate for bibliographic service to academicians.

The purposes of the bibliographical tasks. --In the general category of work done in connection with research, we identified three sub-categories: 1) publication and project, i.e., specifically related to a particular research project or a proposed publication; 2) research-related, i.e., reading and study in the area of the instructor's specific research; and 3) peripheral, i.e., reading and study in the general area of the instructor's specialty. In the general category of teaching, we set up five sub-categories: 1) student reading, i.e., concerned with what might be required or suggested as reading--listening or viewing--for students; 2) library, i.e., checking library holdings, recommending library acquisitions; 3) basic course preparation, i.e., using library resources in preparation for lectures or discussion in connection with Monteith required courses; 4) tutorials, using library resources similarly in connection with tutorials, advanced seminars, etc.; 5) background, i.e., presumably contributing to general background for teaching. (We placed tasks in this last category when they were clearly concerned with concepts--or writers--dealt with in Monteith courses but not specifically identified--or identifiable--as a particular unit in any specific course. Most were probably related to the basic required courses.) The list is completed with two categories: 1) personal, e.g., "a book on outrigger canoes" or "   's new novel;" and 2) academic-professional, e. g. "list of Fullbright scholars for the conference to be held in July" or "get all the articles in the Collegian on political clubs on campus. "

Table 17 shows the number of tasks assigned in each of these categories by instructors in each of the three divisions. The uneveness in the total number of tasks performed for each division is easily explained by the fact that the service was provided for more people and for a longer period of time for the Science of Society staff than for the other two. The difference between the Humanistic Studies and Natural Sciences can be partly accounted for by the fact that for about two months the assistants for the latter division worked as a team on a proposed Monteith student assignment. Further research would be needed to find out whether or not there is also some difference between the two groups in the extent to which they depend on library resources for teaching or in the extent to which they are willing to delegate the job of library searching.

The striking fact that the Humanistic Studies faculty used the service exclusively for teaching, while only about one-half of the total fell into this category is also easily explained. [4] When they were given the service, the humanities instructors were just launching their course; they were presenting the first semester's work and planning the rest of a three-semester course sequence. The other two divisions were winding up their courses, having presented the first year's work before the project began. Apparently, first things do come first. People whose immediate problem is planning a course will use bibliographic assistance for this purpose. When the course is planned, some of them turn their attention to, and use assistance for their own research.

The small total number of tasks assigned by the Natural Sciences staff precludes generalizations comparing them with the social scientists. But it would be interesting to know if the lack of "academic-professional" tasks means that the natural science fields are less conference-minded, less gregarious, more likely to depend on print than people for keeping up with current developments.

The types of bibliographical tasks assigned. --Table 18

Table 17

The Purposes of Bibliographical Tasks
by Division of Instruction

	Science of Society			Humanistic Studies			Natural Science			Total		
	No.	%	Faculty[1]	No.	%	Faculty[1]	No.	%	Faculty[1]	No.	%	Faculty[1]
Research												
Publication & Project	13		5	0		0	0		0	13		5
Related	23		12	0		0	5		3	28		15
Peripheral	9		5	0		0	0		0	9		5
Total	45	48%	16	0	0%	0	5	71%	3	50	38%	19
Teaching												
Student Reading	12		5	7		2	0		0	19		7
Library	1		1	2		2	0		0	3		3
Basic Course Preparation	5		5	15		4	0		0	20		9
Tutorials	8		6	0		0	0		0	8		6
Background	11		3	6		2	2		1	19		7
Total	37	39%	9	30	100%	4	2	29%	1	69	53%	14
Other												
Personal	2		2	0		0	0		0	2		2
Academic-Professional	10		6	0		0	0		0	10		6
Total	12	14%	8	0	0	0	0	0%	0	12	9%	8
Grand Total	94	101%	16	30	100%	4	7	100%	4	131	100%	24

[1]Number of faculty making the assignments. Some made assignments in more than one category.

Table 18

Types of Bibliographical Tasks by Division of Instruction

	Science of Society			Humanistic Studies			Natural Science			Total		
	No.	%	Faculty[1]	No.	%	Faculty[1]	No.	%	Faculty[1]	No.	%	Faculty[1]
Read & Report	15	16	5	0	0	0	0	0	0	15	11	5
Bibliographical												
1. Abstracting	3		2	1		1	0		0	4		3
2. Selective & scouting	25		13	9		4	0		0	34		17
3. Exhaustive	19		12	0		0	1		1	20		13
4. Checking	7		6	6		3	1		1	14		10
Total	54	57%	15	16	53%	4	2	28%	2	72	55%	21
Information												
1. Selective & scouting	7		5	7		2	1		1	15		8
2. General	4		1	2		2	4		2	10		5
3. Specific	14		6	5		2	0		0	19		8
Total	25	27%	10	14	47%	2	5	86%	3	44	34%	15
Selective & Scouting (B2&I1)[2]	32	34%	16	16	53%	4	1	14%	1	49	37%	21
Grand Total	94	100%	16	30	100%	4	7	100%	4	131	100%	24

1. Number of faculty making the assignments. Some made assignments in more than one category.
2. I. e., the total of "Bibliographical 2, Selective and scouting" and "Information 1, Selective and scouting"

presents the tasks assigned in each division, now classified according to the activity they seem to require of the bibliographic assistants. [5] Most of the tasks are bibliographic and more than a third of them are of the "scouting and selective" type. The fact that only the social scientists asked the assistants to "read and report" seems to be partly due to their having underclassmen, particularly Monteith students for assistants. Seven of the 15 tasks in this group were performed by one assistant whose faculty principal frankly valued her as a sounding-board on which he could try out materials he was thinking of using with his other students.

Noting that more than half of the tasks assigned by the Humanities Division were in the "selective and scouting" category, we wondered whether this finding was related to the fact that all of the work in this division was for teaching. Table 19 sheds some light on this question by classifying research and teaching work according to the kind of activity involved. The table shows that while exhaustive bibliographical searching--to be sure that everything is covered--was, as expected, almost exclusively assigned in connection with research and "checking" -- to see what is in print, in the library, available in paperback--was assigned exclusively in connection with teaching, bibliographical tasks in general were more prevalent for research than for teaching. They account for more than half of the tasks in any case. Note, furthermore, that bibliographical expertise, i. e., the ability to locate sources of information is involved also in the category we have identified as "Information, Selective and Scouting. " (We classified these items as "information" only because they did not explicitly indicate that a bibliography was to be compiled.) More than two-thirds of the tasks were of this type, while less than 10 per cent were concerned with the retrieval of specific information. And, returning to the two "selective and scouting" categories, note that we found that at least as many such tasks were assigned for research as for teaching. Apparently the research activities of a faculty member are not confined to those specific subjects where he feels himself fully oriented, fully acquainted with the literature.

Table 19
Types of Bibliographical Task by Purpose

	Research		Teaching		Total	
	No.	Percent	No.	Percent	No.	Percent
Read and Report	3	6	12	17	15	13
Bibliographical						
1. Abstracting	1		3		4	
2. Selective & scouting	15		17		32	
3. Exhaustive	16		1		17	
4. Checking	0		14		14	
Total	32	64%	35	51%	67	56%
Information						
1. Selective & scouting	6		8		14	
2. General	5		5		10	
3. Specific	4		9		13	
Total	15	30%	22	32%	37	31%
Selective & Scouting (B_2 I_1)	21	42	25	36	46	39
Grand Total	50	100%	69	100%	119	100%

Bibliographic service for teaching. --When an instructor
plans a new course he is likely to want a bibliography. One assistant
reported as follows:

> General assignment: Collecting bibliography for a course in
> Personality and Culture, to be given next semester.
>
> Spot assignment: Getting some familiarity with the field of
> personality theory.   Mr._____ gave me his personal copy
> of Theories of Personality, to see what type of ideas are
> concerned with in this field.   I went thru the book quickly,
> noting bibliographies, chapter titles, etc. (The bibliographies,
> especially after Chapter 1, will be helpful later.) Read
> completely Chapter 1, "The Nature of Personality Theory, "
> noting names and key phrases (for vertical file, if necessary).
> Read last half of concluding chapter to get the general spread
> of the work, i.e., just how far this field has advanced...
>
> Spot assignment: Go through Sociological Abstracts and
> Psychological Abstracts to begin listing bibliographies. Hints
> from faculty: Together we made up a list of "give-away"
> terms to look for in abstract titles, e.g., Personality, Self,
> Identity, Ego...Working with abstracts is new to me, but I
> found them fascinating. In addition to listing books and
> articles for the personality course, I have been adding extra
> articles which he might find interesting or useful in his in-
> terests (communication,...) or in his regular classes (Sci-
> ence of Society, which I had last year and am finishing the
> sequence now).
>
> Spot assignment: Mr._____ had originally given me a tenta-
> tive bibliography for the planned course.   At this time I was
> to take certain listed books out of the library...
>
> Spot assignment: To go back through the last 10 years of
> American Journal of Sociology and the American Sociological
> Review checking for the same type of articles (pertaining to
> personality and society).
>
> When I completed tracing ASR for 10 years, I showed the
> results to Mr._____, who checked seven different arti-
> cles for me to abstract for him.

This is our most explicit statement of an overall bibliographical strategy in the development of a new course.   It also
illustrates nicely the kind of bibliographical assignment which we
have classified as "scouting and selective. "   What is wanted is not
complete coverage of "everything on" a subject but presumably selected works which deal with certain key concepts.   Note that the
starting place was a single book (a textbook?, a "state of the art"
summary?) which was used to establish a framework for the search.

From this point, the search moved directly to specialized abstracting services and finally to specific journals.

When the task as reported by the assistant did not state
explicitly that a bibliography was what was wanted, it was classified,
as we noted above, in the general category of "information." But
in most cases of this kind, we believe the instructor probably wanted
a selected bibliography from which he might choose certain items
to be abstracted, certain items to be charged out, and so forth.
We quote a few statements of such assignments:

> Mimesis, and how its meaning has changed through the
> centuries.
>
> The nature of mathematics in the formal sciences.
>
> Information on Christian interpretation of nature.

These tasks, too, would require the development of a conceptual
framework for the search and a technique of scouting and selecting.
Only rarely do we have information about the extent to which the
instructor worked with the assistant in developing such a conceptual
framework or suggested bibliographical tools to be consulted. But
in any case, an effective technique would seem to be that beginning
with an encyclopedia or a guide to the literature of a field. Such
non-selective tools as the card catalog or periodical indexes would
be useful only to locate one or two books or articles which would
serve similarly as a starting place to provide a conceptual framework and perhaps a few leads to a further search. Systematic
examination would be called for only in specialized journals, if at
all.

The development of a bibliography of readings to be assigned
or suggested to students may also involve scouting: "How is the
world put together in terms of autobiographies, forms of autobiography, themes; determine availability, see if in paper." (Here
one could not approach the task through the tools associated with
the academic disciplines. The typically library classification for
"form" is to the point. But this is a rare case.)

The more common bibliographical activity in connection with
student reading is checking:

Find out what is available in paper-bound concerning all aspects of Greek culture (philosophy, history, religion, literature, etc.)

List of all articles in the American Anthropologist, 1948-- which deal with the American Indian value system.

Bibliography of individual dialecticians. Some of these: Plato, Whitehead, Bradley, Hegel, Bosanquet. What they wrote also works about them--available in DPL or Wayne.

Very rarely, identifying reading--or in this case, viewing--for students involves retrieval:

Locate good reproductions and photos of Grunwald and Von Eyck, the Chartres cathedral, Autun, Vezeley, Tournos, Parthenon, Erectheum, Acropolis, Sculpture on Portal Royal at Chartres, the glass windows of Chartres, Goya's etchings.

In preparing for lectures and discussion, the instructor sometimes requires rather general information:

Monastic orders and styles of France (Romanesque): Cluny, Cistercians (Churches and their orders--briefly about orders); differences between orders which are highly structured compared with more hermit.

or quite specific information:

On Friday, Miss_____told me she was preparing a lecture on internal migration and needed the following statistics: number of persons migrating from rural to urban areas each year; yearly total rural and urban population; yearly total of persons employed in farm work and all other types of labor.

Bibliographical service for research. --As we have noted, the exhaustive type of bibliographical task was assigned almost exclusively in connection with research. The most ambitious project in this category was a bibliographic survey, "chronologically and by source of scientific discourse, the nature of American private foreign investment." The faculty member and his assistant, working in a colleague relationship, compiled and organized a bibliography of several hundred items coded on IBM cards, which then could be used for retrieval and print-outs on any sub-category within the general subject.

Other exhaustive bibliographies were more limited in scope but were also needed in connection with projects or publication:

For an encyclopedia article: Compile a bibliography on Roger Bacon of writings available anywhere.

For a dissertation: Find everything written on or by Piaget.

For a possible "collected papers:" Compile, collect works of Herbert Blumer--Xerox copies and compile bibliography.

More frequently, however, the request for exhaustive bibliographies came in connection with the faculty member's need to keep up with new research in his own specialty, and what was sought was completeness after a certain date, the date when the faculty member last felt fully in command of the literature on his subject:

Find all I can on Indians in urban society since 1958.

Calculus of variation: list of different papers on the subject from 1945-58.

Everything published on Durkheim in the past two years.

On the other hand, preparation for a research project or publication did not necessarily produce a request for exhaustive searching; a selective, scouting type of bibliography was often assigned:

To compile a bibliography on the role of the corporation in American society...Dr._____suggested I use the Journal of Business History and simply thumb through their volumes. (He was using the material to write an introduction for a book of readings on the corporation.)

Mr._____pulled three folders from his desk, projects he had been working on in the past, and asked me which I would like to work on. I chose one on American teen-agers, although I noted the other two in case I run across anything on them. We discussed the problem he had formulated on this problem including past work he had found. We tossed the question around with Mr._____who dropped into the office.

The selective, scouting type of bibliography was also assigned in connection with new or peripheral areas of interest, or possible interest, for research:

Collect bibliographical sources that deal with the study of social class in American society, stressing social stratification, distribution of life chances, status groups, class awareness, class consciousness, social mobility.

Compile a bibliography on all aspects of the sociology of art.

Occasionally, but rarely, an assistant was assigned a task which seemed to involve searching for information directly, although the reports do not make it clear that the assistants were not here, again, expected merely to locate and bring books or articles which dealt with the topic:

C. S. Lewis' systems of strict implication.

Kant's ethical views prior to the Critique.

One assistant reported:

> Assignment: To look into the Congressional Record under such categories as "Crime," "Civilian Conservation Corps," "Juvenile Delinquency," "Youth," "Youth Conservation Corps," "Conservation," etc., for all material that related to the proposed Youth Conservation Corps or to its major problem--juvenile delinquency. . . From his conversation I gathered that Dr._____wanted a rather extensive report since he planned to base the last chapter of a proposed book on my research. In view of this purpose of the report, I worked nearly 8 weeks on the subject and handed in a 75 page report which included 50 pages that were reproduced directly from the Congressional Record as illustration of what I had observed.

Quite clearly, this young man was no longer acting as a bibliographic assistant; he was in process of becoming a junior colleague, but, in general, the tasks assigned for research, as for teaching, were mainly bibliographical rather than informational.

Conclusion. --Our analysis of faculty use of bibliographical service suffered from the deficiencies of the reporting of our bibliographic assistants. Our data were neither detailed nor uniform enough to provide substance for analysis of the "faculty's library interests, needs and demands [in terms of their] association with varying subject disciplines, research interests, previous library experiences, educational goals, and concepts of academic library functions."[6]

The reports, nevertheless, do provide evidence, tentative but persuasive, for one hypothesis that we set out to explore: "that providing [the faculty] with bibliographical assistance will result in their making extensive use of library resources for their own course work."[7] The faculty did, indeed, use the bibliographic service as a resource for teaching, several did so extensively.

From the types of tasks our faculty assigned, moreover, we learned a great deal about the kind of training program needed by those who would provide library service to academicians. We were convinced, for instance, that emphasis in such training should be on bibliographies rather than on reference books and that training for specific retrieval of information (i. e. , the use of dictionaries, biographical directories, fact books, etc.) should be minimized. Where service for teaching is the main job, training should give considerable attention to trade bibliographies; where service for research is also provided, training should include the exhaustive national and subject bibliographies. But for either purpose, it is essential that there be thorough coverage of selective bibliographical tools, of scouting techniques, and of the bibliographic network which controls --to a great or lesser degree, depending on the discipline--reporting of the results of research and scholarship.

On the basis of the reports which were, in fact, fully and conscientiously prepared we were also able to identify factors which deserve further study for their potential effect on faculty use of library resources and bibliographical service. We are satisfied that the aspects of faculty purpose and bibliographical activity can be adequately treated in terms of the categories and subcategories used in the discussion above. We are confident that a form could be designed which would provide for recording without too much burden, information on faculty-assistant interaction, on searching procedures suggested by the faculty, on procedures actually used, on the degree of success achieved, on faculty appraisal of the work, and, most important, on faculty use of the resources provided. Complete and accurate reporting on such a form could be ensured through careful training, and interviews with both faculty and assistants could be used to probe for supplementary data.

We have not felt it necessary to quote from the reports to substantiate our claim that all of the factors identified above seem to be significantly related to the effectiveness of a program such as ours. But we should like to close by offering two more quotations which speak to the matter of the effect of the program on our assistants' view of what librarianship is all about.

> I am finding this work great and expect to spend more time than 10 hours a week on it - for my own interest, if not for extra pay.

> I have begun to look upon research work as somewhat akin to an art--where imagination as well as intelligence is required for success.

Notes

1. See Appendix II, The Bibliographic Assistance Program: Excerpts from the Progress Reports, for information on the organization of the program, on the training provided for the bibliographical assistants, and on the methods used for gathering data for this analysis.

2. Monteith faculty are, perhaps, less than most college faculty members subject to the normal academic pressure to engage in research and publish. But they are not, of course, immune to it. We tried to convey the impression that the bibliographical service might be used with equal propriety for either research or teaching.

3. We found that the assistants varied in their reporting on tasks involving picking up and delivering books and getting articles xeroxed. Some reported each item separately, others made such notations as "pick up several books" or "got the articles xeroxed." The "non-library" tasks included checking statistical computations and reacting as a student, e.g., "attend my tutorial and tell me whether the students are getting the ideas I want to get across."

4. If "pick-up" and "non-library" tasks had not been eliminated from our calculations, the proportion of tasks connected with teaching would have been much higher. Of the 35 'pick-up" tasks reported as separate items, 17 were teaching, 8 were for research interests, 8 were personal or academic-professional and 2 were unidentifiable. Of the 14 "non-library" tasks, 6 were in connection with teaching, 5 were concerned with research, and 3 had to do with a professional conference.

5. The classifications are illustrated in the quotations presented later in the chapter.

6. Proposal, p. 7.

7. Proposal, p. 2.

Chapter VII

Summary and Conclusions

Again and again in the preceding chapters we have emphasized the point that the pilot project phase of the Monteith Library
Program was designed as exploratory research. The proposal,
listing several general hypotheses, indicated that we would "explore
ways of investigating" them. We focussed our attention on the
central function of the academic library, that of contributing to the
instructional program of the institution it serves and we addressed
ourselves to basic and fundamental questions about this library function. But these questions were broad and ill-defined. They were
to be asked in the context of a "real life" situation, with all the
fluidity and intransigence that term implies. We were content,
therefore, that our work should be of interest primarily as a
demonstration of methodology.

It seems to us appropriate, then, that this summary chapter
should stress methods of research, indicating how our basic, general questions acquired definition, how variables became identified,
how data were gathered and analyzed. Our conclusions, which are,
often as not, inconclusive, suggest lines of inquiry for further investigation.

The general hypotheses we undertook to explore ways of investigating were stated as follows:

1. That the student is likely to acquire library understanding and competence when his experiences in the library are
functionally related to the objectives and content of his subject courses and when this relationship is made manifest.

2. That the student's library experiences can be so related
to his course work when librarians are involved from the
beginning in course planning.

3. That library staff involvement can stimulate extensive
exploitation of available library resources in course work.

4. That when librarians are closely involved in course
development their contributions, especially in connection with

130

the use-of-materials aspects of course content and objectives, will be valued by the faculty and will be implemented
in the curriculum.

5. That most college teachers lack time and many lack
bibliographical expertise to make the most of the library's
potential contribution to teaching, and that providing them
with bibliographical assistance will result in their making
extensive use of library resources for their course work.[1]

The first four hypotheses rest one upon another. In essence
they say: if librarians participate with faculty in course planning,
they can get student library use built into the courses planned, and
if student library use is built into courses, students will use the
library for these courses, and if students use the library for their
courses they will acquire understanding of the library and competence
in its use. The fifth hypothesis is subordinate; it suggests that if
expert bibliographical assistance is provided to the faculty, the
processes hypothesized in the first four will be facilitated.

The chapters in this report deal with each of these propositions in
turn. Chapter II is concerned with the social structure in which librarians participated in the course planning activities of the faculty.
Chapter III--and the section of the Appendix related to it--deals with the
nature of the student library experiences which resulted from these
course planning activities and, using one sequence of such experiences,
shows how exposure to such experiences might be examined for
its association with certain variables in the background and
achievement of students. Chapter IV reports on our attempt to
analyze and measure library understanding and competence. Chapter
V brings together the results of our investigation in these three
areas. It presents a "model" program of instruction in the use of
the library, a program which stems from our conclusions as to the
nature of library competence needed for academic work and as to
the sort of social structure in which library assignments designed
to further the achievement of such competence can effectively be
planned, implemented, and evaluated. Chapter VI, dealing with the
subordinate hypothesis of bibliographical service as a facilitating
measure, analyzes faculty use of the service provided.

Social Structure

Under the heading "Procedures" our proposal stated:

Planning for use of materials in instruction. --Whenever instructional plans involve materials, the Coordinator [later
called the project director] and the librarian will cooperate
with the faculty in deciding upon materials to be used and
in devising appropriate methods of providing them. They
may be called upon to advise about a choice, for example,
between a film and a reading assignment to convey a particular concept, and to locate good items of each type. They
may be asked to work out special methods for exposing a
large number of students to materials in limited supply, for
example, the census data on a particular community.

The proposal further indicated that:

Data will be collected, through group observation techniques
and interviews, on the relationship between the library staff
and the teaching faculty, the contributions of librarians to
curriculum planning, the acceptance these contributions received from the faculty, and the extent to which they were
implemented in instruction. . .

Data on the relationship between the faculty and the project
and the regular library staff will be analyzed for form and
content of interaction in staff meetings, role expectancies
and roles assumed, agreements and conflicts on goals and
methods, et cetera. . .

The pilot project will produce a preliminary appraisal of the
effectiveness of the social structure established to coordinate
the library and instructional program. [2]

Defining the question and identifying variables. --We began
our work on this aspect of the project with a rather naive view of
librarians' potential participation in faculty deliberations. In a
staff-planned course, we thought, it would be a simple matter for
librarians to attend all course-planning sessions of the staff, to be
alert to those aspects of the plans which might involve books or
other library resources, and to offer suggestions about what materials might be selected, how they might be provided to students,
and so forth. We became aware almost immediately that the
matter of librarians' participation with faculty in course planning
involved a number of complexities concerned with 1) who among the
staff initiated, advocated, or reviewed specific plans; 2) when and
where the crucial moments of decision took place, and 3) how plans
were developed, implemented and evaluated. We found, for example,

that the support of a powerful member of the staff could practically guarantee an initial hearing for our ideas, but that such support could not assure implementation of these ideas by all members of the staff--even when the staff as a group had accepted them. We learned also that staff-planning often turned out to be staff reviewing of plans developed in committees or in informal groups and that our ideas, contributed in the general staff meetings, could, as a consequence, be seriously out of tune with the objectives and style of plans presented or, at best, too late to be implemented. We learned that course planning involves deciding what students should do, how the work should be presented to them, how they should be guided in doing it, how their work should be discussed and evaluated.

As we attempted to define "faculty, " "participation, " and "course planning, " then, we found ourselves dealing with a great many variables. Instructors were, of course, individuals with varying degrees of understanding of the potential contribution of the library to teaching, varying degrees of support for our efforts. And they were also members of small formal and informal groups and members of divisional staffs, as well as being members of the total faculty. "Participation" could be anything from permission to attend a staff meeting to close collaboration with a powerful member of an important sub-committee. "Course planning" processes involved many distinct steps and several different styles of working.

Gathering and analyzing data. --In accordance with the proposal data on this aspect of the study were gathered through intensive interviews and through group observation techniques. The data were analyzed by the project research analyst, an anthropologist, well-trained also in sociology, and she used the methods and concepts of these two disciplines.

The analysis revealed that the social structure of Monteith College has some characteristics of each of three types--or, "models"--of structure often used in analysis of this kind. As a formal institution, and especially as one unit in a large university, Monteith has some of the characteristics of a bureaucracy, which in its pure form is marked by considerable division of labor, and a high degree of specialization and by formalized relationships and stated

rules and procedures. In its internal relationships, particularly in
its emphasis upon the involvement of all faculty in decision-making,
it has some of the characteristics of the collegial structure which
calls for diversity among peers and for decision through consensus.
And in the autonomy it grants the individual instructor in his own
discussion section it resembles the model of the independent prac-
titioner who operates within the framework of a larger professional
or occupational world.

Four social science concepts were particularly useful in the
analysis of the library project's relationship to the College structure:

1.   The concept of "role, " i. e., the idea that people act--
and often even think and feel--in accordance with their perception of the expectations of other actors in a given social
situation.

2.   The concept of "the group, " i. e., the idea that a group
is not simply a collection of individuals but that it estab-
lishes qualifications for members, assigns roles and responsibilities, develops patterns and styles of communication, in
short, that it controls the behavior of its members.

3.   The concept of the "reference group, " i. e., the related
idea that individuals refer to groups of "others"--who may
be generalized others, such as "the profession" or "good
teachers"--for standards of what sort of behavior is proper
or desirable.

4.   The concept of "social distance, " i. e., the idea that interaction between individuals in different roles is much affected
by the social distance between those roles, whether that distance be vertical, a matter of status, power, or prestige, or
horizontal, a matter of communication across boundaries
between equals.

Conclusions and implications for library research. --Analysis
of the relationships of the library project in the social structure of
Monteith College revealed that four characteristics of the structure
were important at each stage of the project's development:

1.   An acceptance of the dual role--one individual carrying
two sets of responsibilities, behaving in accordance with two
sets of expectations.

2.   A strong identification with the subject divisional staff
group, with teaching in that staff as a crucial criterion for
membership in the group.

3. Little social distance <u>within</u> the teaching and administrative groups, but much social distance <u>between</u> these groups.

4. <u>Reference group ambivalence</u> on the part of the individual instructor as he moved from shared responsibility for lectures and overall course planning in the divisional staff to individual responsibility for the students enrolled in his own discussion sections.

Working in the beginning with the social sciences division, the library project staff found easy acceptance of their own dual role responsibilities and behavior, but the two non-teaching librarians were not admitted to full membership in the group. The lack of social distance within the group meant that they had no difficulty getting a sympathetic hearing for the first suggested library assignments, but it meant, also, that objections to later assignments were freely voiced in spite of the fact that they were supported by the division chairman. Instructors' reference group ambivalence appeared in the fact that some agreed to certain assignments in general staff meetings but failed to implement them in their own discussion sections.

The considerable social distance among the three subject divisions became a crucial factor as the project staff began to work with natural science and humanities divisional staffs in the later stages of the project. Because the project librarians were seen as essentially members of the social sciences staff, promoting what was essentially a social science enterprise, their ideas were regarded with a degree of suspicion.

In the final stage of the project we instituted a new structure of relationship, one better adapted to the realities of the structural features of the College. By inviting one member of each teaching staff to serve as library project representative in his own faculty, we preserved the dual role pattern but at the same time made sure that proposed library assignments were properly timed and fully in tune with the plans developed by the faculty, and most important, that they were put forward by a person admitted to full membership in the faculty group. We met the problem of the instructor's ambivalence between his faculty-related lecture and planning responsibilities and his individual discussion section responsibilities

by going into each small section ourselves to present and discuss
every library assignment. In effect we represented a faculty decision by our very presence in the class. We made certain, of
course, that the instructor was present and that he engaged in discussion of the assignment.

Every innovation must make its way against patterns of
relationship and behavior which are firmly established and very
powerful. Although Monteith College had been in existence less
than a year when the library project began and its structure was
still somewhat fluid, we found that our work was considerably
easier and more effective when we modified our own structure to
take into account structural realities of the organization with which
we worked. The methods of analysis used in anthropological studies
of communities and in sociological studies of institutions have rarely
been used in library research. Our experience at Monteith suggests
that such methods could be most fruitfully employed in many library investigations, particularly in those concerned with a changing
library function. And where, indeed, is the function of the library
not changing?

Student Library Experiences

Let us quote again from the section of our proposal which
deals with procedure:

> Planning, guiding, and evaluating library assignments. --The
> development of each assignment which requires library use
> will involve: discussion among the faculty, the Coordinator,
> the Librarian, and the Research Analyst to plan student ex-
> periences in terms of desired objectives and feasible methods
> of evaluation; working through of assignments by bibliographi-
> cal assistants and consequent revision; briefing of regular
> library staff on objectives of the assignment and procedures
> to be used with students; briefing of students; individual
> guidance of students in the library; evaluation by faculty
> through examination, analysis of the product of the assign-
> ment, or other such evidence.
> . . . .
> A third type of data obtained through observation and inter-
> views will deal with students' experiences in the library.
> Attempts will be made to answer questions such as the
> following: What problems did this kind of library use create?
> How were they handled? What difficulties did students
> have? Were they overcome? The project research librarian

and the bibliographical research assistants will keep logs on
what happened in the library. Under certain circumstances
these will be supplemented through reports from regular
Wayne library staff.

Exploratory evaluations of the student response to library
instruction will provide a fourth type of data to be used in
the preliminary work. They will include performance on
certain course examination questions and possibly on tests
of library competence, analysis of sources used for papers,
circulation records, reading diaries, and the logs of the
process of searching for materials, and questionnaires with
faculty and student participants.

Data on students' library experiences will be analyzed in
terms of the library personnel, organization, and facilities
required for library assignments and in terms of the kinds
of briefing and guidance which are associated with successes
and difficulties students encounter in carrying out library
assignments. The exploratory evaluations of student response to library instruction will be directed toward the attainment of library competence and for examination of the
importance of such competence for general academic achievement.

[The pilot project will] attempt to produce a series of instruments such as observation schedules and tests, for evalua—
ting student attainment of library understanding and competence, and a research design with hypotheses to be tested
in the second phase of the program. [3]

Defining the question and identifying the variables. --Obvi-
ously, in this aspect of our investigation we were quite frankly prepared to adopt a shot-gun approach. We did not know what kinds
of library assignments might be appropriate--and accepted--for
courses which had never been offered and were still being planned.
Our views about what sorts of student library experiences might
lead to high-level library competence were largely negative; we
were convinced that traditional instruction in the use of the library
was limited and ineffective, if not downright harmful. We were
not even clear about what we meant by the term "library competence, " and we had only vague notions about the kinds of knowledge
and understanding and skill it might involve. And finally, on the
matter of the possible contribution of library competence to general
academic achievement, we were conscious of the fact that there is
little agreement in the academic world on how such achievement
should be defined and measured.

In short, we "explored ways of investigating" innumerable variables involved in a series of ill-defined questions. As we explored, the questions gradually took shape:

> 1. What kinds of assignments work? i. e., what should their objectives be, how should they be related to courses, how should they be presented, how discussed, how evaluated, how ordered in a sequence, etc.
>
> 2. What sort of library competence is appropriate for academic work? How can it be measured? What factors in the student's capacity, experience, and training are associated with his attainment of it?
>
> 3. What are the measures of general academic achievement which might be suitable to use in the attempt to examine any possible contribution of library competence to such achievement? How is library competence related to other contributing factors?

Gathering and analyzing data. --In gathering data on the library assignments we used every technique indicated in our proposal: questionnaires, interviews, logs, products of assignments, and so on, depending on what we hoped to find out about each specific one. In our attempt to analyze these data, however, we encountered a number of difficulties. When we depended completely on instructors for implementation of assignments, for example, our returns were incomplete. In some instances, when the assignment was individualized, permitting the student great freedom in his choice of topic and search procedure, we found it difficult if not impossible to arrive at reasonably uniform standards of performance. We had insufficient staff to make thorough evaluation of sources used for papers. Such an evaluation would call not only for full command of the literature on the topic of the paper but also for thorough familiarity with the library's holdings in the area. In order that students not waste time on some assignments, we scheduled ourselves to be in the library to assist them; this meant that the products of these assignments were biased in favor of those students who, for whatever reason, made use of this assistance. Only once did we succeed in getting the faculty to accept a question concerned with a library assignment in a final examination.[4] And, even here, we were somewhat concerned that the question might

have measured sheer memory of certain reference tools rather
than the desired capacity to select a type of tool appropriate for a
given purpose.

The small sample studies reported in Chapter IV gave us
the opportunity to gather data under conditions of better control.
We could design performance tests, controlling steps to be taken,
time allowed, standards for evaluation--all without concerning ourselves about relating the work to any specific course objectives or
content. Interviews, questionnaires, and paper-and-pencil tests
could be administered to all students under uniform conditions. And
the fact that the sample was chosen on a random basis made it
possible for us to use nonparametric, small sample statistics to
analyze the data gathered.

The Monteith Program Study[5] provided us with data on such
measures of academic achievement as class status, honor point
average, and scores on Graduate Record Examinations, on such
background factors as parents' education and rating of high school
attended, and on such personality measures as the Omnibus Personality Inventory. Here, again, we found nonparametric statistics
useful for analysis.

Conclusions and implications for library research. --The most
important conclusion we arrived at as a result of our small random-
sample studies, reported in Chapter IV, was that the technique, itself, is most promising. There are so many variables involved in
the use of library tools and resources that it would seem wise for
investigators to make the most of methods which provide an opportunity for studies in depth of a small number of cases. Through
such studies it should be possible to develop hypotheses worthy of
testing with a larger number of respondents. We were struck for
example, by the high correlation we found between performance on
our library tests and scores on the Terman Concept Mastery Test
--recommended as a good measure for the capacity to determine
quickly the probable odds in favor of a particular search strategy.
Most of our performance tests were devised as measures of what
we assumed to be the skills needed for common library-use problems
rather than as measures of the achievement of the objectives set for

our own library assignments. The one test which did measure
such achievement, the test of rapid book evaluation skill, did show
large enough correspondence with the exposure to the assignment--
and small enough correspondence with scores on a standard library
test--to justify the conclusion that small sample studies might be
useful in evaluating the effectiveness of non-traditional instruction
in the use of the library.

Our analysis, presented in Chapter III, of the association
between exposure to a series of library assignments and other
variables in the background and achievement of students was mostly
inconclusive. But the negative correlation between exposure to library assignments and attrition suggests further investigation of
some sort. The gains--significantly greater than that of other
groups--made by the exposed sample on the Theoretical Orientation
factor in the Omnibus Personality Inventory also suggests a point
worth further exploration. We were gratified, too, by the fact that
our "exposed sample" were active participants in the group life of
the campus.

In short, our experience with small samples and with nonparametric statistics leads us to recommend wider use of such
methods in library research.

But the major conclusions resulting from our work with student library experiences are reflected in the model program presented in Chapter V. The program consists of a sequence of ten
library assignments related to the Monteith curriculum. The assignments are coordinated with the three basic subject fields covered in the curriculum and they extend through the full four years
of the student's undergraduate work. The sequence derives unity
and coherence from a theoretical framework which encompasses
our conclusions concerning the nature of library competence needed
for academic work. In brief, this framework presents the library
as a complex, but unified system of "ways" or paths to library resources. The part of the system which is particularly important
for academic work is the machinery through which the results of
scholarly and scientific work are reported, organized and communicated. The assignments are designed to give students

experiences with the total library system, and particularly with the scholarly-reporting part of it, such that they can discover empirically certain general principles about the way the system is organized and about the choices and decisions one must make in order to use it effectively.

Plans for implementing the program take into account what we learned from our analysis of social structure. Plans for evaluation and for continuing research take into account not only our work in connection with the assignments presented in the pilot project but also some insights which stem from our small sample studies of library performance.

The program as a whole, then, resulted not from any individual experiment nor from any comprehensive set of "findings." Rather, it developed gradually from our explorations into the many different aspects of the whole project, from discussions with our faculty colleagues, and from our own reflections upon our experiences. We are satisfied, nevertheless, that the program meets the goal stated in our proposal:

> The pilot project will produce records which will serve as the basis for an accurate and detailed plan for the second phase of the Monteith Library Program. It will enable us to base proposed staff, budget, and procedures on actual experience. In planning the second phase, we will know something of what happens in the library when large numbers of students are given certain kinds of library assignments. We will have some tentative ideas about what students learn from these assignments and about how such learning can be tested. We will be able to propose a research design through which the results of this kind of library program can be subjected to more rigorous scientific achievement. [6]

Faculty Use of Bibliographical Service

Although the bibliographical assistance program was a subsidary part of the pilot project, three aspects of it are of sufficient interest to be considered in this report. The part played by the assistants in the total social structure is presented in Chapter II. The Appendix includes excerpts from our progress reports which describe the activities we carried on, the difficulties we encountered, and our conclusions with regard to training and supervision of the

assistants.   And Chapter VI reports, in accordance with our proposal, "a tentative analysis of patterns of faculty use of library
resources. "7

Defining the question and identifying variables. --We were
concerned first of all with learning what the faculty used the
bibliographical service for.   In the major category of teaching we
were able to identify such sub-categories as basic course preparation, general background reading, and identification of references to
be recommended as student reading.   We found that research tasks
could be classified as being related to specific publications or
projects, to keeping up with one's own field, and to study in new
or peripheral fields.

Next, we were concerned with finding out what sorts of tasks
were assigned.   Here the major categories were "bibliographical"
and "informational, " and we were able to identify tasks which called
for abstracting, exhaustive bibliographical searching, scouting and
selective work, and so forth.

We were able to analyze data on each of these two major
questions in terms of the other and in terms of the subject divisions
of the College, but our data were not sufficiently detailed to permit
analysis in terms of specific disciplines, previous library experiences, or other such individual attributes of the faculty.

Gathering and analyzing data. --We were obliged to rely on
the assistants themselves to provide the data on their work.   This
caused difficulties because most of them were far more concerned
with the job of serving the faculty than with the research work of
the project   and, in any case, they were not experienced in the
matter of keeping proper "field work" records.

In our analysis of the reports of the assistants, therefore,
we contented ourselves with presenting gross statistical description
and focussed our attention on the sub-categories of purpose and of
task we were able to perceive.

Conclusions. --The analysis indicated, in the first place, that
the faculty did, indeed, use the bibliographic service as a resource
for teaching.   A second and more interesting general finding was

that whether the tasks assigned were for teaching or for research, they were much more likely to be bibliographical than informational. And of the bibliographical tasks, most called for selective and scouting activities. We concluded, therefore, that training for bibliographic service to academicians should minimize retrieval of specific information and should stress, instead, bibliographies and indexes, particularly selective bibliographical tools, scouting techniques, and the apparatus of reporting and communication in the academic disciplines.

Notes

1. Proposal, p. 2.

2. Proposal, p. 5-8.

3. Proposal, p. 5-8.

4. See "Independence Assignment," Appendix I, p. 180-181.

5. Project No. 1455, Cooperative Research Branch, Office of Education, Department of Health, Education and Welfare.

6. Proposal, p. 2. Actually, the model program proposed in Chapter V is based on ideas which are considerably less tentative than the above would suggest. Furthermore, a research proposal including plans for implementing procedures, staff, budget, and suggested research design, has been prepared for use in connection with the program if and when funds become available to put it into effect.

7. Proposal, p. 8.

Appendix I

Library Assignments in the Pilot Project

Sequence A: Experienced by Students Who Entered in the Fall of 1959 and the Spring of 1960

Assignment 1 (Fall, 1959, Science of Society I)

Nature of the course assignment. -- The first unit of the Science of Society course was built around a popular account of the conduct of the United States prisoners of war in the Korean War. The faculty wished to begin with a relatively self-contained unit of work which would introduce the student to several social science disciplines so that the student could see that different disciplines can be used to study the same social phenomenon but that they will formulate different questions, use different methods to pursue these questions, draw on different sources of parallel and comparative data, come up with different insights and answers.

The book of readings reprinted for the unit included items selected to represent six different disciplines and, for each discipline, a list of further readings was provided. Each discussion section of 12 students was divided into six teams of two students responsible for an oral or written report on one of the six approaches to the problem.

Purpose of the library component. -- The library component was seen as introduction of these freshmen students to the general topography of a large university library. They were to use the card catalog to find the call numbers of the references listed, use the directory to find the location in which the books were to be found, and find the books on the open shelves.

Administration of the assignment. -- There were about 320 students enrolled in the course, so that, in the six weeks provided for the unit, 50 to 60 students would be using the references on one of the six bibliographies. The library purchased extra copies

145

of many of the books and xeroxed extra copies of the journal articles listed.   One copy of each reference was put on "special reserve" behind the circulation desk, but the others were shelved in
their customary places, available for short-term loan.

In order to provide guidance for those students who might
be interested in exploring beyond the references listed in the text,
the library project director-to-be was asked to write an article to
be included along with the readings reprinted in the text.   This
article identified potentially useful reference tools, indicated locations of certain kinds of information, suggested tools which might
help the student understand some of the more technical items on
the bibliographies.

Evaluation. --Eight of the nine faculty members who had
experience with this unit were interviewed in the summer and fall
of 1962.   All reported, directly or indirectly, that they were
pleased with the integration of the library component of the assignment with the course.   We quote one:

> ...that the entering students should have been sent to the
> library in connection with brainwashing seemed a matter of
> course, and it might even have seemed that way to the stu-
> dents insofar as anything in that kind of wonderful edentate
> condition seems to be normal in the matter of course.

Three people, however, would not have wished to repeat the library
work as given: one because "the students didn't learn much, "
another because he would rather make the assignment more demand-
ing by introducing the students to the similarities and differences in
the literature of the disciplines involved, and a third, because he
would rather spend this time teaching the students to read critically.

Fourteen of the sixteen members of this class who appeared
in the small samples studies conducted in the summers of 1961 and
1962 reported that they had indeed gone to the library and secured
some of the items on one of the bibliographies.   Nine of them had
done reports based on materials from the library.   Five more had
used this work to contribute to class discussions.   One could not
remember anything except that there had been such a unit of work.
One did not report.

These individual discontents did not prevent the faculty from repeating this unit, including the library component, without essential change in the Fall of 1962.

The circulation records of the "last" copy of each reference, i.e., the copy on special reserve, showed no circulation for many items. From this, we infer that most of the students did not read all of the sources listed on any one bibliography.

Conclusions. --The assignment seems to have served its purpose of getting the students to actually use the library during his first few weeks on campus and thus to become acquainted with its general organization. The fact that the assignment was not required with uniform strictness by all of the instructors meant that the readers among the students read everything on the list, the non-readers only enough to get by. In this sense, our experience with the assignment was commonplace. Also commonplace was the division of labor between the faculty and the librarians; the faculty selected the references and the librarians facilitated students' use of them. The assignment was somewhat unusual, nevertheless, in that it introduced freshmen to the library not in the context of an orientation tour and lecture but in the context of a real need for a real course.

Assignment 2 (Spring, 1960, Science of Society II)

Nature of the course assignment. --The second semester of the Science of Society course was designed to bring the student to understand the characteristics and quality of such complex social organizations as institutions and cities and to learn through experience what is involved in the scientific study of such phenomena. He was required to design and carry through a semester-long research project on one of a list of 113 topics concerned with some aspect of the work of one of 22 cooperating social agencies in Detroit--such agencies as the Urban League, the Humane Society, Travelers' Aid, etc.

As a first step in this research project, the student was expected to use the library to find materials to help him in his work.

Purpose of the library component. --It is usually assumed
that the first step in any research is the "search of the literature."
The library assignment, then, demonstrated this assumption. Since
this was to be an assignment for freshmen, however, the library
exploration was thought of not as an exhaustive search to see that
the proposed investigation had not already been carried out, but as
a way of getting ideas about promising approaches and useful methods. And it was also expected to be a highly motivated experience
in the subject approach to library resources.

Administration of the assignment. --In preparation for the
assignment, librarians of the University Library staff carried
through preliminary searches of the literature, trying to identify
fruitful search patterns for each of the topics on the list. Three
of these librarians and the project director-to-be conducted four
resource meetings for the students. They discussed the use of
certain reference tools, especially those in the social sciences, and
they drew on their own experience in conducting the preliminary
searches.

Each student was required to hand in a report on his library
research, including a) a log of the search process in the library--
subjects searched in the card catalog or in indexes, titles of items
sought, whether or not these items were found, were useful, etc.
--b) responses to a questionnaire designed to summarize the search
experience--number of items in bibliography so far, reference tool
most useful, etc.--and c) an essay on the library search as an
experience--problems encountered, most useful sources, etc. We
hoped that preparing these reports would make the student aware of
the pattern in his search.

Students who entered in the Spring of 1960 were enrolled in
the first two semesters of the Science of Society course simulta-
neously, so that they were also involved in the research project assignment. The resource meetings conducted for this group introduced the students to three "state of the art" bibliographical
summary works: Hoselitz' Readers Guide to the Social Sciences,
Lindzey's Handbook of Social Psychology and Shils' The Present
State of American Sociology. The students were advised to use

these works to orient themselves to the general area of the topic
of their proposed research and to follow a chain of inquiry from
one cited work to another.

Evaluation. --Faculty members reacted to this course assignment and its library component so articulately that quotations from
the interviews offer revealing evidence:

> ...The research project--here my impression is that while
> we make a how to the library, I would swear it is pretty
> much pro forma. In my own case I feel it's slightly hypo-
> critical inasmuch as I would say, "go look up things" and
> yet I don't think I could actually help them look it up...

> ...Many of the students, for their research projects, were
> able to collect a great deal of relevant material in relation
> to their topics. Only a few of them were able to express
> what they had gained from it, and how it had influenced
> their thinking, how they had selected what was important to
> it or useful to it, and left the things which would have
> driven them in another direction. Most of the time I had to
> ask them to add a little bibliographical note to their paper
> in which they were doing precisely that, this kind of critical
> appreciation of the books they had read. But the fact is
> that more than half of my students were able to get inter-
> esting material which I myself had not suggested to them.
> One of the useful things we have done was what we did for
> the very first research project, which was to have them
> keep a log of their search and their findings. Another was
> what we did for the students who entered in the spring that
> year (the smaller class). This was to assign them to some
> sort of wide review of the literature in an area and ask
> them to start from there for their search in the library...
> I think that keeping the log for the search was probably a
> good idea, except for the format which was used; it was far
> too complicated, and it tended to hide, actually, the inter-
> esting.

This instructor was not satisfied with the bibliographic work
of his students, as a result, the next year for the similar assignment:

> I gave them a list of sources. And then I said, you find
> articles and look over the last ten years relating to this
> subject...And whatever the project was associated with, I
> gave them the possible reference sources for them and told
> them to look for this...And to be able to write up and come
> in the following week with a summary statement for each
> of the articles.

> ...an attitude, I suppose, which balks a little bit at the

notions of retrieval, organization of the library, research
paper, what you will.   Let me say what may be a defect,
although I would probably nurture it as a very dear defect,
in that I have never in my life been able to collect cards
and write a "research paper" from them...I can tell and I
think that I could say that the library project has, in many
cases shown the students their way around, yet I'm always
sad when a student writes a paper obviously that way.
Namely, that cited subject went to the library, went through
card catalog, and approved sources of information, labori-
ously composed research paper, and I suppose I say 'fine
work,' but I still probably prefer the one who cites subjects,
writes on a subject, introduces corrections, if any, in terms
of what he may find out.   I think you can tell the difference.
It's a difference between...passive research and what I
would like to call active research...Active research: I suppose I retain a notion that research is the advancement of
knowledge."

...their research papers have enough field work that they
don't really get to use the library...

I wouldn't want the library project people working with the
students at all.   I'd have them working only with the faculty.
And have the faculty work with the students.   And I wouldn't
have any set of library assignments...Now you might have
the instructors give library assignments in connection with
research projects.   But I'd tie the library assignment to a
research project.

...that first conversation (with the student about his project)
usually results in my giving bibliographic hints...

...One of the things that annoyed me, disturbed me a little
bit about the assignment the first semester, where they
went to the library, and they worked out a bibliography, I
think on their research project...it seemed to me that there
were a whole set of assumptions lying in the minds of the
people on the library project about how the library should
be used which didn't match anything in my head about the
way I use the library.   It seemed to be loaded with these
assumptions which are not evident when you teach kids.   To
learn how to use reference books, what resources are available in the library, specifics like that, seem to me to invade
the teaching function.   I was trying at the same time as
these (library) project people to teach these kids how to do
research projects.   And one of the ways to do a research
project is the way outlined in the library thing.   But that
was just one way, and for some kids it was a very bad, ill-
adapted way to begin their particular research.   They had to
go out and get their feet into some data, and they had to
sit down in an armchair and think and begin to crystallize
and formulate problems, and so on.   At which point, then,
they were ready to go to the library.   But to go prematurely
would have been bad for them.

Whatever you do after this, let it be something which does
not involve me in collecting millions of pieces of paper...

The interviews indicated, also, that a majority of instructors were less than pleased with some or most of the items students found in their library search. They felt that the required
library search had given the students opportunity to find and use
books or articles which were seriously unsuitable. Some instructors objected, in addition, to the fairly strict time table the students and faculty were required to follow. They felt that each instructor is better able to decide if and when a student should use
the library, show a sample of the analytic procedures he is using,
and so on. Within this general objection they objected to the library search required at a given point for all students.

From the interviews we would conclude, in general, that
the faculty saw the research project as primarily an assignment
leading a student to understand the process of research, a process
in which the "search of the literature" plays a strictly subordinate
and not highly valued part. And with freshmen, whose "research"
could not realistically be expected to push back the frontiers of
knowledge, there is also the danger that a search of the literature
will be interpreted as not the beginning but the end of research.

We hypothesized that faculty advisers--each student was
assigned to an adviser for his research project--who were not
favorably disposed toward the library project might have influenced
negatively the performance of their students in the library component of the assignment. We found, first, that we had received
many more library reports from the pro-library project faculty
than from the anti-library project faculty. (This does not mean,
necessarily that more of the students of the pro-faculty did the
assignments; the anti-faculty may simply have neglected to forward
the reports to us). For purposes of study, we then assumed that
the students of the "pro" instructors had probably done their library
work more carefully than the students of the "anti" instructors and
that this might have helped them earn higher grades on the total
research effort. (Since we had more reports from students of

"pro" than of "anti" advisers, the groups were of unequal size).
Using the median test we found that there was a difference significant at $p < .05$, between the grades of the two groups, with the students of the "pro" advisers receiving, as expected, the higher
grades. We found, also, that 11 per cent of the students of the
"pro" advisers but 22 per cent of those of the "anti" advisers received a grade of "F" or "I"--incomplete.

Plans for full analysis of the three-part student reports were
modified because, in spite of every effort, we were unable to secure
complete reports from all students, and because the great variation
in topics and, therefore, in appropriate search strategies--made
evaluation of the students' search patterns almost impossible. From
analysis of partial reports we were able to arrive at some general
conclusions. (We had at least one of the three parts from 250 students, i. e., 66 per cent of the class, but full reports from only
33).

Most of these freshmen were rather unaware of the general
organization of the library. Some spoke of finding items "by accident" in their properly classified place on the open shelves. All
students used the card catalog more than any other bibliographic
tool, though it was not as suitable as periodical indexes for some
of the topics they were concerned with.

They did not, however, confine themselves to the card catalog. Forty per cent reported that some material they wanted was
not in the Wayne Library. Since we wondered whether they had
just not been able to find what they wanted on the shelf, we made
a special check of the logs of these students. We found that they
had used bibliographic tools other than the card catalog more than
their fellow students. We concluded, therefore, that they had come
upon items which were, indeed, not in the University Library collection and that an assignment as unrestricted as this--and given to
380 students--strained the capacity of the Library.

To compare the larger Fall class with the smaller Spring
class, we used reports from 48 students, 24 from each class,
matched as closely as possible as to topics of research. The
Spring students, who had begun work with a bibliographic essay,

used fewer bibliographic tools than did the Fall students. They
used the card catalog 2 1/2 times as frequently as did the Fall
students, but primarily to find specific authors or titles. As expected, use of the bibliographic essay leads to specific references;
lack of such a tool leads to a subject approach to the card catalog.

From the interviews and questionnaires with students in the
class who appeared in our small samples studies, we learned that
all had used library materials for some aspect of the assignment,
most for background information, some for help in formulating a
research problem, a few for data, a few for methodology.

Conclusions. --Clearly, the research assignment led students
to use the library. But neither the faculty nor the students saw
the library component as very important either as a contribution to
the research project or as an experience in dealing with a bibliographical problem. The log did not prove to be a good teaching
device; we found no evidence that it helped students perceive the
search patterns they were using or might better have used. It was,
moreover, complex and time-consuming. Students varied in their
interpretation of the directions for recording the steps they took.
Thus it did not lend itself to detailed analysis of the students' search
processes.

In short, what we learned from the experience of this assignment was mostly negative. The sink-or-swim approach to the
library is a hazardous experience for freshmen. The "search of
the literature," while a respectable part of research procedure,
must be explained and modified when it is used in connection with
research as a teaching-learning experience.

Assignment 3 (Spring, 1960, Science of Society III)

Nature of the course assignment. --The third semester of
this course in the Science of Society was designed to carry the student further in his understanding of complex social organization,
especially of some of the characteristic ways such phenomena change.
Each student was required to undertake the study of some aspect of
a social movement, --a movement to bring about, for example,

national independence, universal education, or religious reform. He
was given a month to complete the required research paper for
which he was expected to gather his own bibliography, though he
could and would then receive help from faculty, the project librarian,
Wayne University librarians. He was expected to use his resources
creatively to reflect on one of the theories of social change he was
studying in the course.

Purpose of the Library Component. --The project staff considered this work a reasonable library assignment. It was expected
to be simple to the extent that social movements are historical
events and thus are unambigiously located in time and space, since
the organization of the library is straight-forward with regard to
historical events. It was expected to be challenging, however, in
that it would require the student to use several kinds of material.
A simple historical account of the Russian Revolution and a good
biography of Lenin would not be sufficient to make a study of Lenin's
leadership in the Russian Revolution, for example. Rather, the student would have to use his imagination to conceive of the letters,
newspaper accounts, possible sources of good journal articles, etc.,
he would need, and then find and use bibliographic reference tools
to help him find these things. Both the cenceptualization and the
search would be difficult.

Administration of the assignment. --We saw the bibliographical problem of the student to be one of the   types depending
upon the social movement he chose to study. If he chose one of
the great revolutionary movements, he would be obliged to find his
way about in a voluminous literature and to select valid sources
relevant to a specific aspect of that movement. If, on the other
hand, he preferred to work in territory less crowded, for example,
an obscure movement or a social change not ordinarily thought of
as a social movement, he might have difficulty locating enough materials. In order to help the students along with both types of
problems, we assigned the bibliographical assistants to the task of
compiling bibliographies, identifying the "best" sources on the great
revolutions and ferreting out whatever they could on the obscure
social movements. They were oriented to this task by way of a

briefing on social movement theory from the chairman of the social
sciences staff. The bibliographies they compiled were collated and
organized by the project librarian and made available to students
in his office in the library.

Evaluation. --Since in this semester the student had his first
opportunity to meet the Monteith requirement that he work semi-
independently the last semester in one of this three basic courses,
the project staff decided to analyze the papers of all of these students (35) as against a sample matched on the basis of College
Placement scores and grades received in the preceding two semesters of the social science course.[1] We were able to match thirty
pairs. We planned to analyze these papers not only to check the
effectiveness of the assignment, but also to test our hypothesis that
students who have attained a level of bibliographic control feel
themselves able to work semi-independently, i.e., that the semi-
independent students would do better bibliographical work.

For a number of reasons, however, we were unable to carry
out this comparison. Some students were permitted to report
orally, some faculty members, in spite of repeated requests, did
not provide us with the written reports. A sample of 17 papers--
from both groups--were, however analyzed for 1) number of items
in the bibliography actually used in the paper, 2) the inclusion of
theoretical and historical materials, 3) the inclusion of primary
sources, the appropriateness of sources included. Out of a possible
15 points on these criteria, 10 of the 17 students in the sample
earned 10 or more. When we compared the scores on this analysis
with the grades on the paper as a whole given by the instructor we
found little correspondence, though no student with a score of less
than eight received a grade higher than B.

The faculty liked the assignment as a whole and approved of
the idea of a paper based on library resources at this point in the
course. But all of them expressed dismay with the number of inadequate bibliographies their students presented. They were particularly concerned with the students' lack of discrimination in their
choice of books and journals.

From the interview and questionnaire responses of the students in the small sample studies, we found that eight of the fourteen who had had the assignment were exceedingly vague about what the assignment had required of them. None saw the assignment as primarily bibliographic though all but one remembered including a bibliography. Of those who remembered the library work, only one reported using any tool other than the card catalog.

The bibliography which had been compiled was consulted very little. Only ten students in the class actually used it.

Conclusions. --It would seem that the use of library resources for the assignment of a paper on a social movement is most appropriate. To be an effective experience in learning how to use the bibliographical machinery of the library it would have to be modified in several ways. Students need preliminary training in the appraisal of library materials. They need to arrive at an understanding of the idea that books and articles can be used as evidence upon which one bases one's own conclusions, rather than as ready-made conclusions which one merely finds. They need, also, to understand the techniques involved in selecting from great masses of material, on the one hand, or tracking down elusive information, on the other. And they need to be made fully aware of the extent to which sources of information are important--and reflected in grades--as part of the total product.

Assignment 4 (Fall, 1960, Science of Society III)

Nature of the course assignment. --The final semester of the three-semester Science of Society course was designed to take the student further in his understanding of complex social organization, finally focussing his attention on civilization and civilizations. He was expected to do a final paper on the "nature of civilized society, and/or...what it is to be a human being in a civilized society." Several themes were suggested as topics he might develop, for example, social mobility and its dilemmas, the relationship between communication and society. He was directed to use his own observation and experience in modern-day America primarily, to draw selectively on relevant texts in his possession secondarily,

and to use "additional materials which you select from the library"
should he need them.   He was told that this assignment was not
meant primarily to be a research paper.

Purpose of the library component. --Although the two project
staff members who worked with the committee which planned this
assignment saw it originally as involving library work for all students, they were, at the same time aware that the social movements
paper, given in the same semester, had been more difficult and
time-consuming than had been anticipated.   They proposed, therefore, that use of the library for this paper be optional. They hoped
that the student would begin his work with reflection on his own experiences, with use of his own books, and that he would think of
the library as being a potential source of materials which would
enrich and extend his own thinking, but as a source to be used only
after that thinking had produced some real questions.

Administration of the assignment. --Because the social movements paper had been difficult, several of the instructors decided
to make this paper optional for their students.   The library component was optional for all, so no special preparations were made
for it.

Evaluation. --Interviews with the faculty revealed that none
of them considered this assignment to be a bibliographic problem,
though three of the six students in the small sample studies who had
had the course, felt that their instructors considered bibliographic
work in grading their papers.

Conclusions. --Clearly the library part of this assignment
was insignificant.   Not all students were expected to use the library
and apparently few did.   We, ourselves, were vague about what
contribution library resources might make to the student's thinking
and about what he might learn about the organization of the library
from the experience of locating such sources.   We have reason to
think, however, that our difficulties were due at least partly to the
fact that the assignment was presented so soon after the difficult
social movements paper and that it was developed by a small committee and not discussed at all adequately in the total staff.   It

simply suffered from the typical academic end-of-the-term rush.

Assignment 5 (Spring, 1961, Humanistic Studies I)

Nature of the course assignment. --The student began his
three-semester-long basic course in Humanistic Studies in his
fourth semester in college. This semester's work was designed to
give him understanding of "man's symbol making in the arts"
through the study of selected musical, artistic and literary works
of Western culture. [2] In the third unit of the semester's work the
students were required to write a "research paper in which they
investigated the social and intellectual milieu of one of the artists
they had studies. "[3] They were to see whether information about
the artist and his milieu contributed to their understanding of one
of the artist's works.

Purpose of the library component. --We saw this fourth assignment as a relatively simply library problem because an artist
has a name and because he can be placed in time and space. The
organizing tools of the library emphasize name, place, date, and
form. They tend to stress literature and the arts.

Administration of the assignment. --To brief the students for
the assignment the project librarian prepared a leaflet, "Notes on
the Use of the Library, " which stressed the biographical approach
to library materials. A short questionnaire was distributed with
the directions for the paper. The questionnaire called for comments
on how the student used the library--where he entered the system,
what tools he used. whether or not he had read the Guide we prepared for him; and on his reaction to the various parts of the total
assignment--the study of the artist's work, the library search, the
writing of the paper.

The project staff also asked that the faculty include questions
on the library work in the final course examination that semester.
The faculty expressed doubt that the questions suggested were really
on as high a level as questions on the content of the readings and
lectures and artistic experiences the students had had. One of the
questions we suggested was included among those given to the

students to help them prepare for the examination, but none was actually used in the final examination.

Evaluation. --In interviews, three members of the four Humanistic Studies staff members expressed dissatisfaction with the bibliographic assignment because they felt that it was not sufficiently challenging for these particular second semester sophomores. [4] They all indicated that they were pleased that the bibliographic component of the assignment had actually led to a required paper, and expressed the hope that all future bibliographic assignments would be as closely integrated with the aims of the course. Although the faculty had themselves proposed that no paper be accepted without our library questionnaire, we actually received only 70, approximately thirty-four per cent return. Judging from these reports, we should say that the library component was imbedded in a difficult course assignment. Fifty-nine per cent of these students had found the actual writing of the paper the most difficult part of their work, thought most reported that studying a specific work of art took the least amount of time and was the easiest part of the task.

The bibliographic component of the assignment was most time consuming for seventy-one per cent of the student respondents. Indeed, fifty-six per cent of them felt that they had insufficient time to do this part of their work properly. On the other hand, doing the research was the most valuable part of the assignment for fifty-six per cent, and the most enjoyable part for thirty-seven per cent of them. Thirty-one per cent of those reporting had found the project librarian's "Notes" helpful to them in some way, and these students earned slightly higher grades on their research papers.

Of the sixteen students in the small sample studies who had completed this course, nine were unable to give a clear statement of the course assignment; eight were not able to describe the method of development of their own work. These findings support our observation that the assignment as a whole was difficult. Ten of the students in the sample did not see the library work as an integral part of the assignment although all but one did use library for his work.

Conclusions. --The assignment did bring almost all of the

students into the library. That many of them did not perceive the
bibliographical aspect as part of what was required could mean that
the assignment was not set clearly, or it could mean that the bibliographic component was so completely a part of the course assignment that students did not feel that it needed to be mentioned
specifically.

As a problem in the use of bibliographic organization, this
assignment was less difficult than those the students had already
encountered, thought it did introduce them to the literature of new
fields of study. The faculty were not enthusiastic, being concerned
primarily that the challenge of responding to a work of art not be
diluted by what seemed to them the rather high-schoolish task of
finding information in the library.

Assignment 6 (Spring, 1961, Natural Science IV)

Nature of the course assignment. --In the fourth and last
semester of the basic course in the natural sciences, the philosophy
of science constituted one of the three units of study. The faculty
committee responsible for this unit of work assigned a paper in
which the student was expected to demonstrate his ability to see
and to work with a genuine problem in the philosophy of science.
The project staff proposed that this paper be based on sources the
student would find for himself in the library.

Philosophy of the library component. --This library assignment was designed to introduce the student to a new area of literature, an area which is thoroughly organized but for the specialist
rather than the layman.

While the project staff wanted the student to find and select
his own materials, the faculty committee responsible for the assignment felt that he would need some help, because finding suitable
materials and discriminating against unsuitable ones is unusually
difficult for the non-scientist. Much of the material in the philogo-
phy of science is beyond the comprehension of the non-specialist,
and much of the popularization in the area is not acceptable on the
college level for several reasons. The project staff suggested a

procedure which the committee agreed to.

    <u>Administration of the assignment.</u> --The faculty committee planned that the student would select one of fifteen broad areas such as cybernetics, probability, the relationship between technology and culture. He would then have about ten days to use the library to do preliminary searching, reading and thinking which would result in a prospectus of the paper he wished to do. This would include his statement of a specific problem he had set for himself in the area, his bibliography, and the details of his plan for developing the topic. His instructor would review the prospectus, make suggestions as needed. The student would then have four to five weeks to complete his paper.

    In order to test pathways to the kinds of sources the faculty might find acceptable and be sure that the Wayne State Library could cope with this number of students, the six bibliographic assistants who had just been engaged to work with the natural sciences staff did a preliminary search for library materials usable by a sophomore student. Under the direction of the project librarian, the assistants, all of whom were majors or graduate students in scientific disciplines, began their search with a) the card catalog, or b) an encyclopedia article, or c) a bibliography included in the course text. Before the Monteith students were given the assignment, the bibliographic assistants had submitted to the faculty committee the bibliographies they had compiled to date. They had reported that the students could find adequate sources by entering the library system from any of these three starting points, and that there were sufficient materials to accommodate the number of students enrolled. Before the prospectuses were due, all of the bibliographies the assistants had prepared were in the hands of the faculty to use in making suggestions to students. We requested that faculty refrain from referring a student to specific titles unless the student was hopelessly lost.

    In order to help the student begin his search, the project director wrote a leaflet "Suggested Library Procedures for your Term Paper" which was put in the hands of the student along with the list of the fifteen areas in which he could work.

The project staff also worked out a short questionnaire to
check the effectiveness of the bibliographic work in relation to the
course assignment, the effectiveness of the administrative procedures, and the capacity of the Wayne State Library to handle this
number of students involved in such work in this period of time.
Faculty members distributed these questionnaires to students shortly
before the research papers were due.   The students were expected
to turn in the completed questionnaire along with the final paper.

Evaluation. --In interview with five of the seven faculty
members who had taught this course, three expressed satisfaction
with the assignment as such and with its bibliographic component as
it was planned. 5   Two of them were dissatisfied--one felt that the
students should have learned to build an adequate bibliography before
the second semester of the sophomore year and one felt that the
non-specialist student was not capable to do so in this particular
area.   The three who were satisfied liked not only this specific
assignment but this type of assignment--one which calls for the student to select his own problem and build his own bibliography. All
five were unhappy that students had relied entirely on books and
ignored periodical literature.   No one felt that the bibliographic
assistants' work had contributed anything significant to student or
faculty in this unit of work.

Forty-five questionnaires, less than twenty-five per cent,
were returned.   Judging from the reports from this group of students, this course assignment was somewhat difficult, though sixty-
six per cent were satisfied with their work.   Fifty-six per cent
found writing the paper was more difficult than doing the research
for it and fifty-five per cent found writing the paper more difficult
than either selecting a problem or doing the necessary research
for it.   Most reported that doing the research for the paper was
at once more valuable, more enjoyable and more time-consuming
than writing the paper.

Forty-two per cent of the respondents reported that the
"Suggested Library Procedures for your Term Paper" was useful
to them in this work.   These students used significantly more

references discussed in this leaflet than those who reported that the leaflet was not helpful to them.   Whether or not the student had used the "Suggested Library Procedures..." had no noticeable relationship with his overall satisfaction, his difficulty or ease in selecting a research problem, or with the problems he encountered in his work.

Under the method of administration and preparation we used, the resources of the Wayne State Library were strained.   Over seventy-five per cent of the respondents reported that needed materials were out or unavailable.   This may have been caused by lack of ability to identify and locate useful materials, though any such lack less than three per cent perceived.   The responses of the sixteen students in the sample studies who had completed this course also indicated that the assignment was difficult.   Only two of this group were able to give a clear statement of what the assignment was; only three were able to describe the process of development in their own work.

Only one of the sixteen perceived the assignment as involving a bibliographic problem, though all used the library for this work and six mentioned their work in the library when describing the process of developing their paper.   None reported difficulties getting necessary library materials.   Three, out of eleven asked, had found the "Suggested Procedures in the Library" helpful.

Conclusions. --Though there is no doubt that this assignment caused students to use the library, as it was administered, it resulted in feelings of frustration.   The Wayne State Library was not able to cope with so many students searching for materials with so little guidance or preparation.   Since the questionnaires from the forty-five students were written just as the class was finishing this work, we consider their information about library problems to be more reliable than the reports of the small sample students who reported two weeks or a year after completing the course, and whose problems getting materials may have faded from memory.   The work of the bibliographic assistants did not alert us to the inadequacy of the library for this assignment because neither they nor the faculty committee coordinated their bibliographies; many of the same books appeared in the bibliography of more than one bibliographic assistant.

The fact that the three starting places suggested in the briefing statement did not lead the students to periodical literature deserves further study. Perhaps a quite different approach is needed if the literature of science is to be used by the non-specialist.

Sequence B: Experienced by Students Who Entered in the Fall of 1960

Assignment I (Fall, 1960, Science of Society I)

Nature of the course assignment. --When the Science of Society course was presented for the second time, in the Fall of 1960, it was introduced by a unit which dealt with three different concepts of what man is: 1) man, the species homo sapiens of the physical anthropologist, 2) the man of tribal tradition, and 3) man, the actor and builder of culture whom the social scientist sees. The first assignment was designed to conceptualize man as homo sapiens. The student was asked to work out a visual presentation of the man in geological time, a device such as those which use a clock diagram to show the brevity of man's history on earth. The presentation was to be understandable to a young child.

Purpose of the library component. --As a library experience, we saw this assignment serving exactly the same purpose as that which had been used in the previous year--it would introduce the freshman to the general topography of a large university library. He would use the card catalog to find call numbers, the directory to find locations, and the open shelf arrangement to locate specific titles.

Administration of the assignment. --The project staff drew up a bibliography of sources of information on the topic and distributed this to them. The project staff also prepared an exhibit entitled Ontogeny Recapitulates Phylogeny which was placed prominently in the library. The exhibit, which included books open to appropriate charts was designed to capture the interest of the entering freshmen in the assignment and also to give him clues about the appropriate parts of the books on his bibliography.

Evaluation. --The library component of this assignment made little impression on the faculty. None of those interviewed had any comments to make on this aspect. Nine of the twenty-two students in the small sample studies who had this assignment did not remember it at all. Of the seven who did the work and remembered it, two did not use the library for it.

Conclusion. --Although this assignment was designed to provide the same library experience as that presented to entering freshmen in the previous year, it appears not to have been as effective. Several factors may have helped to bring this about. The faculty felt that there were too many assignments made in this semester and some deleted at least one of the set proposed by the committee responsible for the semester plan. At least one instructor deleted this assignment. The fact that all students were referred to the same list of sources meant that none needed to feel responsibility for the showing of his "team" as had the students the previous year. And, most important, the information for which the sources were recommended was not too hard to find elsewhere--in a home encyclopedia, for example.

Assignment 2 (Fall, 1960, Science of Society I)

Nature of the course assignment. --The third unit of this semester's work was devoted to explaining and demonstrating some of the much used analytic concepts in the social disciplines: relation, role, small group. This unit extended also through the second and third semesters of the course. The students read relevant work done by two specialists in the study of the small group. One of these authors had written about the same piece of work for three different journals directed to three different audiences. All three articles were included in the student's basic texts. The student was expected to write a short paper entitled: What is this scientist's audience for each of the three selections? Alternatively the student would write a short paper on "The Structure of Street-Corner

Society as a Book. " The alternate paper was expected to direct
him to observe and reflect upon the physical organization--Title
page, Table of Contents, Introduction, and especially, the methodological Appendix of this book, which constituted a basic text, and
to think about what this physical organization itself tells the reader.

Philosophy of the library component. --We saw this assignment as moving the student to the other end of the scale in his library experience, i. e., from the gross organization of the library
to the detailed characteristics of the book. If the student developed
the habit of thinking critically about the relationship between a writer
and the audience he is addressing, and about the significance of the
organization of a published work, he would be taking a step toward
overcoming the common student affliction of adhering to belief in
"the democracy of books--one book is as good as another"--to quote
one of our Monteith instructors.

Administration of the assignment. --Reponsibility for implementing the assignment was left entirely with individual instructors.

Evaluation. --Only two of the fifteen instructors were sufficiently impressed with the assignment to be able to comment on
it when they were interviewed two years later. One had omitted
the assignment because he felt his students were overloaded with
written work. Another reported that he "got no feedback at all, "
although his students had done the work. Students questioned in the
small sample studies were equally vague.

Conclusions. --In spite of all this apparent lack of impact,
we gathered, from informal conversations with the faculty at the
time the assignment was given, that the assignment suffered not
from any intrinsic lack of merit but because it was placed in the
midst of a very crowded list of assignments. All the faculty feels
strongly that students should early and continuously be helped to
sharpen their critical faculties and thus their ability to build bibliographies of appropriate, reliable items. All agree that this sort
of assignment is a step in this direction.

Assignment 3 (Fall, 1960, Science of Society I)

Nature of the course assignment. --The last unit in the first

semester of the basic course in the social sciences was devoted to
the study of socialization--the process whereby the young of _homo
sapiens_ becomes a language-speaking, tool-using, role-taking,
socially and ethically dependable human being. The student had
been asked to read an autobiography, one of his own choice. He
was now asked to write a paper analyzing the adolescence of the
subject/author of this autobiography, using the conceptual framework proposed by Erik Erikson in "The Problem of Ego Identity"
(_Psychological Issues,_ vol. I, no. 1, 1959). Because no autobiography tells the whole story, he was expected to use the library to
find materials which might shed light on the adolescent pattern of
the socialization process of the autobiographer.

Philosophy of the library component. --The library problem
involved in the assignment called for a subject approach, the first
this class had encountered. We considered it an appropriate introduction to the subject approach because the materials to be sought
would be concerned with a person--a person who has a name and
who exists in space and time. Biographical dictionaries and encyclopedias would be obvious starting places for the search and they
are easy to use. Catalogs and indexes emphasize names, the
names of people and places and periods. The assignment seemed
a good one to introduce the student to the idea of using clues to
lead from one source to another.

Administration of the assignment. --To help the students get
started on their search for materials, the project librarian wrote
a guide to the reference works in biography, and both the project
director and the project librarian offered to come to the small
discussion sections to discuss with students the organization of biographical reference sources and to show these sources in the library
if time allowed. Seven of the fourteen instructors accepted the
offer. Others indicated that they would have liked to have done so,
had they not already made plans for other work.

Evaluation. --The instructors opinions on this assignment,
expressed in staff meetings, in informal conversations, and in
formal interviews, were almost unanimous. With one exception all

agreed that the Erikson framework was conceptually too difficult for the freshman student. For that reason, they felt, the biographic work, which only a minority of students did in any case, was without point, and therefore an additional source of frustration. Each instructor was asked to turn over to the Project Research Analyst one "average" paper. Out of the fourteen papers collected, eight included bibliographies. The eight showed that the students had used bibliographies and/or periodical indexes, and/or encyclopedias in their library search. Further, there was internal evidence in the papers that the bibliography was used in every case. One of these eight papers had a very poor grade, however, and a note to the student pointing out that her conceptualization of the socialization process is inadequate and faulty. The six papers without bibliographies attached or used were graded "A," "B," "B-" and "C." The instructor appended a note asking for bibliography in two of the six only. We concluded, therefore, that the inclusion and use of a bibliography was not an important factor in the instructor's grading of the assignment.

The responses of the nineteen students in the small sample studies who had finished this semester indicated that this assignment was indeed difficult. Only five of the nineteen could give a good, clear statement of what was expected in the assignment. Six students reported trouble in understanding the concepts involved, two more trouble applying the relevant concepts to the data they had. Ten did not report the specific sources of difficulty and one did not answer.

Only two reported that they saw this assignment to involve a bibliographic problem, although eight had been in discussion sections in which either the project director or project librarian had given a briefing on biographical reference organization. Of the fourteen who remembered receiving the written guide to sources, only five had used it to get hints about where to find biographical information.

Conclusion. --The lesson we learned most vividly from this assignment was that the library component of an assignment shares in the reaction earned by the assignment itself. We are still convinced that a biographical problem offers a suitable introduction to the subject approach to library resources. But in this case, the conceptual difficulty of the host assignment was so great that it made the library problem seem more difficult than it was. The students were inclined to blame the library for not helping them with their conceptual problem. And the faculty, knowing that the library could not help them at this point, were inclined to slight the library problem altogether. Some did not require it. Most did not give it much weight in grading.

Assignment 4 (Spring, 1961, Science of Society II)

Nature of the course assignment. --The second time the Science of Society course was offered, students were once again required to plan and complete a research project in the second semester. This time, however, they were not given a list of topics to choose from but were encouraged to enroll in the discussion section of an instructor whose research concerns lay in an area they were interested in, e.g., underdeveloped countries, ethnic relations, early childhood, etc. The change meant that the students had greater latitude in their choice of topics and that they were not necessarily involved in field research.

Philosophy of the library component. --The Library Project Staff saw this research assignment as one, like that given in the previous year, which naturally and inevitably called for the use of library resources. The student would be obliged to orient himself to the problem he had chosen to work on, to see what kinds of approaches and concepts had been used to study it, to investigate various methods and instruments which might be used to gather and analyze data pertaining to it. In order to find such library resoures, he would need to use the bibliographic organizing tools of the library and would thus learn how to use them.

Administration of the assignment. --As a result of our experience the previous year, the project staff had been convinced that students needed more direct guidance in their approach to the library. We were gradually becoming aware of the fact that the organization of the typically "library" tools, i. e., the card catalog, the periodical indexes, the "types" of reference books, was not as well suited to the needs of this assignment as would be an organizing framework which would fit the social science disciplines. Each discipline, we felt, was "bibliographically controlled" to a greater or lesser degree by special encyclopedias, bibliographies, indexes, abstracting services, journals which reported original research, series which summarized research, etc. An understanding of this bibliographical machinery would facilitate the students search for materials relevant to his own research problem.

We hoped, however, that we could do more than just introduce the student to specific tools he would find useful. We wanted him to understand that certain kinds of tools perform certain kinds of functions for each discipline. In collaboration with the chairman of the Division, therefore, we worked out a chart which listed types of publications and then asked the student to identify the type he might find useful, and name specific titles if he knew them. The object of this exercise, as we saw it, was to focus the student's attention on bibliographical functions, as well as to find out how much he knew about specific tools.

The students were given a week to fill in the chart and then were given a list of the sources, for each discipline, which served the functions indicated on the chart. (The specialists on the social sciences staff had been asked to recommend items for inclusion on this list).

Evaluation. --A minority of the faculty objected vigorously to the use of the chart and the recommended list of sources, apparently on the grounds that it over-structured the student's approach to resources, that it suggested that any statement on a topic could be described as "definitive," that sources were recommended in a wholesale fashion rather than in terms of the individual student's need and development, and that--in the final analysis--recommending sources was the business of faculty, not of librarians. Since most of the staff did not feel strongly about these matters,

the chart and the list were distributed to students, but we received
only a ten per cent return on the chart.   In interviews and through
conversations we gathered, moreover, that none of the faculty saw
the experience in locating and using library resources as figuring
prominently in the research project assignment.

Nevertheless, an overwhelming proportion of the students
did, in fact, use the library for the assignment.   The research
analyst used questionnaires to investigate student experiences with
the assignment, administering one questionnaire four weeks after
the beginning of the semester and designing a second to be handed
in with the completed paper.   Two hundred five of the 275 students
registered in the course completed the first questionnaire, 141
handed in the second, and 132 completed both.   Eighty-seven per
cent were using the library by the end of the first four weeks and
slightly more did so before they were through.   Thirty-two per
cent were using only library materials for their work, while 55 per
cent were doing a combination of field and library research.

From the questionnaires we learned also that students used
the library to get oriented to the area of their research problems
and to get ideas about limiting their work to a specific topic more than
for any other purpose.   The major reference tools used, in order
of frequency checked were: the card catalog, course materials,
the Readers' Guide, general encyclopedias, and scholarly journals.
A number of students used such reference tools as historical and
biographical indexes, Dissertation Abstracts, and abstracting
services in the scholarly disciplines, but most used only the standard reference tools.

Of the 214 students who responded on one or the other of
the two questionnaires, 15 per cent reported some difficulty in getting help from the University librarians in their work.   Forty-one
per cent reported that they sought help from librarians "only as a
last resort. "   About half of the students saw the project librarian
as a helpful or potentially helpful resource person, but only a
small per cent actually availed themselves of his service.

The questionnaire data were not sufficient to show to what
extent the resources of the library were adequate to meet the

demands put upon them by the assignment. By the end of four weeks, however, 57 per cent of the students responding reported having experienced problems of one sort or another. By the end of the semester, 82 per cent reported problems, 33 per cent indicating that materials they needed were charged out, 13 per cent referring to frustrations with library rules and regulations.

Asked about their own library skills, 75 per cent indicated that they felt their library skills were "adequate" for the research project, though, at the time of the first questionnaire 60 per cent and at the time of the final questionnaire, 41 per cent had felt that they needed more training. Only 2 per cent indicated that they would be interested in a course to develop library skills.

The responses from the students in the small sample studies indicated that somewhat less than half considered the library work an important aspect of the research project assignment and that even these considered it less important than such other aspects as analysis of findings, formulations of problem, etc.

Conclusion. --In one sense, our experience with the library aspect of the research project the second time was much what it had been the first time. The assignment did get students to use the library and use it rather extensively. At the same time, this class seemed no more than the former one to perceive their library work as a significant part of the total assignment nor to acquire a greater comprehension of the organization of library resources. This time, however, hostility to the assignment came more from faculty than from students. The students were less burdened, less confused by the questionnaires than the previous had been by the log, questionnaire, and report. The faculty, however, expressed their objection openly and vigorously to what they saw as our attempt to take a more active part in structuring the experience of the students. Our morale suffered as a result of the attacks upon our proposals, but on later reflection we came to the conclusion that our attempt to identify and describe the functions of tools in the academic disciplines had contributed to our own thinking, particularly in making us conscious of the characteristics of the organization of scholarly literature as distinct from the characteristics of the organizing tools of the library world.

Assignment 5 (Fall, 1961, Science of Society III)

Nature of the course assignment. --The second time the
faculty offered the final semester in the Science of Society basic
sequence, they opened with the study of the Sacco-Vanzetti case as
a focal point through which to study: 1) the legal system, 2) social
conscience, 3) civil rights, 4) integration of the immigrant, and 5)
radicals and radical movements--all in the context of the complex
society.

Philosophy of the library component. --This assignment
occurred in the third semester of the library project, after the
changes instituted as a result of our reflections of the summer of
1961.   We had learned from the faculty's dissatisfaction with the
sources used by students in their research project reports and from
the performance of the students in the first small sample study on
the "quick book evaluation" task that most students lack discrimination and sophistication in their choice of materials for academic
work.   We decided, therefore, to present an exercise deliberately
planned to help them acquire the skill and knowledge needed for
effective use of the large open-shelf collection of books.   The Sacco-
Vanzetti problem offered a convenient vehicle for the exercise,
since the students were using only a casebook of primary documents.
Collateral readings concerned with the five aspects of the problem
to be stressed would contribute to the discussion.

Administration of the assignment. --We assembled five sets
of ten books, one on each of the five areas to be discussed.   Each
set was selected to demonstrate the great variety of materials to
be found on the open shelves of the library.   Each included at least
one bound scientific journal, with at least one relevant article, at
least one primary document, at least one book which would be
difficult to find through the card catalog--a book in a series for
example--at least one book which had a comprehensive bibliography,
at least one obviously secondary and superficial book--a high school
text, for example--at least one book by an apparently unqualified
author, at least one outstanding monographic study.   In general, the

assignment was planned in such a way that the student would encounter different kinds of easily recognizable "junk" and different
kinds of easily recognizable and probably reliable books and articles.

The assignment was spread over a period of four weeks,
with each discussion section given one week to complete it.   One or
another member of the project staff visited each discussion section,
where he gave each student a briefing statement prepared by the
project librarian.   At the same time, the student chose a particular
time to do the assignment, so that traffic jams could be avoided.

The five sets of books were assembled in a room in the
college and placed under the supervision of a student assistant. The
assistant gave each student a checklist to use in doing the assignment and collected it when the student was finished.   At the end of
the week, a project staff member returned to the discussion section
to lead discussion of the problems involved in rapid appraisal of
books for academic work.

Evaluation. --In interviews, the faculty expressed mixed
reactions to this assignment.   Three members were enthusiastic
about it; they thought it was the kind of thing we should do and
want it repeated.   Two instructors thought the assignment was a
worthy cause, but they noted that this particular assignment did not
result in better bibliographies than those produced by former students.   One of these felt that the assignment was too sophisticated
for the sophomore student.   Two faculty members indicated their
view that all bibliographic assignments should be so designed that
the student doesn't realize he is doing them.   They did not like
this particular assignment, though both saw the need to help students develop reliable criteria to use in selecting sources for their
studies.   One instructor, who would prefer that all direct instruction
about bibliographic work be done by the faculty, did not like the
assignment at all.   Two instructors felt that the whole library
project effort in library education is a waste of student and class
time, though one of them considers it a worthy research project.
The assignment was done by only 79 students out of a class of 185.

(The students of the instructors who were unfavorable to the assignment were over-represented in the group who did not do it.)   The

checklists completed by these 79 students were examined for criteria used in evaluation and for discrimination in deciding whether or not a book was "worthy of further consideration." Thirty-two per cent of the students used only criteria from the comprehensive list suggested to them. Thirty per cent used their own criteria, most often that the book was "relevant" or "not relevant" to the topic-- in spite of our statement that every item in each set was chosen for its relevance.

The student's final decision that a book was worthy of further consideration accorded with our own judgement 77 per cent of the time, though in considering specific criteria, e.g., qualifications of the author, date, etc., his judgement coincided with ours in a range between 62 per cent and 75 per cent of the time.

As a further check on the assignment, the project research analyst conducted a test and interview study approximately two months after the assignment was completed. Seven students who had done the assignment well, seven who had done it poorly, and seven who had not done it at all were asked to evaluate quickly a set of five books not used originally. The students who had done well originally performed better on this follow-up test than did either of the other two groups, but the students who had not done the assignment at all performed better than those who had done it poorly. The students who had done the assignment poorly reported that they had not found the briefing statement useful or had not read it. Most of the students in all three groups remembered the class discussion of the assignment, however, and felt that it had been beneficial to them.

From the small sample study conducted in the summer of 1962, the most interesting finding was that reported in Chapter IV, where we noted that the sophomores who had done the assignment scored better on the book evaluation test than did those who had not. From the questionnaire we learned that about half understood the purpose of the assignment, about half used the briefing state-ment and found it helpful, and, again, most remembered the class discussion and thought it useful.

Conclusion. --We are certain from our analysis of student bibliographies, and from our analysis of a book evaluation task we administered to the 1961 Summer Sample that students need specific work in this area. Students tend to judge a book usable for a term paper if it is easy to read, written in a pleasing literary style, and seemingly exactly relevant to the topic at hand. In the light of this knowledge, we were gratified with the overall performance of those students who did the work. Nor are we overly concerned about the faculty's comments that the assignment did not produce better student bibliographies, since no systematic analysis of student bibliographies has been made. We are certain that the book evaluation work we gave the student at least gave him the opportunity to think explicitly about what a useful set of criteria would be in this area, and to begin to use them. It seems to us that it takes time to break old habits and form new ones. Perhaps the skilled habits which this assignment endeavors to instill in the undergraduate are not mastered quickly. They may be observable only a year or more later.

Assignment 6 (Spring, 1962, Humanistic Studies I)

Nature of the course assignment. --In the student's fourth semester, he had just completed his sequence in the social sciences. Now he began his studies in the humanities. An early unit of work in this semester was designed to demonstrate to them that richness and depth of understanding of a work of art which is attained through using systematically several frames of reference to study it. Thus the student approached Joyce's Portrait of the Artist as a Young Man biographically--as a product of an individual man--ethnographically--as a product of a social milieu--philosophically--as an expression of ideas and values--and formally critically[6]--as an aesthetic event.

Philosophy of the library component. --In association with the member of the Humanistic Studies Faculty who acted as liason between the project staff and faculty in 1961-62, the project staff planned an assignment to contribute to the Joyce study and to make the student aware of the range and potential usefulness of

various sources of bibliographic information, the exhaustive and the
selective listings, those which provide information directly and
those which do not, those which are organized and evaluative and
those which are not.   The assignment called for the student to
write a short paper comparing and contrasting three bibliographies
--a comprehensive, non-selective one, such as a volume of the
Annual Bibliography of English Language and Literature; a general
and selective one--such as a volume of Abstracts of English
Studies; and a book on Joyce's life or work.   Each student was required to look over one of the five such sets we made available
to him from the three points of view: 1) that of a scholar preparing
an exhaustive bibliography on Joyce, 2) that of a scholar seeking
an esoteric bit of information, and 3) that of a general reader or
neophyte beginning a study of Joyce.   We suggested that he compare these bibliographic tools on the basis of comprehensiveness,
informativeness, selectivity, usability, and general value in order
to arrive at his conclusions.

Administration of the assignment. --Each instructor scheduled
the assignment during one of the four weeks which The Portrait of
the Artist was under discussion.   A member of the project staff
visited the class once to distribute the directions for the assignment and return the following week to lead a discussion of the
completed work.   These discussions were concerned particularly
with the general principle that the usefulness of a bibliographical
tool depends on the amount of information the user has at his command.   The scholar is equipped to use an exhaustive, non-informa-
tive bibliography; the neophyte would be well advised to begin his
work with a source which is selective and which offers information
along with its references.

When the assignment was completed, we distributed to the
students a list of all of the bibliographies the students had examined.
The list was classified in accordance with the functional categories
we had discussed.

Evaluation. --Of the five humanities instructors concerned
with this assignment only one found it entirely satisfactory both as
a course assignment and as a step in the bibliographical education

of the Monteith student. He felt that it functioned well in terms of the course because it not only dealt with course content, but actually brought the student to study the Portrait from more than one viewpoint. He advised his students that he expected them all to do the assignment and that their work on it would be included in his computation of the final grades in the semester. Three other instructors would have preferred the students to use bibliographies to write a paper on Joyce rather than an essay on the bibliographies themselves, though two of these found it a valuable assignment, nevertheless, because it taught students something they should know about bibliographic organization. The other two instructors took the position that any bibliographic assignment should be so couched in a course assignment that the student doesn't realize that he is learning something about the library. They thought that the sheer mechanical aspects of this work actually blocked the student's bibliographical education. Four of the five instructors did not include the student's work in this assignment in his semester grade.

The essays written by the students were evaluated in terms of two questions: 1) did the student perceive the functional variation among the three bibliographical tools he examined and 2) did he perceive the significance of these variations for different users with different purposes? Only 85 out of the 169 students enrolled in the class did the assignment. Performance on the two factors varied together and 26 per cent of the essays were scored "good, " 35 per cent scored "fair" and 39 per cent scored "poor. "

Conclusion. --Despite the mixed reaction of the faculty, we are persuaded that this assignment is appropriate for sophomore students beginning work in the humanities. It introduces them to the organization of the scholarly and critical literature of this area at the same time that it stresses the point that not all bibliographical tools are equally useful to all people and for all purposes. It may be, however, that the assignment would have made this point even better if the students had been required to use sources from the tools they examined for a paper on one of the four aspects from which the Portrait was to be considered.

Sequence C: Experienced by Students Who Entered in the Fall of 1961

Assignment 1 (Fall, 1961, Science of Society I)

Nature of the course assignment. --The first unit of study of
the sequence in the social sciences was designed to bring the student to think critically about the related ideas: individual, nation,
citizen, community, government, state, society.   The faculty hoped
that in so doing he would develop a conception of the kind of thing
which is the relationship of the individual to his society.   The readings included selections from Plato, Rousseau, Thoreau, and
Jefferson.

Philosophy of the library component. --When the chairman
of the division suggested that the students might be asked to write
a paper based on library resources in connection with this unit, we
immediately recognized the difficulty the student would have with
such an assignment because we knew that the tools these freshman
students would be familiar with, the card catalog and the Readers'
Guide, would be very difficult to use in the search for references
on such abstract ideas as those to be discussed.   It occurred to us,
then, that we might design an exercise which would demonstrate
in vivid terms the limitations of these tools and at the same time
introduce other tools.   The understanding we hoped the student
would acquire as a result of his experience was concerned with the
fact that there are very many entries to the resources organized in
the library and that the user must choose his entry in terms of the
sort of information he wants.

Administration of the assignment. --The project staff drew
up fifteen series of questions about fifteen concepts such as those
cited above.   The answers to these questions were to be found in
the Oxford English Dictionary, the Syntopicon of Great Books of the
Western World, the International Index of Periodical Literature, the
Reader's Guide to Periodical Literature, and the card catalog. Each
student was to find the answers to one set of questions and he was
also asked to invent a metaphor for the concept he had been working on.   The metaphor was designed to demonstrate to the incoming
freshman that he must do some thinking strictly independently in

his college work. As a model for the assignment an article "Independence in the Library" was included in the students' basic text. Using the word "independence," it described what one might find in the tools assigned and it also included reflections on the general uses and limitations of such tools. In order that the library might deal with over 300 students using the same bibliographic tools, we assigned the exercises to five discussion sections each week over the six week period in which this part of the course was taught.

A member of the project staff went to a meeting of the discussion class to give out the list of questions, to draw the students' attention to the article "Independence in the Library," to tell them that a member of the project staff would station himself in the library on two different days at specified periods during that week to give help as needed, and to say that this work would be discussed in class the following week.

We stationed ourselves in the library to give help because the Library Advisory Committee and the project staff felt it would put an impossible strain on the Wayne State Library Staff to deal with sixty new freshmen doing this kind of work each week for six weeks and because we did not want any student to spend too much time on the assignment, perhaps because he misunderstood a question or because he got lost on a false trail.

Evaluation. -- This assignment was the only one which we were able to evaluate on the basis of a question in any objective final examination given to the whole class. This multiple choice question was as follows:

Each of the items listed below presents a topic on which you might want to write a paper. For each topic you are to select the one source which would be most efficient in providing references to give you a start in your work:

    A. Oxford English Dictionary
    B. Syntopicon
    C. Readers' Guide
    D. International Index
    E. Card catalog

1. The idea of "community" as a basis for social relationship.

2. "Community organization" as a branch of social work.

3. The development of the idea "community" as the expression of common interests, values, etc.

4. The recent publicity concerning alleged abuses in the community welfare program of Newburgh, Mass.

5. Recent research on the disintegration of urban communities resulting from urban renewal programs.

6. The utopian communities founded in the 19th century.

   Key: 1-B, 2-E, 3-A, 4-C, 5 ·D, 6-E.

The per cent of students who answered each part correctly was as follows:

```
1 . . . . . 52
2 . . . . . 57
3 . . . . . 56
4 . . . . . 83
5 . . . . . 31
6 . . . . . 47
```

The 206 students who took the final examination answered the question as follows:

```
all six parts correct . . . . . 9. 2
five parts correct . . . . . 13. 1
four parts correct . . . . . 27. 2
three parts correct . . . . . 26. 7
two parts correct . . . . . 13. 6
one part  correct . . . . . 10. 2
no part  correct . . . . . 4. 4
```

These figures would indicate that the question does discriminate among students, showing something in the nature of a normal curve. We compared performance on this question with performance on the examination as a whole and found that it discriminates in the same fashion, i. e. , that students who scored well on it scored well on the total examination.

In interviews, six out of eleven faculty indicated that they liked it. One considered it valuable because she was assured that this work had introduced the student to the university library and had given him some skill in using it. Others felt that the assignment had widened the students' horizons, had given them an appreciation of the fact that important ideas change and grow through generations of use. Another was pleased with it because it developed skills he considered necessary for the undergraduate. Five of the faculty reacted negatively, two objecting to its "exercise" form which they considered poor pedagogy, and three because they considered all requirements in the courses a professor teaches should be his responsibility alone. These three, perhaps, should not be considered negative toward this assignment per se, but rather toward any special program in library education. This same faculty, including two professors who had originally reacted negatively to this effort, repeated essentially the same assignment when it was once again relevant to the course materials being taught in the Fall of 1963. At this time they led the discussion in their own sections and helped with the job of assisting students in the library.

Conclusion. --The "Independence Assignment" as it has come to be known was clearly successful. The fact that the faculty asked that it be repeated after the project was terminated and were willing to assist in its administration and take complete responsibility for discussing it with their students is sufficient evidence. It seems to us to be both challenging enough to be a college assignment and realistic in its estimation of what freshmen understand about the organization of the library.

Assignment 2 (Spring, 1962, Science of Society II)

Nature of the course assignment. --The third time the Science of Society course was presented, the semester-long research project was again assigned in the second half of the freshman year. It was handled as it had been in the previous year with each student selecting his discussion section on the basis of the general research interests of the instructor.

Philosophy of the library component. --In this, our third experience with the research project, we focussed the student's attention on the bibliographic review or essay. Students floundered and were frustrated, we had found, when they were left completely free to find in the library whatever they could which might be helpful in their work on their research problems. In the second year, we had met hostility from some of the faculty when we attempted to introduce students to a general structure for

approaching the literature of a discipline. We decided this time
to introduce students to one genre of bibliographical tools at the
same time that we put into their hands an example of that genre
which we hoped would be useful for their specific research problems.

Administration of the Assignment. --Each student was asked
to select one from a list of concepts, such as "role," "pattern,"
"social class," etc., which he thought would pertain to the research problem he planned to work on. For each of these concepts we had located a bibliographic essay and devised a set of
specific questions whose answers were contained in the essay. The
questions were intended to lead the student to discover what sorts
of information is usually presented in a bibliographic essay, how
such essays are usually organized, how one can use them to begin
developing a search strategy.

Once again, the project staff scheduled the assignment so that one
of us could attend each discussion section, first, to present the assignment and, second, to lead discussion of it. Discussion centered on the
series of publications which report on scholarly work and scientific research: the original report, the index, the abstract, the annual review,
and the bibliographic review which summarizes work done in connection
with one aspect, one concept, or one methodology. We noted that the
disciplines vary widely with regard to how well they are "controlled"
bibliographically. And we stressed the point that the exhaustive and
unselective bibliographies and abstracting and indexing services, necessary as they are for the scholar, are less useful for the neophyte than
is the bibliographical review which, in a sense, lays out a field of study.

Evaluation. --The instructors' reaction to this assignment
paralleled their reaction to the "Independence" assignment given in
the previous term. Most thought it highly useful in developing
students' awareness of the organization of the literature of a discipline in increasing their sophistication about historical social, and
political factors which affect that organization. Others objected to
the fact that librarians participated directly in carrying the assignment out, since they believe all bibliographic instruction should be
left entirely to the teaching faculty. And, once again, there were some
whose objection was to the while idea of a library instructional program.

Judging from comments and behavior in the discussion sections, most of the students were interested in the assignment, but almost none of them reported finding the bibliographical essay helpful in providing useful references for their specific research projects. One-hundred-thirty-six students out of a total of two-hundred-eighty-five, registered for the course completed the assignment. There were some returns from every one of the instructors. Since the answering of the questions merely required reading the essays, the number of correct answers probably indicates only the care with which the students did read them. The students had an average of 83 per cent of the answers correct.

Conclusion. --The bibliographical review appears to be a most appropriate starting place for a research project assigned to freshman students. It alerts them at once to the kinds of sources the faculty expect them to use, to the concepts which are characteristically used for approaches to social science research, and to methods and instruments which have been found useful.

The rather artificial questions we devised in this case, however, did not seem to help the student discover these values in the essay. We think now that an exercise based on a hypothetical research problem of the student's own choice and formulation would be more effective.

Notes

1. In a basic course the student normally attends two lectures per week, two small discussion classes, completes the required reading, the required papers, reports, etc., and sits for an examination each semester. The semi-independent student attends two lectures, may attend one discussion class, must complete the reading, may submit his own plans for papers, reports, etc., to his discussion group faculty, may solicit and receive limited help from faculty, librarians, project personnel.

2. "A Report on the Humanistic Studies Sequence at Monteith College," Wayne State University, 1961.

3. Ibid.

4. The fourth staff member left Monteith to take the chairmanship of the department elsewhere before he could be interviewed.

5. Two faculty members had left the staff before they could be interviewed.

6. Drury, George, Introduction to Humanistic Studies, Lecture I,
    Locating Humanistic Studies.   Detroit, Michigan: Monteith
    College, Wayne State University, 1962, (Mimeographed).

Appendix II

The Bibliographical Assistance Program: Excerpts from the
Proposal and the Progress Reports

From the Proposal

III.   Objectives

The pilot project will explore ways of investigating the following general hypotheses:

. . . .

5.   That most college teachers lack time and many lack
bibliographical expertise to make the most of the library's potential
contribution to teaching, and that providing them with bibliographical
assistance will result in their making extensive use of library resources for their course work.

V.   Procedures

. . . .

2.   Procedures and methods.

. . . .

Provision of bibliographical research assistance to the faculty.
--Graduate assistants recruited primarily from the social sciences
and natural sciences departments in Wayne's Graduate School, will be
assigned to work with individual members of the Monteith social
sciences staff.   After careful and systematic training in library
skills, they will provide the faculty with the kind of bibliographical
services commonly provided by librarians in special libraries.   They
will prepare bibliographies and abstracts, do literature searches,
and gather materials on four designated topics: (a) current developments in those areas of social science and natural science research
which are given particular attention in the basic courses; (b) the
particular research interests of individual members of the faculty,
so that frontier developments will find a channel into teaching; (c)
particular topics used as unifying points of emphasis (The topic suggested for the first semester of the social science course: Detroit
as a Laboratory for Social Analysis.); (d) current developments in

the teaching of the social science and natural science programs of
general education.

These bibliographical research assistants will be supervised
by the project librarian. They will keep careful records of their
activities and will meet regularly in seminar sessions to analyze
and discuss their work to the end of discovering something about
the nature of faculty use of library resources for teaching and
about student responses to library experiences.

Specific functions of pilot project staff. --

The Project Librarian will train the bibliographical research
assistants, supervise their library activities, and collect and organize their reports on the faculty's library needs and requirements...

The Bibliographical Research Assistants will locate and prepare materials for Monteith library assignments, and will assist
the students in accordance with plans developed by the librarians
and faculty in carrying them out. They will conduct bibliographical searches, as assigned, for the faculty, the Project Coordinator,
and the Project Research Librarian, and they will report regularly
to the latter on developments in the kinds of searching tasks
assigned to them and on the students' responses to their library
experiences.

The Project Research Analyst... will work with the Project
Research Librarian in developing methods for collecting, organizing,
and reporting data on faculty use of library resources for instruction and on student library experiences;... and she will work with
the Project Coordinator in maintaining, organizing, and reporting
data produced by the pilot project and in formulating plans for the
second phase of the Program.

B. Data

A second type of data will be produced as a result of the
work of the bibliographical research assistants. The assistants
will note the kinds of materials the faculty were interested in, the
kinds of materials they used, how and when they decided what to
use, what kinds of library services they required, what kinds of
library services they wanted and did not get, et cetera. This

information will be reported to the project research librarian...

C. Methods of analysis.

...Data on the faculty's library interests, needs and demands will be analyzed for association with varying subject disciplines, research interests, previous library experiences, educational goals, and concepts of academic library functions.

E. Expected end-product and publication plans.

The pilot project will produce...a tentative analysis of patterns of faculty use of library resources.

From Report Number 1, April 1-June 30, 1960

Bibliographical Assistants. --We plan to hire graduate students to serve as bibliographical research assistants to the faculty. Actual appointments will not be made until school begins in September, though we may use two or three to assist with the bibliographical searching required in connection with course planning this summer. In the meantime, we asked each member of the teaching staff, who will be involved with the project, to indicate the particular knowledge and skill, e.g., foreign language, subject specialization, that would be important for his work. As these preferences have been forwarded to us, we have contacted appropriate faculty members and department chairmen in the College of Liberal Arts for recommendations as to qualified graduate students. Some applications have already been taken and filed for future decision.

Organizational Pattern. --...It is particularly important that the Monteith instructors understand that bibliographical assistants will not be just additional student assistants. They will provide a particular kind of service--bibliographical--for the specific purpose of maximizing the contribution of the library to the teaching process. The instructor, of course, will determine what bibliographical services he thinks will contribute most to his teaching effectiveness, but the project librarian will be responsible for the way in which these services are performed. The instructors must understand, moreover, that planning, preparation, and guidance of student library assignments have first claim on the bibliographical research assistants' time. The faculty will determine the problems, but the project librarian will train and supervise the preparation and guidance activities the problems entail.

<u>From Report Number 2, July 1, 1960-January 30, 1961</u>

Bibliographical Assistance to the Faculty

The plan for the project called for the assignment to every faculty member of those divisions with which we were working a graduate student to work nine hours per week on bibliographical assignments. This service was designed primarily to increase the instructor's awareness and facilitate his use of library resources to the end of increasing his exploitation of them in his teaching.

Sixteen bibliographical assistants have worked for the project during the first semester of its operation, twelve assigned to members of the social sciences faculty, four assigned to the project director and the project librarian. At the beginning of the second semester we plan to employ ten more bibliographical assistants, six for the Natural Sciences staff and four for the Humanities staff. As noted above our original plan did not call for our working with the Humanities staff. Since the project began late, however, members of the Humanities faculty arrived on the scene in time to be involved. They had great need for bibliographical service, while certain members of the Natural Sciences staff doubted that the available graduate students would have sufficiently specialized training to handle the literature of the sciences. We decided therefore, to limit the Natural Sciences quota and assign assistants to the Humanities staff. We are certain that the Humanities staff will make good use of their assistants. If the Natural Sciences staff also find the service very beneficial we expect to ask for additional funds to provide them with the complete coverage originally contemplated in the plan.

Recruiting

Recruiting graduate students for bibliographical service proved to be more difficult than we had anticipated. The Wayne Graduate School is young, and, in many departments, not strong. A large proportion of graduate students have full-time jobs and are students part-time. In several instances, therefore, we settled for well recommended undergraduates.

Some of our faculty, moreover, expressed a preference for good, bright, Monteith students over graduate students from other colleges at Wayne. We resisted this pressure because we were afraid that Monteith students might have difficulty in maintaining what we considered the appropriate sense of being on the "Project Staff. " We felt it important that the bibliographical assistants should represent an out-reach of the library, an extension of library services, rather than services of the College, such as the typing, filing, and errand-running duties of the regular student assistants. We made a few exceptions to this rule, however, in cases in which the faculty member was able to demonstrate that a particular Monteith student had special qualifications equivalent to the subject knowledge that might be expected of an upper classman or a grad-uate student. Our experience with these deviations from our orig-inal plan have led us to conclude, not surprisingly, that brains and intensity of interest are more important than subject knowledge, but that our fears about ambivalence in the definition of roles were at least partly justified.

Training

The project staff has met with the bibliographical assistants in regular bi-weekly seminars. In general these meetings have served three purposes. They provided the opportunity for briefing on roles and relationships, for instruction on particular assignments, or particular types of bibliographical tools, and for feed-back on relationships with faculty and on experiences in the library. Specif-ically the following items have been covered in the Agenda:

1. An explanation of the special privileges of the biblio-graphical assistant. (Each assistant was provided with a special identification card entitling him to faculty privileges while on the job).

2. Discussion of the role of the bibliographical assistant as an intermediary between the faculty and the library, respon-sible for interpreting the needs of the faculty member to the library on the one hand and the exigencies of the library system to the faculty member on the other.

3. Presentations by the Chairman of the Social Sciences Division, by the Director of Monteith College and by the Director of the Libraries, of their respective views of the potential values of the project in general and of the services

of the bibliographical assistants in particular.

4.   A briefing on the assignment on Social Movements.   All
the bibliographical assistants were assigned for a two-week
period to the identification of social movements and to the
location of some references on them.   The product of their
work was a bibliography on cards which was made available
to the Monteith students when the Social Movements assignment was made.

5.   A critique on the Social Movements assignment.

6.   Library Orientation Test for College Freshmen (New York:
Columbia Teachers College, 1955).

7.   Training in the use of national and trade bibliographies.

8.   Instruction in reporting on bibliographical work.

These reports on bibliographical work, devised by the project
research analyst, were turned in weekly.   The assistants were instructed to report verbatim on the assignments they received from
their faculty principals, on the purpose of these assignments, on
faculty suggestions as to procedures, on the actual procedures they
employed, on the nature of what they produced, on the difficulties
they encountered in the library, on the nature of all contacts with
librarians, and on their own reactions to each assignment.   The
reports were prepared in the form of a detailed diary.   This form
was conceived as an experiment and a new more concise reporting
form has been developed for the coming semester.   It will be ac-
companied by a bi-weekly individual interview.

The work of the bibliographical assistants has ranged all
the way from plain leg work of picking up books in the library and
bringing them to the faculty member to the preparation of elaborate-
ly organized, exhaustive bibliographies on certain topics.   Some
assistants have been assigned the on-going task of regularly scanning
a list of scholarly journals, searching for articles on particular
topics and writing abstracts of these articles on these topics according to a carefully planned formula.   Some have been asked to
look for references suitable as suggested readings for the Monteith
courses, some have translated, some have verified references. We
shall be interested to learn whether the Natural Sciences staff and
the Humanities staff use their bibliographical assistants in as

varied a fashion. At present the Natural Sciences staff plans, at least temporarily, to pool their bibliographical assistants and assign them as a group to the task of doing a kind of dry run on the assignment planned for the Monteith students in the fourth semester of the Natural Sciences course. Members of the Humanities staff have in mind the preparation of bibliographies on topics which cut across the arts, such as symbolism, form, style, etc.

The Work of the Bibliographical Assistants. Most of our questions on this aspect of our program, as indicated above, center upon relationship and role. We had envisioned bibliographical assistants providing a service such as that provided by the library staff in a special library or a small college library. In some instances this seems to be what has happened. In others, however, the lack of frequent, informal, association or communication keeps this kind of relationship from developing. The alert librarian in a special library or a small college library is atuned to the interests and concerns of his patrons. He can pick up ideas about what materials will be interesting to them, and, without being asked, produce these materials for examination. The bibliographic assistant, on the other hand, works on the basis of the specific assignment. His success may very well depend on the extent to which the faculty member is able clearly to formulate and communicate his interests.

Instructors are used to working with student assistants and with research assistants. Attempting to define a new role for bibliographical assistans, we said that they should not be assigned typical student assistant duties such as typing, filing, or running errands nor research assistant duties such as designing experiments or observing the behavior of rats. We set no closer definition because we wanted the jobs to be defined by the library and bibliographical needs the faculty themselves felt. But the previous experience of the faculty still carries weight, and, in any case, the lines are hard to draw. The organization of a bibliography on cards may require typing and filing. Reading the Congressional Record may be the equivalent for a historian, of observing a rat for a psychologist.

Analysis of Data

The Work of the Bibliographical Assistants. --The reports of
the bibliographical assistants are the chief source of data as to both
the kinds of services asked, the nature of the relationships which
develop, and any problems in the use of the library. The research
analyst attends all of the bibliographical assistant seminars and has
frequent individual interviews with the assistants.

II. Problems, Questions, and Tentative Conclusions

The three-way relationship among the instructor, the bibliographical assistant, and the librarian is another to be viewed in
light of this problem. Our diagnosis here is just the opposite. The
bibliographical assistants are not generally skilled in the use of the
library, they are, more or less, in command of the literature of a
field. We had hoped to make them both, by having them work from
the beginning under close supervision of the librarian. But we have
encountered two difficulties in carrying out this plan. First, in our
earliest seminars, we urged each bibliographical assistant to work
hard at developing good communication with his faculty principal so
that the fruits of his work would really meet a need. The result of
this emphasis has been a strong person-to-person tie between the
assistant and his principal and a weak tie between the assistant and
the project. As a consequence the work of the bibliographical
assistants is probably not as efficient as it might otherwise have
been, though it is highly satisfying to most instructors. The second
difficulty is lack of time. The assistants work a total of ten hours
per week, but one hour is set aside for the seminar and consultation with the instructor may take another. Regular individual consultation and supervision from the librarian seems to cut too deeply
into time already extremely limited.

To overcome these difficulties we have thought of using a
smaller number, a kind of pool, of bibliographical assistants, each
working perhaps twenty hours per week and allocated to individual
faculty members only for specified assignments. This arrangement
would strengthen the tie between the assistant and the project, and

presumably, increase the efficiency of the assistant's work. Most important, it might provide time for the Librarian to develop ways of using the assistant to communicate to the faculty the concept of the library-as-system. The disadvantage of this solution is that it rules out those cases in which the provision of the service stimulates the instructor to create worthwhile biographical enterprises.

Obviously in all this we are still dealing in speculations. It may be that our fears about the lack of implementation of student library assignments are unjustified. At any rate we plan no deliberate change in the structure we have set up. For one thing, we are about to start work with two new groups of instructors and two new groups of bibliographical assistants, so the different feelings of relationship may emerge naturally. For another, slight modifications of relationship have grown up within the present structure. As a small experiment in the "pool" idea, for instance, the project librarian and the director have made their assistants available to instructors for certain specified assignments.

The effects of such variations will be worth watching. Indeed, our experience so far has underlined the general need for examining carefully the effects of the complexities of relationship in our structure.

From Report Number 3, February 1, 1961-January 30, 1962

Bibliographical Assistance to the Faculties

All but two of the bibliographical assistants employed to serve the Social Sciences faculty continued their work for individual faculty members. In addition we hired six assistants for the Natural Sciences staff and four for the Humanities staff. The new assistants were given much the same training and orientation as that presented to the earlier recruits. The bibliographical seminar program was expanded to include sessions for the new recruits alone, for assistants in each subject division, and for the whole group together.

Assistants for the Humanities staff worked for individual faculty members as had those assigned to the Social Sciences staff, but they worked exclusively on collecting and organizing materials

for lectures, and for readings, recordings and prints to be assigned.
As anticipated, the assistants assigned to the Natural Sciences staff
worked as a group on a dry run of the assignment in the philosophy
of science. After this assignment was prepared, one or two individual tasks were assigned, but, in general, the Natural Sciences
staff tended toward group assignments.
. . . .

Reflection and Revision Summer 1961

The Bibliographical Assistance Program

From the beginning we had experienced certain difficulties
with our plan to provide bibliographical assistance to the faculty.
We noted in Report No. 2, for example, that our emphasis upon
the development of good communication between the bibliographical
assistant and his faculty principal resulted in "a strong person-to-
person tie between the assistant and his principal and a weak tie
between the assistant and the project. As a consequence the work
of the bibliographical assistants is probably not as efficient as it
might otherwise have been though it is highly satisfying to most
instructors. " With a larger number of assistants, furthermore,
we discovered more instances in which one faculty member felt
burdened by the responsibility to assign ten hours of work regularly
each week while another needed far more than the ten hours budg-
eted.

As we reviewed our two semesters of experience with the
program, we found more and more appealing the idea of a pool of
assistants assigned not to individual faculty members, but to specific bibliographical tasks under the close supervision of the project
librarian. We decided to try this procedure in the third semester.
. . . .

The Bibliographical Assistant Program

Having decided to try using our bibliographical assistants as
a pool upon whose services the faculty might draw for particular
assignments, we cut the total number of assistants from twenty-five
to fourteen, at the same time increasing the normal hours from ten
to fifteen. (We made the cut by not replacing most assistants who
had left in June, and by dismissing those whose work was least

satisfactory. We employed three new assistants to provide subject coverage in areas in which we were weak). The increase in hours was partly required to provide for an expanded training program. This program consisted of a series of eight weekly seminars, each requiring the assistants to perform certain tasks in preparation. The series covered a) the three principal entrances to the library as a systematically organized storehouse of literature--the card catalog, special reference works, the reference librarian; and b) the library as a storehouse of literature which the library user organizes and reorganizes to suit his purposes.

In the one seminar on the card catalog, we stressed the organization of the Wayne card catalog, the organization of the Library of Congress book of subject headings, the Dewey Decimal System and the relationship between the three organizations. A member of our Library Advisory Committee who works in cataloging took part in this discussion.

In the first of two seminars on special reference works we were guided by relevant chapters in Louis Shores', Basic Reference Sources, and in Carter Alexander and Arvid Burke's, How to Locate Educational Information. The project librarian gave a lecture on the general field of reference works. Then in a discussion we worked with the various types of reference works there are and the kinds of information each type supplies. In the second, aided by a library advisory committee member who is a professional bibliographer, we focussed on the fine points of bibliography--the detective-like characteristics of the work.

The seminar on the reference librarian was built around an experience each bibliographic assistant had acquired the previous week. Each had taken the same question to two different reference librarians at the reference station best equipped to handle the particular question. The bibliographic assistant wrote up his experiences in the same way he would write up any interview experience. Since all of the reference stations in the library were covered, the seminar in which the bibliographic assistants pooled their experience revealed the function of the reference librarian generally and also the variability that actually exists in carrying out the function.

The first of the three seminars on organizing the library to suit one's purposes included a member of the library education staff who had charted from conception to solution the steps through which a problem goes which can be solved by use of information stored in the library. The bibliographic assistants had had this chart in hand to use and to think about in relation to the problem of making clear to themselves precisely what they are doing in their work in the library. The speaker made a point of the many kinds of microprint now used in the library. The last two meetings were organized around construction of a "guide to the literature" of a field. The bibliographic assistants themselves led these meetings by bringing out for the seminar's consideration the problems one or another of them had run into in their work on the particular guide to the literature he had essayed. At the end of the first of these seminars the project librarian gave an introductory lecture to a detailed set of suggestions he had drawn up to help the bibliographic assistants in this task. He stressed that the guide to the literature is a specific bibliographic form itself, whose characteristics emerge from the particular problematic situation.

We chose this particular organization of the seminars for two reasons. At one time or another all of the bibliographic assistants had worked out the Columbia Teachers' College Library Orientation Test. Their performance indicated that as a group they were not as sure as they might be about what reference tool to choose for specific purposes. We also wanted our bibliographic assistants to get firmly in mind the idea that the library is organized, that it is a system, that the user either recognizes the organizing principles and uses them, or he is lost in a maze.

With this organization of the seminars, also, we were able to make of the preparatory tasks the assistants did jobs which the program needed to have done. Thus the questions the bibliographic assistants took to the reference librarians were questions we needed to begin work on for one or another purpose. Likewise, the guides to the literature that the assistants worked out are of particular use in a college of general education like Monteith.

It is our impression that the pooling of bibliographical assistants has had the several advantages we anticipated and at least two more. It did, indeed, result in an evener work load among the assistants and in more efficient procedures for their work, and it produced a much closer sense of identification with the project. It created, moreover, a quite unexpected degree of esprit de corps among the assistants. And, because the group was smaller and better selected, it furnished the stimulus and opportunity for a more systematic and thorough training program.

It is clear, on the other hand, that some faculty members were less moved to make use of the service than they had been when assistants were individually assigned. The total number of bibliographical requests decreased markedly. One can assume, of course, that the requests we did receive represented real needs as opposed to some make-work assignments given previously. Evidence from reports of work done during both periods would seem to indicate that this assumption is well grounded for some, but not for all, cases. The project, however, benefited from the time released, because we were able to make greater use of the bibliographical assistants in the preparation of assignments. The new assignments required so much preparation that they might not have been developed at all had we not had the help of our bibliographical assistants.

Collection and Analysis of Data
The Bibliographical Assistant Program

The Research Analyst improved her collection of data on the work of bibliographical assistants by developing a new reporting form. She continued holding bi-weekly interviews with the assistants, dictating from extensive notes on these interviews. She worked closely with the project librarian in planning and conducting the training program, collected the students' preparatory work for these seminars, and kept notes on the seminars themselves.

Appendix III

Exhibits: Selected Instructional Materials used in the Pilot Project

Monteith College - Science of Society 132
The Library Assignment for Spring Students

Friday, April 8, 1960

Readings

Hoselitz, Bert, ed. A Reader's Guide to the Social Sciences.
Glencoe, Free Press, 1959.

Shils, Edward.   The Present State of American Sociology.
Glencoe, Free Press, 1948.

Lindzey, Gardner, ed. Handbook of Social Psychology.
Cambridge, Addison-Wesley, 1954.   Vols. I and II.

Purpose: to introduce you to important studies which, by virtue
of author, concepts and terms, or methodology, will provide you
with a starting place for your library search.

Procedures for Library Search

The purpose of the library search is to help you:

        a.   understand the social context in which your
            problem occurs.

        b.   translate your "topic" into a "researchable
            problem."

        c.   learn how to decide on and use appropriate
            research methods.

1.   Read one or all of the items listed above.   (All of these
     titles are on special reserve, kept behind the circulation
     desk, in the Social Studies Division, third floor of the
     General Library.)

2.   As you read, be alert to:

        a.   The names of authors who have worked in
            areas which are in any way pertinent to your
            own problem.   Do not expect to find topics
            which are right on the nose.   But if, for

example, your problem might involve the
relationships among individuals in a small
group, and you ran across a discussion of
Street Corner Society, you should note the
name of the author, W. L. Whyte, not only
for what insights you might derive from
reading this study in particular, but also so
that you could check to see if Mr.
Whyte has
reported on other studies, perhaps more recent or more specifically relevant to your
problem.

b. Concepts, ways of looking at data, and the
terms used to identify them. If for example,
your problem suggests that one factor involved may be cultural differences between
groups, you might note such terms as
"ecological approach, " "cultural differentia-
tion, " etc.

c. Methods, instruments, techniques used in the
studies described. Be alert to the variety of
ways to gather data. You may want to check
on certain studies which are pertinent to your
problem only in that they use methods or
instruments which might be useful in your
work.

3. Search further, using: these names of authors, terms, etc.

a. the card catalog

b. the shelves

c. the International Index to Periodicals

Consult your WSU Library Guide for specific instruction about
using the card catalog and about locating materials of all kinds
in the WSU Library

Suggestions

A. About using the card catalog:

1. Use the catalog on the main floor. Catalogs in the divisions include only books in that one division, they enter
books under author and title only. There are no subject
cards, no cards for editor, associations, etc., unless
the association happens to be considered the "author" in
a particular case.

2. Look under the names of the author or editor of the whole
book. An article in a book of readings is not listed

separately in the catalog.

3. If you happen to know of one particular book on the subject you want, look under the author of that book. Note
that at the bottom of the card for that book there are
usually terms under which other books on that subject
will be listed.

4. Be alert to "see" and "see also" reference cards, and
be persistent about following the leads they give you.

5. When you find that several books listed under a particular
subject heading have the same call number, note that
call number and look on the shelves for other books with
the same or almost the same call number. In this way
you may find other studies which are more recent or
more pertinent than the book you started with.

B. About using the shelves:

1. Browse. Have a look at all the books in the neighborhood
of the one you came to find.

2. Having a look means scanning the title page (to find out
something about the qualifications of the author or sponsor
of the work), the table of contents (to get a notion of the
organization and scope of the work), the index (to see if
there is something especially pertinent to your problem),
and the bibliography (to see if there are any good leads).

C. About using the International Index to Periodicals

1. When you are looking for articles by a given author, check
systematically every volume of the index.

2. When you are looking for articles on a given subject,
start with a recent fat volume. In that volume,

a. For every subject (or concept or approach or idea)
you have, scan the entries under as many different
terms as you can think of which might have been
used.

b. When the term, i.e., subject heading, you look under
turns out to have page after page of entries, scan,
first, the entries under the main term, and then
check all the subdivisions to see which look promising. Scan the articles listed under these subheadings.
Watch out for cross references, and scan the entries
under these.

c. Having in this way identified the headings which produce, then check only these headings in all the rest
of the volumes in the series.

3. When you find articles you want to have a look at, be
sure to note author, title, date, volume and page. Use

the list of abbreviations, and the list of code symbols
in the front of the index to help you decipher the references.

Procedures for Keeping Your Log

The Log of Library Search is planned to help you to be
systematic in the library part of your Detroit Project assignment.
It provides you with an easy method of recording your progress.
And, finally, in the interests of the Monteith Library Program, for
which we have recently received a grant from the U. S. Office of
Education, it will provide data on the efficiency of certain library
tools for identifying and locating materials on various kinds of
problems.

As you conduct your search for library materials useful for
your project, record your steps following the directions for each
column presented below.

The professional librarians of the Social Studies Division, on
the third floor of the General Library, will assist you, not by
telling you what to read, but by helping you identify and locate useful reading.   Do not hesitate to ask for help nor to return for
further help when you hit a dead end.   But indicate with an * where-
ever in your search you receive assistance from a librarian.   We
are interested in learning what sorts of dead ends you meet and
what the librarian can contribute to your search.

Fill out your log as follows:

Column 1.   Estimate the total amount of time you spent on each
                particular task of your search, e. g., author, concept,
                etc.

Column 2.   Indicate the source of the lead, i. e., the reading in
                which you found the reference or a term to look un-
                der, e. g., Hoselitz, Shils, or other, or instructor,
                librarian, etc.

Column 3.   Indicate cat (catalog), shelf, or I. I. (International
                Index to Periodicals).

Column 4.   Indicate the name of every author, and each of the
                major terms you scan.   If you have been referred
                to a name or a term by a cross reference, put an
                arrow in front of it.   When you check the shelves,
                indicate the call number.

Column 5.   A "promising reference" is one which, as far as you
                can judge from its author, title, source, etc., seems
                worth looking at.   Indicate how many you found, e. g.,
                6x.

Column 6.   Indicate how many you located, e. g., 4x.   For those
                you did not locate, indicate as follows: 0=did not try,
                O WSU = not in Wayne library, 0 shelf = not on
                shelf, 0 out = charged out, 0 locate = could not find.

If you find that a promising reference is not in the Wayne library, please make out a bibliography card for it, mark the card "not in WSU library" and turn it in with your other bibliography cards. The library will try to obtain these items for the use of future generations of Monteith students.

Column 7.   If, having located the item, you find it useful in some way, or if you expect to find it useful, mark an x in the column and make out a bibliography card.

Column 8.   Enter in this column anything which leads you to another reference or on another task in your search. It may be a footnote. It may be the name of a person or an organization that could be helpful.

The Library Report

Your report on your library search, due April 28, will consist of:

1. The log of Library Search, completely filled out. (Note that your log will be evaluated <u>not</u> on the basis of your familiarity with library tools and your experience in using them, but rather on the extent to which your procedures are sensible and ingenious).

2. The 3 x 5 bibliography cards for all references you find useful, indicating for each:

For a book:

  author
  title
  publisher
  date
  source of reference, i. e.,
    books, cat., shelf, I. I.,
    <u>and</u> author, subject heading,
    or call no.

For an article:

  author
  title of article
  title of journal
  issue number and date
  source of reference, i. e.,
    book, I. I., and author,
    subject heading, or call no.

Note, also, that the "source of reference" may be your research advisor, an instructor, another student, or it may be the card catalog, the shelf, a bibliography or index. (If it is a bibliography, an index, or any other library book, name it).

(Keep a copy of your bibliography to turn in with your final report on the Detroit project assignment).

3. Similarly, bibliography cards for promising references that the Wayne Library does not have.

4. Answers to a short questionnaire (to be distributed later) and a brief summary of your library search. Your summary should include the following:

  a.   A general estimate of what has been written on your topic. You may find that much has been written advocating study of your problem or proposing solutions but that little actual field research is presented.

b. A brief analysis of your own experiences in conducting the library search, noting where you got off on a wild goose chase, where you came unexpectedly upon a treasure, which library tools were particularly useful, which were a waste of time, etc.

c. Comments on those items in your bibliography which were most helpful indicating _how_ they helped, for example in providing you with some background understanding of the nature of your problem, in defining its scope, in suggesting a research technique, etc.

Monteith College

Log of Library Search   Name_____   Science of Society 132   _____Problem No._____

(1) Time Spent	(2) What Sought	(3) Where Looked (e.g., card catalog, shelf, Readers' Guide)	(4) Under What Term or in What cate- gory	(5) Found Prom- ising References x = yes 0 = no	(6) Located Item x = yes 0 = no*	(7) Item Proved Useful x = yes** 0 = no	(8) Item Provid- ed Promis- ing Lead***

*If no, indicate why not. See Procedures.
**If yes, include among your 3x5 bilbiography cards.
***For example, footnote, bibliography, new term to look up, etc.

Questionnaire to be Filled out by Students as Part of Library Report

1. How many items in your bibliography?_____

2. How many promising items not located, because:

    a. not followed up_____

    b. not in WSU library_____

    c. not on shelf_____

    d. charged out_____

    e. other (explain)_____

3. If you used any other library, indicate which.

4. What was the source for most of the items in your bibliography?

    a. Card Catalogue   d. Librarian

    b. Index   e. Other

    c. Faculty

5. What was the source for the one most useful reference in your bibliography?

    a. Card Catalogue   d. Librarian

    b. Index   e. Other

    c. Faculty

6. What library tools (card catalogue, index, etc.) did you find easiest to use?

7. What library tools were the hardest to use?

8. Did you ever have a course in using the library?_____

9. Were you ever a student assistant in the library?_____

10. How much experience using a library have you had?

    much_____some_____little_____none_____

Date_____   Project Number_____

Name_____   Name of instructor_____

Name of research advisor_____

January, 1961

One Intellectual Use of the Autobiography of Your Choice

We had many purposes in mind in asking you to choose an autobiography as one of your intellectual companions in this course. Certainly what a person has to say about himself and his life ought to be appealing in itself. Certainly a felicitously written autobiography gives an immediate aesthetic reward. Without losing these values, an autobiography may also be looked upon as a rich source of data for further analysis, just as good conversation, rewarding in itself, brings further reward in the form of new thoughts which reverberate long after the conversation itself has ceased.

In your reading selection by the psychoanalyst Erik H. Erikson you have an excellent example of an analysis of data provided in an autobiographical essay by George Bernard Shaw. It is Erikson's purpose not only to make illuminating statements about Shaw, but to explain his concept of ego identity formation and other related concepts and to help make these concepts available as intellectual tools.

Intellectual tools exist only in the minds of people and it is an important purpose of ours, of course, to help you equip your minds with such implements. Thus we are asking you to take the data your autobiographer provides you with and subject it to an analysis using Erikson's concepts. We hope that in that way these concepts will become more a part of your usable intellectual equipment. We also hope that this exercise will help make you a more sensitive listener to what that unique person, your autobiographer, has to say.

Now Erikson happens to be a very skilled, experienced, and sensitive listener. As a result he sometimes is able to say penetrating things about people which it would be difficult for another person to duplicate. We therefore thought that it would be helpful to you if you had some explicit suggestions from us about what sort of things to listen to with special sensitivity in your own autobiographical material. These suggestions will be cast in the form of questions. Some of them Erikson discusses quite explicitly. Not all of them will have equal value for _different_ autobiographies.

1. Since people change over time, who is the man _writing_ the autobiography? How old is he? Has he been successful in the eyes of the world? In his own eyes?

2. What range of his total life history does he concentrate on as being of crucial interest to him?

3. What groups of people, what part of the world does the author see himself as belonging to? As not belonging to but not opposed to? As opposed to?

4. What are his areas of deliberate conformity and non-conformity?

5. Is he able to maintain continuity in his identify in the face of important changes in his life situation?

6. What are the major crises of his life? Do they seem to have been resolved? If so how have they been resolved with regard to the way in which the person changes as a result of the particular resolution? What identity conflicts remain unresolved?

Although a person can always tell us things about himself that no one else can, he is by no means a complete informant. Some of the questions above may be very valid questions to ask your autobiographer. You may nevertheless not receive very clear answers to very appropriate questions. Think of an area of information pertaining to your autobiographer which you think could add valuably to your knowledge of the formation and content of his identity, but which the autobiography slights or is silent on. Use other materials from the library, such as biographies or collections of letters, to get a more satisfying answer to your question. Our librarian, Mr. Donahue, 325 General Library, can be consulted should you wish or need his help. A bibliography, in proper form, should be appended to your paper. All materials you use in this paper should be included in your bibliography. This includes materials from your Readings as well as materials you abstract from the library.

To summarize, then, your task is to write a paper using Erikson's general concepts and propositions about ego identity to analyze the ego identity of your autobiographer. The second part of your analysis should be the formulation of a question from your reading. Attempt to answer these questions by reference to other sources you find in the library, either with the help of Mr. Donahue, or by yourself. The primary reason for finding and using additional, relevant sources is to write a good paper. The secondary and very important reason is to carry forward your technical and imaginative use of the library. The independent student must be highly skilled in finding relevant documentary evidence of at least minimal quality. We are committed to nurturing the independent student.

On the Intellectual Use of Your Autobiography:
Some Supplementary Library Techniques
and Tools

Gilbert E. Donahue
Monteith College
Library Project

In the assignment, One Intellectual Use of the Autobiography
of Your Choice, dated January 5, 1961, some explicit suggestions
were given about what sort of things to which one should pay special
attention in your own autobiographical materials. Your task in this
assignment is to write a paper using Erikson's general concepts and
propositions about ego identity to analyze the ego identity of your
autobiographer. The second part of your analysis should be the
formulation of a question, i. e., to find an area of information pertaining to your autobiographer which you think could add valuably to
your knowledge of the formation and content of his identity, but
which the autobiography slights or is silent on. In other words, use
the Erikson framework of concepts and propositions to find what
seems to you to be a significant gap in the information which your
autobiographer reveals about himself. Having discovered this gap,
the second part of your task becomes one of filling this gap by the
use of supplementary materials which you can uncover in the library.
At this stage, the problem becomes how does one find this supplementary material in the library?

The basic step in the successful use of the library is already
implicit in the above paragraph. Go to the library only after def-
initely deciding just what is the question on which the information
or data is required. The assignment sheet listed six general question areas upon which you might concentrate, but they do not exhaust
the possible areas which may be relevant to the unique situation of
your autobiographer.

Assuming that you have read your autobiography critically and
perceptively, you will already know important clues which can help
you find supplementary materials in the library. You will know,
for example, the time period in which your subject lived, something
about his family, his education, his associates at various times
during his life, his occupation, his avocations, interests and hobbies
and his membership in various religious, professional, social or
perhaps political organizations. In other words, from his autobiography you already know many of the dimensions in the network of
social relationships which give structure to his ego identity. Since
social relationships are in large part reciprocal, in those deimensions
in which a particular autobiographer may, for various interesting
reasons, be silent--the other "partner" in the reciprocal relationship may not be so reticent.

As the Introduction to the Readings on Socialization indicated,
the process of socialization implies that the individual learns about
objects, meanings, values, and also about himself, bv being involved in other people's behavior. This "involvement" in other

people's behavior, while much of it may remain private and unre-
corded, generally gives rise to various types of primary records
and ultimately to a fairly extensive set of documentation which finds
its preservation in libraries. Thus, the individual autobiographer
may not only have written an autobiography, but he may also have
kept a diary, written extensive personal letters, journals or memoirs. Likewise, it is possible that other people who were involved
in the social relationships of our autobiographer may, themselves,
have written autobiographies, memoirs, personal letters and thus
commented upon our original autobiographer. Not only such personal materials, but also local histories of the city or region in
which our autobiographer lived may provide information relating to
him or to his family. Similarly, histories of schools, churches,
or other organizations with which he was "involved" may yield
further insights. A recent paperback book, for example, This
Little Band of Prophets: The British Fabians, by Anne Fremantle
(Mentor, MT266, 1960, 750), gives a fascinating picture of the
activities of George Bernard Shaw which might well be read in conjunction with the Erikson reading.

It is not only a George Bernard Shaw, however, who creates
an extensive set of documentation for himself. Every individual,
no matter how humble or unnoticed he may think himself to be, is
constantly creating a series of public and semi-public records concerning his own existence. At birth, there is his birth certificate.
If he participates in religious organizations, there are various
records of the degree of his activities. Attendance at schools
means another extensive set of public records. Military service
adds further documentation. When he enters into the economic
sector of society, either into the labor force or as a credit-using
consumer, there are many more records established. Marriage and
family life add further records and, of course, with death there
is the death certificate. With these and many other social relationships, the process of socialization leaves in its wake a constantly increasing amount of records which document virtually every
phase of our existence.

Essentially, then, your task in filling in some gap in the life
of your autobiographer is similar to the task that the social historian or biographer faces in creating some coherent account of a
particular facet within the life of a subject they investigate. Dr.
Jesse H. Shera in his work, Historians, Books and Librarians, has
described the bibliographic tools available in libraries which are
appropriate for answering many of the questions involved in your
task. Such questions may be broadly classified as in the following
columns:

Questions	Bibliographic Aids
Agents	
Individuals	Directories, biographical dictionaries, genealogies, biographies, personal journals, correspondence, memoirs, etc.

Organizations: Governmental, industrial, financial, professional, religious, etc.

Directories, histories of the particular organization or of the field to which it belongs, general histories of the place and period, official records, both public and private, etc.

Events

Dates, places, participants, accurate recital of the course of action, relation to other happenings, consequences, etc.

Chronologies, general histories, newspapers, diaries, biographies, official records, compilations of legal decisions, etc.

Interpretation

Opinion as to causes, influences, underlying forces, larger consequences, psychological or philosophical explanations.

General histories representing different points of view, biographies of participants, philosophies of history, etc.

Quantitative Description of

Population, production, trade, social conditions, etc.

Statistical compilations and handbooks, special statistical analyses in monographs, journal articles, theses, etc.

In this assignment we are, of course, focusing upon locating individual biographical information. There are two types of library tools available for such information: 1) indexes to sources of biographies, such as the Biography Index, and 2) source books of biographies, such as the Dictionary of American Biography.

The Biography Index is a cumulative index to biographical materials in books and magazines. It includes current books in the English language wherever published, biographical material from the 1500 periodicals now regularly indexed in the Wilson indexes, plus a selected list of professional journals in the fields of law and medicine as well as obituaries of national and international interest from the New York Times. All types of biographical material are covered and works of collective biography are fully analyzed. Portraits are indicated when they appear in conjunction with indexed material. The index is in two sections 1) name alphabet with dates, nationality, and profession or occupation; and 2) an index by profession and occupation. Much retrospective and current biography appears in books and periodicals and the Biography Index is the best tool for such sources which have been published since 1945, the date this index was established.

Some other indexes to biographies are: Edward Hayes O'Neill, Biography by Americans, 1658-1936, A Subject Bibliography, (Phila.: University of Penna. Press, 1939. 465 p.) It attempts to record all known biographies written by Americans. Also to be noted is Phyllis M. Riches, Analytical Bibliography of Universal Collected Biography. (London: Library Association, 1934. 709 p.) It is an index to biographies in collected works, arranged alphabetically by the names of the persons, followed by a bibliography of the books analyzed; a chronological list of the biographies; and a list arranged by profession or trade. The Essay and General Literature Index contains a large amount of analytical material for biography and criticism of individuals and so often serves as an index of biography. For biographies in foreign countries, the U. S. Library of Congress, General Reference and Bibliography Division, Biographical Sources for Foreign Countires, no. 1-4, (Washington, D. C. 1944-45) should be consulted.

The second type of library tool for biographical information, the source book of biographies, is quite varied in content. These source books may be grouped in three main types:

1) the universal type, such as World Biography, is most likely to contain data on the very notable of all times and places;

2) the retrospective type, such as Who Was Who, is useful for finding biographies of persons no longer living; and

3) the current type, such as Who's Who in America, gives data on persons still living.

The current type may be very general and very selective. If so, the source is useful for locating information on key persons who are notable enough to achieve international or national importance. There are also similar works for regions, such as Who's Who in the Midwest, some states, and some localities. The current type may also be very specialized. With the development of specialization within our society, a wide variety of biographical dictionaries have become available for such fields as art, education, library science, engineering, law, medicine, music, science and particular industries. If a person is outstanding in a geographic area or in a field of specialization, these dictionaries generally are the best sources of information.

Given these two general types of biographical tools, how do we use them? The first step is to have the person's name spelled correctly. Since in this assignment, we are dealing with already selected autobiographies, this should be no problem. Secondly, is the person alive or dead? Again, this should be no problem in this assignment. In general, however, it does make a difference because different biographical tools become usable depending upon whether the subject is alive or dead

For famous deceased persons, a brief biography of any famous person long dead can be found in any decent encyclopedia. Large dictionaries include famous people in the main alphabetical list or in a separate list, giving a few facts like birth and death dates, nationality, chief grounds for fame and pronunciation of the name.

There are universal biographical dictionaries, the most widely accessible and important, for names of all periods and places, is the Webster's Biographical Dictionary (2nd ed., 1953). Its thumbnail sketches are far less detailed than a good encyclopedia.

Biographies of notable deceased Americans up to 1935 may be found in the twenty volumes of the Dictionary of American Biography or in the many volumes of the National Cyclopedia of American Biography. Both have indexes. The two volumes of Who Was Who in America also may be used for the period 1897 to 1950.

Biographies of British and Irish individuals may be found in the Dictionary of National Biography, 1885--

For regular separately issued biographies, which usually give more details and fuller interpretations than the biographical dictionaries, the searching procedure depends upon the publication data. Such biographies published before 1946 should be sought in the Cumulative Book Index with the person's name as the subject heading. To cover practically all biographical items on persons long dead, in books and periodicals published since 1945, only the use of the Biography Index is necessary.

For less well known deceased persons who died more than a generation ago, try Webster's Biographical Dictionary and the Riches and O'Neill compilations. For persons who died within the last thirty or forty years, the appropriate specialized Who's Who book should be used. This requires a knowledge of the approximate data of death and some idea of the person's occupation and/or geographic area of residence.

For biographical information on contemporaries, (i. e., living persons or those who have died so recently that their names are not yet included in biographical dictionaries or encyclopedias) if only a few facts are needed, try Webster's Biographical Dictionary. Other sources are:

1) World Biography, for internationally known contemporaries in various professions and occupations;
2) for American notables, the latest volumes of the National Cyclopedia of American Biography;
3) the proper Who's Who, according to geographic area or field of specialization;
4) Current Biography, established in 1940, it is a source book of biographies for national and international names that receive much attention in the current news;
5) Facts on File, for immediately current facts about persons in the news rather than a systematic biography;
6) The New York Times Index for obituary notices which will give a systematic biography;
7) Biography Index, valuable as a current index to sources of biographies of contemporaries as well as for retrospective biography;
8) Libraries of newspapers;

9) Indexes and other files maintained by reference departments of public and university libraries;

10) Headquarters of professional societies, corporations, and other organizations with whom given individuals may be associated.

Monteith College
Science of Society

November 9, 1960

The Paper for the Social Movements Section.

We have some suggestions:

1. Read carefully the "Working Paper" in your Readings, Part
    Five.

2. Think about your own interests. (See p. 1465 for examples
    of the way social movements may be identified as related to
    areas of interest.)

3. You may want to discuss your ideas with your instructor.

4. The Monteith Library Program staff has prepared a file of
    suggested references. This is necessarily incomplete, but it
    may be helpful in providing you with (a) examples of social
    movements, or (b) a few suggested references. Attached is a
    list of some of the areas covered by this file.

    The file is in Mr. Donahue's office, Room 325, third floor of the
    general library. You are invited to consult it and Mr.
    Donahue.

5. In your first discussion group meeting during the week of
    November 13, you will be asked to indicate what topic you
    have chosen for this paper. Be prepared.

Additional suggestions about finding materials:

1. Use your Wayne State University Library Guide. (If you do
    not have a copy, ask for one at the General Circulation desk
    on the main floor of the library.)

2. You may wish to have a second look at the "Library Notes"
    included in your readings for Problem One, (p. 319-323). The
    context is different, but the principles are the same.

3. For quick orientation to your topic, try encyclopedias and
    follow up for references they suggest. We recommend partic-
    ularly the Encyclopedia of the Social Sciences and the Encyclo-
    pedia Britannica.

4. The Journal of Social History is a likely source for journal
    articles. Along with other scholarly journals in the area, it
    is indexed in the International Index to Periodicals.

5. The Public Affairs Information Service is a useful index to
    ephemeral materials - pamphlets, documents, etc., the forms

of publications characteristic of the "message" of the social
movement once it is organized.

6.   Note that materials on very recent social movements will not
     have been published in book form.   The periodical indexes
     and the New York Times Index may be the only clue to infor-
     mation about such topics.

About writing your paper:

     Have a good hard look at chapter 13 of the Writer's Guide and
     Index to English.   Follow its recommendations for form of
     footnotes and bibliography.   (Note that your instructor will
     expect your paper to be documented with footnotes and bibliog-
     raphy.)

And a Reminder:

     When you take a book out of the library, please indicate
     Monteith in the space which asks for the course.

     (The following is a list of broad subject areas for which some
     references are available in room 325, General Library. They
     are not necessarily meant as specific topics for your term
     paper).

Africa--

          Freedom movements in South Africa
          Struggle for Algerian independence
          Liberia: A Century of Survival
          Social and political change in the Gold Coast
          The Agadir Crisis
          The Moroccan Crisis
          European imperialism in Africa
          Social reforms in Egypt
          Formation of anti-slavery societies
          Development of African political societies
          Anti-Jewish movements in South Africa
          Missionary activities in Africa
          Fundamental education in Africa
          African nationalism

Asia--

     India:

          The Montagu-Chelmsford Reforms
          The Civil Disobedience Campaign
          Labor and Socialist movements
          The Swadeshi movement
          Asian churches in the Ecumenical movement
          Social and religious movements of the 19th century

China:

    Religious movements in China
    The Chinese labor movement
    Disaster relief and spring cultivation movement in China
    Chinese student movement
    Revolutionary movements in China
    The Nationalist Revolution
    The Chinese Renaissance or New Culture Movement

Japan:

    The Japanese Labor Movement
    Nationalism in Japan
    Japanese National Essence Movement
    National Reconstruction Movement
    The "Revere the Emperor" Movement or "S-No Movement"

Europe--

    Romanticism and Classicism as factors in the social move-
        ments of Europe
    The Socialist movement in various countries of Europe
    Utilitarianism in England
    Religious movements in Europe, e. g., the Reformation, Coun-
        ter-Reformation, Jansenism.
    The French Revolution and its various movements, such as
        Jacobinism
    Development of Existentialism
    The Enlightenment as a social movement
    Nationalism in Europe
    Women's rights and suffrage
    Social Welfare movements
    The French labor movement
    Anarchism and syndicalism in Europe
    Utopian thought and movements

North America--

    The Agrarian revolt of the 1800's in the U. S.
    The Abolitionist movement
    Secessionism in pre-Civil War America
    The Progressive-Muckraking movement
    Socialist movement in America
    American Trotskyism
    The populist movement
    Bimetallism in the U. S.
    Criminal Syndicalism
    Development of social legislation in the U. S.
    Suffrage and women's rights movement
    The American Labor Movement
    Utopian community movements in the U. S.

South America--

> The labor movement in South America
> Religious movements in Latin America
> The colonization process in the early history of S. America
> Colonial elites in Central and South America
> Political reform movements
> 19th century dictators and revolutions
> 20th century dictators and revolutions
> Development of Latin American culture
> Contemporary cultural movements
> The Mexican Revolution
> Industrial Revolution in Mexico
> Labor political parties in Latin America

Library Project: Humanistic Studies 231   Spring, 1961

Discover whatever evidence you can find in the personal life, the social milieu, or intellectual environment of an individual that might account for the values you find in one of his works which you have dealt with this semester. Annotate your paper properly and include at the end a bibliography of all material which you have used. Be prepared to justify in conference that your use of the library has been intelligent.

Notes on the Use of the library

Gilbert E. Donahue
Monteith Library
Project

The assignment you have just received poses a two step process for its successful completion. In the first place, it calls upon you to make a judgment as to the values you find in one of the works with which you have dealt in this course and, secondly, it requires that you find evidence to support your judgment. Breaking down the assignment into its various components, it requires that you:

1) find evidence from: a) the personal life of an individual
                        b) his social milieu, or
                        c) his intellectual environment

2) which might account for the values reflected in

3) one of his works with which you have dealt in this course, which may be: a) a literary work, b) a painting, or c) a musical composition.

Your judgment of the values to be found in the works utilized in this course depends upon your personal reflection and interpretation. Finding evidence to support your judgment, however, requires you to obtain external, objective data which complement your viewpoint. A primary source from which to obtain such data is the library.

The library, in its most general sense, is a systematically arranged collection of books and other materials which record a major portion of the world's knowledge. As such, the library cannot give you a personal interpretation of the work you selected for this assignment, but its system, as you learn it, can lead you to the sources of evidence to support or modify your viewpoint. It can provide data relating to the personal life of an individual and to his social milieu or his intellectual environment.

The library can do this because it is an organized system: a set of physical facilities, books and other materials and trained personnel, such as the reference librarians, whose common purpose is to facilitate your access to the information you require for academic success. A key point at which to start using the library system, although not the only possible starting point, is the first

floor card catalog. What can it do for you? In the first place,
under the name of the individual whose work you have selected, the
catalog will have cards listing first any books written by him and
secondly cards listing books which have been written about him,
such as biographies. Thus any autobiographies or biographies in
separately published form which are in the library can be readily
located through the use of the card catalog.

Biographical materials, especially autobiographies, can give
you important clues not only about the personal life of an individual,
but also about his social milieu and intellectual environment. From
them you will know, for example, the time period in which your
individual lived, something about his family, his education, his
associates at various times during his life, his vocations, interests
and hobbies, and his membership in various religious, literary,
artistic or perhaps political organizations. In other words, from
these biographical materials you can know many of the social relationships which gave a structure or pattern to his career and which
may, or may not, have had a direct impact on the work you have
selected for comment.

These clues which you can find in biographical materials provide a way for discovering additional subject headings in the card
catalog which, in turn, will disclose more information relating to
your subject. You will know by now, for example, whether he is
an author, a painter or a composer. For biography of a special
class of men, the card catalog tells us, see the name of that class.
In other words, in addition to checking under the personal name of
your subject, look up the specific type of artist or literary figure
which most closely approximates his work, e.g., not only: 1) Authors, but also Dramatists, Humorists, Novelists, or Poets, 2)
Artists, but also Painters, etc., and 3) Musicians, but also Composers, etc. These subject headings are made even more specific
by the addition of nationality or geographic subdivisions. Thus, we
have subject headings for "Authors, America," "Composers,
European," and the like.

The clues from biographical data also enable you to place
your subject in time and in geographic location. With this information, you can find subject headings in the catalog which will list
materials on the social and intellectual conditions of his time and
place. If your subject were a 19th century English novelist, the
heading, "Gt. Britain--History--19th century," would list general
English histories of that time which would provide background reading. For materials specifically on the social conditions or intellectual environment, the respective headings would be "Gt. Britain--
Social Conditions" and "Gt. Britain--Intellectual Life." For discussions of the English novel of this period, the heading would be
"English fiction--19th century--History and criticism." Materials
giving a more general picture of the state of English writings during
this period would be found under the heading, "English literature--
19th century--History and criticism."

Similar patterns of subject headings may be found in the card
catalog for the fields of art and music. In the field of art, for

example, general works about the subject are listed first, followed
by an alphabetically arrayed group of subject headings behind which
the art literature relating to various countries, historical periods,
schools or styles of art, bibliographic form (bibliography, biography,
dictionaries, etc.), relation to other disciplines and social phenomena, etc. may be found. Thus a sample of the headings under art
may be in the following sequence:

    Art
    Art, Abstract see also Modernism (art)
    Art--Addresses, essays, lectures
    Art, American
    Art, American--Exhibitions
    Art, Ancient
    Art--Asia
    Art, Baroque see also Painting, Baroque
    Art--Bibliography
    Art, British
    Art, Buddhist
    Art--Criticism see Art Criticism
    Art--Dictionaries
    Art--History
    Art--History--Bibliography
    Art--History--19th century
    Art--History--20th century
    Art, Jewish
    Art, Medieval
    Art, Modern--20th century
    Art--Philosophy
    Art--Psychology
    Art, Renaissance
    Art, Rococo
    Art--Study and teaching--U.S.
    Art--Techniques
    Art--U.S.
    Art--U.S.--History
    Art and history
    Art and industry
    Art and literature
    Art and morals
    Art and mythology
    Art and society
    Art criticism

    In music, the subject headings are naturally different but the
logic of their formation and organization is the same. Thus, a
sample sequence of the headings in this field might look as follows:

    Music
    Music--Addresses, essays, lectures
    Music, American
    Music, American--History and criticism
    Music--Bio-bibliography
    Music--Chronology

        Music--Collections
        Music--Dictionaries
        Music--Discography
        Music--History and criticism
        Music--History and criticism--Theory, etc.
        Music--History and criticism--Ancient
                                    --Medieval
                                    --Modern
        Music-Interpretation (Phrasing, dynamics)
        Music-Performance
        Music--Philosophy and Esthetics
        Music--Psychology
        Music--Theory
        Music and architecture
        Music and color
        Music and literature
        Music and morals
        Music and society
        Music and art
        Music in churches

   The point of these remarks is that the subject headings in the
card catalog, whether they relate to a person, the history or conditions of a country, a field of literature or art, can furnish you
with many leads to the information you require for your Monteith
courses.   The card catalog is not always an easy tool to use, but
in case of difficulties consult the reference librarians.   It is part
of their job to facilitate your work.

   After an imaginative use of the card catalog, your end products
should be a list of references relating to various aspects of your
interpretation of the work you have selected for this assignment.
One word of warning: if an item in the catalog seems relevant to
you, make a complete citation of it on a separate 3 x 5 card or by
whatever system you follow the first time you see it. By complete
citation is meant its call number, full name of author, title, publisher and place and date of publication.   A complete citation the
first time will save a lot of time rechecking later when you are
compiling your bibliography.   If you do not follow any system in
your note taking and scanning of references, you should consult one
of your instructors or a member of the Library Project for assistance.   Again, it is simply a matter of making your work easier
and more fruitful if you develop such a system.

   After you have a complete list of references, what do you do
with it?   The process is only partially finished; you need to find
them on the shelves next.   For this purpose use the Library Guide
you were given last year for its book location directory to guide
you to the appropriate sections indicated by the call numbers on your
references.   Each floor has its own directory.   If you are in doubt
and if you continue to have difficulties in locating your materials,
consult the reference librarian on duty on that floor.   If an item is
not in its place on the shelves, ask about it at the divisional Circulation Desk where assistants may be able to supply answers by

checking files which are kept there.

While the card catalog is an essential element in the library system it is not the only tool which must be used to gain access to the information you need for this assignment. The card catalog deals only with books; it does not give access to the contents of periodicals and journals. While the catalog lists the titles of periodicals received by the library, it cannot provide any indication of what information they contain. It is for this reason that we indicated that the card catalog was not the only starting point of your search for information in the library.

Another starting point, consequently, is the use of the indexes and abstracts which analyze the contents of periodical literature by a set of headings similar to those used in the card catalog. While the adequacy and completeness of coverage vary, the information in the journals of each subject field may be found in the appropriate index or abstract. Knowledge and use of these tools is an important element in your program of general education at Monteith.

How do you find an appropriate index or abstract? A general source which lists indexes and abstracts, as well as other reference tools, is Constance Winchell's Guide to Reference Books (Chicago: American Library Association, 1951). A more specialized tool for art is M. W. Chamberlin, Guide to Art Reference Books (Chicago: American Library Association, 1959). Another way of locating indexes and abstracts is through the use of Ulrich's Periodical Directory: A Classified Guide to a Selected List of Current Periodicals, Foreign and Domestic (New York: R. R. Bowker, 1959). This directory not only lists the principal journals in each subject field, but also indicates what index or abstract, if any, analyzes them.

The periodical literature in literary studies is too extensive for any one index or abstract, but the principal tools for this area may be found in John W. Spargo's A Bibliographical Manual for Students of the Language and Literature of England and the United States (New York: Hendricks House, 1936] or in Clarence Gohdes' Bibliographical Guide to the Study of the Literature of the United States (Durham, N. C.: Duke University Press, 1959). The Music Index, the key to current music periodical literature (Detroit, Michigan: Information Service, 1949--) provides for coverage of over forty American and English periodicals representing various aspects of the music field. Likewise, the Art Index, a cumulative author and subject index to fine arts periodicals and museum bulletins (New York: H. W. Wilson, 1933--) covers the various fields in the fine arts.

Much of the biographical information which will be useful in this assignment will appear in periodical literature. For access to such material, the Biography Index is the appropriate tool. It is a cumulative index to biographical materials from over 1500 periodicals as well as to biographies in book form. The index is arranged alphabetically according to the names of the biographies, so the task of finding any specific individual, if he has been included, may be accomplished easily.

The use of all these suggested bibliographic procedures and tools may or may not be necessary in this particular assignment. They have been indicated at this time, however, so as to encourage you to give systematic attention to their mastery in preparation for becoming an independent and mature student.

Monteith College
Natural Science 232
Spring, 1961

Suggested Library Procedures for your Term Paper

You have received a list of subject areas within which you may find topics suitable for the long research paper which you have been asked to write for Natural Sciences 232. This statement has been prepared to suggest ways in which you can use the library to get your bearings within any of these subject areas, and to find an interesting topic and suitable information for your paper.

I.   The approach through the Card Catalog.

A.   Recommended when you are fairly clear about the meaning, scope, and dimensions of the subject area you are interested in exploring.

B.   Starting with the subject area as it appears on your list, you are likely to find a good many cards with the term on your list (or a term very similar to it). You must, therefore, look for clues that will help you select the appropriate few from the many. Here are some clues:

1.   Language. Obviously you must omit books written in languages you are not familiar with.

2.   Technicality. The title, the subtitle, alternate subject headings (listed at the bottom of the card) may provide clues as to the level of the book.

3.   Classification (or call number). You will save time by paying attention to the class number assigned to the books. When you find that most of the books are classified in one or a few classes of numbers, go to the place where that class of books is shelved.

C.   Having found the place in the stacks where most of the books on the general subject area you are interested in are shelved scan them quickly, looking at:

1.   Title page. Any indication of the qualifications of the author? Where does he teach, etc.? (Note that you may also check on the qualifications of the author by consulting a biographical directory such as American Men of Science.)*

2.   Back of the title page. The latest copyright date probably indicates the latest revision of the text (although this is no guarantee of extent of revision).

3.   The preface. Does the author indicate the scope and purpose of the work? What are the qualifications of those whose assistance he acknowledges? With what institutions are they associated?

4.   Introduction. Is it written by a "name" in the field?

If so, does it sound like a thoughtful evaluation of
the contribution of the work or like a chore assigned
by the publisher to a member of his stable of authors.

5. The text.   How is it organized?   How fully does it
cover?   Where is the bibliography?   Is the style
reasonably comprehensible?   Are there chapter summaries or conclusions?

6. The appendix.   What kinds of information does it provide?   Is it understandable in itself?   Does it indicate the sources of this information?

7. The bibliography (or list of references).   Is it keyed
to the text so that it provides clues to further searching?   Are the references timely?   Do you recognize
the authors as authoritative?

8. The index.   Can sub-topics within the area be found
readily?   Are sub-topics grouped to show their inter-
relationships?

D. Scan similarly the books listed in the catalog, but classified elsewhere.   (The scope of such books may be broad-
er, narrower, or tangential to the subject.)

E. As a result of this scanning you should be able to select
a few books which are authoritative, relevant to your
interests, and at a level of technicality appropriate for
your background.

F. From a more thorough examination of these few books,
you may be able to settle on one or more specific topics
that interest you.   The bibliographical references related
to these specific topics then provide you with clues for
further exploration of the topics.

G. At this point you may find it helpful to return to the card
catalog to see what titles are listed under the specific
topics you have tentatively chosen.

H. Probably you will want to check these topics also in the
Readers' Guide, the International Index to Periodicals, or
perhaps, one of the specialized periodical indexes.

II.   The Approach through an Encyclopedia.

A. Recommended when you are not sure you understand the
full meaning, the scope, the development, or the relationships of the subject area you are interested in.

B. General encyclopedias, such as Britannica or Americana
can give you a good start by providing well-organized,
succinct, often scholarly, statements which, characteristically, define the scope and dimensions of a subject, trace
its development, and cite important references in its
literature.   (The Americana has the better reputation for
its treatment of science, but the philosophical emphasis of

the subjects assigned you may make the Britannica a
better choice in this case.)

C. The Dictionary of Philosophy and Psychology, by James
Mark Baldwin (New York: Macmillan, 1901-1905) is old
but excellent and still authoritative for the early history
of many topics. It offers two volumes of concise articles
written by specialists and two volumes of bibliographies.

D. McGraw-Hill Encyclopedia of Science and Technology: an
International Reference Work, (New York, 1960) is current
and comprehensive, published in 15 volumes, the 15th
volume being a detailed index to the set. The articles
are initialled and they include bibliographies.

E. The bibliographies included in such encyclopedias will give
you a good start toward further exploration of any aspect
of the subject you are interested in. But you should also
be alert to terms, names of people, institutions, etc.
which may provide valuable clues for further searching
in the card catalog, periodical indexes, or even the table
of contents and indexes of books on the shelves.

III. The Approach through Books on Your Reading List.

A. Recommended when your interest has been caught by the
particular treatment or point of view on a subject area
which one or more of your readings presents, and when
the book also provides a generous bibliography and/or the
names of scholars or scientists who have worked in the
area.

B. Use any such reference as the first link in a chain,
locating the books cited in it, and the references in their
bibliographies, etc., until you find the same major scholars and works cited again and again. You can then be
reasonably sure that you have identified the figures of
major importance in the subject area.

IV. Some other sources you may find helpful.

A. Scientific American, the leading popular scientific journal
is usually both readable and dependable. It is indexed in
Readers' Guide.

B. Van Nostrand's Scientific Encyclopedia (Third ed., Prince-
ton, N.J., 1958) leans a bit toward applied science, but
it is recent and comprehensive. It does not have bibliographies, however.

C. George Sarton's Introduction to the History of Science
(Baltimore: Williams & Wilkins, 1927-48) and his Horus:
a guide to the history of science (Waltham, Mass.,
Chronica Botanica, 1952) are both valuable sources of
information and bibliographies for historical topics.

D. The Bibliographic Index: A cumulative bibliography of

bibliographies, is published quarterly, cumulated annually, and cumulated again at four-year intervals. The entries are arranged by subject and they include both separately published bibliographies and bibliographies included in books and periodicals. Between 1000 and 1500 periodicals are examined regularly for this compilation.

E. A "Bibliography of Symbolic Logic," compiled by Alonzo Church appeared in Vol. 1, No. 4 of the periodical Symbolic Logic. It covers (December, 1936) this field from 1666 to 1935.

F. The following books of readings contain in addition to the readings, generous and helpful bibliographies:

H. Feigl and W. Sellars. Readings in Philosophical Analysis. (New York: Appleton-Century-Crofts, 1949).

H. Feigl and Brodbeck. Readings in the Philosophy of Science. (New York: Appleton-Century-Crofts, 1953).

L. Linski. Semantics in the Philosophy of Language. (Urbana, Ill.: University of Illinois Press, 1952).

* Note that another way to check on the authoritativeness of a book is to check book reviews. You can locate these reviews through the Book Review Digest.

Monteith College   Science of Society 131
                                                         (Used October, 1960)

Assignment on the Biological Prehistory of Man

The books listed below contain illustrations of history of the verte-
brates. The starred titles have been placed on special reserve (for
use in the library only) in the Kresge Science Library and in the
Social Studies Division of the General Library.   The other titles
and additional copies of the starred titles are on the open shelf.
You can locate them by consulting the card catalogue in the library
on the main floor and by using the location chart and then proceed-
ing to the shelves in these two divisions.

The library will reproduce any material at the cost of 5¢ per page.
This service is available until 4:30.   After 4:30, it is necessary
that a more expensive process be used so that the cost is 15¢ per
page.   If you wish a chart reproduced, take the book to the general
circulation desk on the first floor of the General Library.

1.	Foster, Nathan	Origin Through Evolution
2.	Gregory, W. K.	Man Among the Vertebrates
3.	Hoebel, E. Adamson	Man in the Primitive World
4.	Hooton, E. A.	Up From the Ape
5.	Howells, W. W.	Mankind in the Making*
6.	Howells, W. W.	Mankind So Far*
7.	Lull, Richard Swain	Organic Evolution
8.	Place, Robin	Finding Fossil Man
9.	Romer, A. S.	Man and the Vertebrates*
10.	Sanet, Andre	Man in Search of his Ancestors
11.	Simpson, G. G.	The Meaning of Evolution*

Science of Society 132, Spring 1961

Page 1

FOR THE SUBJECT OF YOUR PROJECT WHICH WOULD YOU LIKE TO HAVE?	Check	For each item checked tell us how you see this as fitting in with your current research project.	If you could only have three items, what is your 1st, 2nd & 3rd choice?	If you could have any of these 3 items which would you use first, which would you use later on?	If you happen to know a book or magazine which has this sort of information please list its name.
1. A definitive article by an eminent scholar on the general subject, written some years ago.					
2. Summary by a competent scholar of the best articles and books in the field which were published last year.					
3. A list of very short synopses of articles and books on topics within the general field, published frequently.					
4. A discussion by eminent researchers of the steps of various research methods in the social sciences.					

Page 2

5. A summary of research findings, statistics, relationships, etc., that have been established.

6. A report on each of the several major theoretical positions in the area.

7. Brief statements on the age, training, professional affiliation, publications, etc. of well-known scholars in the area.

8. Very brief summaries of theses written in the area.

9. Information about where to find full reports on research projects in the area.

10. A summary of classic studies in each of the general fields of the social sciences by a scholar in that field.

Page 3

11. A guide to the various kinds of publications in the general area of your project.			
12. An annotated list of reference books covering all subjects and arranged by subject.			
13. A list of articles in popular magazines listed by author and by subject matter, published frequently.			
14. A summary by an outstanding scholar in the area, of the most important research studies in the area, with a long bibliography.			

Can you think of any subject of information you would like to have that we have not listed?

Monteith College
Science of Society 132
Spring, 1961

Some Suggested Sources for
the Research Project

A few days ago we asked you to fill in a chart indicating
what kinds of articles, books, journals, etc. you thought might provide information useful to you for your research project. We were
interested in learning what kinds of publications might be considered
relevant to what kinds of research problems at what stage of development. Now we want to give you a list of publications which contain these kinds of information.

You should understand that the publications listed below vary
in quality one from another, and often within any one, from chapter
to chapter, article to article, or year to year. They vary, also,
in their relevance to any particular research problem of method.
Furthermore, the list is not exhaustive. For each of the types of
information listed on the chart we gave you, there is at least one
example. Sometimes there are others which do not fit the description exactly but which serve a similar purpose. Obviously, however,
no one publication is relevant to every subject. In filling out the
chart, you, of course, realize that some kinds of works were relevant to your project and some were not. Your instructor can advise
you about the relevance of the reference tools listed below. He may
want to suggest others more specifically to the point.

1. A definitive article by an eminent scholar on the general
    subject. Written some years ago.

    The Encyclopedia of the Social Sciences. New York:
    Macmillan, 1930-35. 15v.

    Comprehensive, aiming to cover all important topics in
    the social sciences. International in scope but fuller for
    the English-speaking world and western Europe. Consists
    of articles by specialists, signed, with bibliographies.
    Many biographical articles. Note that it is approximately
    30 years old.

    Encyclopedia Britannica. 1st ed. 1911.

    Note that this is not the current Britannica. Essentially
    a collection of important monographs on large subjects by
    specialists, often very scholarly.

    Cambridge Ancient History. New York: Macmillan,
    1929-39. 17v. Cambridge Medieval History. New York:
    Macmillan, 1911-36. 8v. Cambridge Modern History.
    New York: Macmillan, 1902-26. 13v.

    Reference histories, chapters written by specialists, full
    bibliographies.

2. Summary by a competent scholar of the best articles
   and books in the field which were published last year.

   Annual Review of Psychology.   Stanford, Calif.; Annual
   Review, Inc., 1950-

   Chapters, by specialists, reviewing the year's research
   in various areas of the field.

   Yearbook of Anthropology, 1955, 1955-   . New York:
   Wenner-Gren Foundation for Anthropological Research,
   1955-   . v. 1-

   Series of papers by scholars summarizing recent scholarly achievements, with extensive bibliographies.

   Review of Educational Research.
   This is a quarterly which aims to cover in the course of
   a three year period the major fields of educational research.   Each issue deals with one of these fields, con-
   taining articles summarizing work done on one aspect,
   with bibliography.

3. A list of very short synopses of articles and books on
   topics within the general field.   Published frequently.

   Psychological Abstracts, 1927-   Lancaster, Pa.:
   American Psychological Association, 1927-   v. 1-

   Bi-monthly journal which summarizes most of the material of psychological interest published in the western
   world.   Subject classification.

   Economic Abstracts, 1952-   v. 1
   Sociological Abstracts, 1952-

   Both published by the Graduate School of Arts and Science
   of New York University.   Abstracts are written by students from various universities sponsored by faculty
   members.   Fairly limited coverage.

   National Research Council.   Committee on Child Development.   Child Development Abstracts and Bibliography.
   1927-

   Bi-monthly, with subject arrangement and author index.
   Annual cumulation with subject and author index.

4. A discussion by eminent researchers of the steps of
   various research methods in the social sciences.

   There are so many discussions of research methods in
   the social sciences, that it may be well for you to refer
   to comments about them in A Reader's Guide to the
   Social Sciences, which is described below under category
   No. 5.   Among those mentioned are:

   Jahoda, Marie, Deutsch, Morton, and Cook, Stuart W.
   Research Methods in Human Relations.   1951.

Festinger, Leon, and Katz, Daniel. Research Methods
in the Behavioral Sciences. 1953.

Gottschalk, Louis. Understanding History.
A particularly comprehensive coverage for one area, appears in chapters 7-15, of Vol. 1 of:

Lindzey, Gardner, ed. Handbook of Social Psychology.
Cambridge, Mass., Addison-Wesley Publishing Co.,
1954. 2v.

5. A summary of research findings, statistics, relationships,
etc. that have been established.

Hoselitz, Bert F., ed. A Reader's Guide to the Social
Sciences. Glencoe, Ill.: Free Press, 1959.

Articles by specialists on the social sciences, history,
geography, political science, economics, sociology,
anthropology, psychology. Intended as "a general introduction to the literature of the social sciences that would
deal with the differences in the literary output in the
major disciplines, and the nature of the available tools...
that are consulted... An attempt has been made in each
chapter to refer to the more important "classics"...

Some attention has been paid to including not only works
incorporating substantive contributions, but also those
discussing methodological questions.

Because of this breadth, this collection serves in a number of the categories we set up. Note, however, the
lack of a subject or title index limits its usefulness to
some extent.

Monroe, Walter Scott. Encyclopedia of Educational Research. 3d ed. New York: Macmillan 1960.

Longish articles, by specialists, summarize and evaluate
the literature of educational research, each with a generous but selective bibliography.

Anthropology Today; an Encyclopedic Inventory, prepared
under the chairmanship of A. L. Kroeber. Chicago:
University of Chicago Press, 1953.

Articles by individual anthropologists, with bibliography.
Includes articles on "Method" and on "Results."

Third Mental Measurements Yearbook, ed. by Oscar K.
Buros. New Brunswick, N. J.: Rutgers University Press,
1949.

Not a yearbook. A new edition is much needed. One
section lists tests with reviews from various viewpoints.
The second edition reviews books on testing. Covers
educational, psychological, and vocational tests.

Annual Review of Psychology. (See no. 4, above)

6. A report on each of several of the major theoretical
    positions in the area.

    Hoselitz, op. cit. (See 5, above)

    Encyclopedia of the Social Sciences. (See no. 1, above)
    Vol. I includes a section titled "Development of Social
    Thought and Institutions. "

    Monroe, op. cit. (See no. 5, above)

    Lindzey, op. cit. (See no. 4, above)
    Volume 1, chapters 2-6 deal with contemporary system-
    atic positions.

    Shils, Edward A. The Present State of American Sociol-
    ogy. Glencoe, Ill.: The Free Press, 1948.

    Monroe, Ruth. Schools of Psychoanalytic Thought. 1955.

7. Brief statements on the age, training, professional affil-
    iation, publications, etc., of well-known scholars in the
    area.

    American Men of Science; a biographical directory, ed.
    by Jaques Cattell. 9th ed. New York: Bowker, 1956.
    Vol. 3.

    This volume covers the social and behavioral sciences.

    Cattell, Jacques. Directory of American Scholars. 2d
    ed. Lancaster, Pa., Science Pr., 1951.

    International Directory of Anthropologists. 3d ed. Wash-
    ington, 1950.

    Note that there are numerous directories, lists of mem-
    bers of learned societies, etc. Consult Winchell (see
    no. 12, below) for those in particular disciplines.

8. Very brief summaries of theses written in the area.

    Dissertation Abstracts (formerly Microfilm Abstracts); a
    guide to dissertations and monographs available in mico-
    form. Ann Arbor, Mich., University Microfilms, 1938-

    The arrangement is by large subject areas - essentially
    by academic department - and the abstracts are furnished
    by the authors. Note that since 1956, one issue lists all
    dissertations for which doctoral degrees were granted in
    the United States, including those not available on micro-
    film. (A key indicates which universities make them
    available on inter-library loan).

9. Information about where to find full reports on research
    projects in the area.

    a. Indexes.

    Public Affairs Information Service. New York, 1915-

Weekly, with five cumulations a year, the fifth being a permanent annual volume.

A subject index, covering books, government documents, pamphlets, articles in periodicals, multilithed material, etc.

International Index to periodicals.   New York: H. W. Wilson, 1916-

Indexes scholarly journals by subject and author.   Published quarterly with annual and triennial cumulations.

Education Index.   1929-   New York: H. W. Wilson, 1932-

Indexes educational journals, and includes references to articles in collections of proceedings, books of readings, pamphlets, and many government documents.   Indexed by subject and usually by author.   Book reviews listed only under "Book Reviews."

Bibliographic Index: a cumulative bibliography of bibliographies.   New York, H. W. Wilson, 1937-

Issued quarterly, cumulated annually and quadrennially. Subject index covering bibliographies published in books and periodicals.   Between 1000 and 1500 periodicals are examined regularly.

Besterman, Theodore.   World Bibliography of Bibliographies and of Bibliographical Catalogues, Calendars, Abstracts, Digests, Indexes and the like.   3d ed. Geneve, Societas Bibliographica, 1955-   v. 1-2 (in progress)

In four volumes, it will include 80,000 separately published bibliographies.   Vol. 4, author index.

London Bibliography of the Social Sciences.   London: British Library of Political and Economic Science, 1931- (in progress) 9v. to 1955.

Called the "most extensive bibliography in its field" lists, by subject materials in nine London libraries and special collections.

Note that Winchell (see no. 12, below) lists and describes many bibliographies on individual subjects.

10.   A summary of classic studies in each of the general fields of the social sciences, by a scholar in that field.

Hoselitz, op. cit. (See no. 5 above)

Encyclopedia of the Social Sciences.   (See no. 1, above)

11.   A guide to the various kinds of publications in the general area of your project.

Hoselitz, op. cit. (See no. 5, above)   Not in all fields

covered.

Alexander, Carter and Burke, Arvid, J. How to Locate
Educational Information and Data. 4th ed. New York:
Bureau of Publications, Teachers College, 1958.

Describe sources of information in all areas of education, how to use them, and how to locate them.

Daniel, Robert S. and Louttit, Chauncey M. Professional Problems in Psychology. New York: Prentice-
Hall, 1953.

Includes an annotated bibliography of reference books,
a list of journals, sources for books, tests, apparatus,
etc.

Harvard Guide to American History. Cambridge, Mass.,
Belknap Press of Harvard University Press, 1954.

Selective guide to books and articles on methods, resources, materials of American history. Some articles
arranged by period.

Channing, Edward, Hart, A. B. and Turner, F. I.
Guide to the Study and Reading of American History.
Rev. ed. Boston: Ginn, 1912.

Classified bibliography, with author, title, and subject
index, serves as a guide to "best" reading - for its
day.

12.   An annotated list of reference books covering all sub-
       jects and arranged by subject.

       Winchell, Constance M. Guide to Reference Books.
       Chicago: American Library Association, 1951. Supple-
       ments 1-3, 1952-58.

       There are other guides to reference books, but none is
       as complete, thorough, and accurate as Winchell.

13.   A list of articles in popular magazines listed by author
       and by subject matter. Published frequently.

       Readers' Guide to Periodical Literature, 1900-
       New York, H. W. Wilson, 1905-

       Indexes by subject, author, and title popular magazines.
       Note that the definition of "popular" may vary, so that
       journals have shifted from time to time from RG to
       the International Index or vice-versa. Note also that
       there is a 19th Century Readers Guide, covering the
       1890's and that Poole's Index to Periodical Literature
       covers 1802-1890.

14.   A summary by an outstanding scholar in the area, of the
       most important research studies in the area, with a

long bibliography.

Hoselitz, <u>op. cit.</u> (See no. 5, above) Except that the bibliographies must be inferred from an author index.

Monroe, Walter Scott, <u>op. cit.</u> (See no. 5, above)

Lindzey, Gardner, <u>op. cit.</u> (See no. 4, above)

<u>Anthropology Today,</u> (See no. 5, above)

Using the Anatomy of a "Book":
Or Learning to Browse Intelligently

Purpose and Function of this Assignment

The purpose of this assignment is to provide a systematic framework of the external characteristics of written materials; such as books and journals, which can enable you to make a quick preliminary judgment of their probable merit as you encounter them in using the open stacks of the library. This assignment, consequently, is directed toward increasing your sense of selectivity and discrimination within that democracy of books, the library. Because they are based solely upon the visible evidence contained within a particular book or journal article, the principles of evaluation in this framework cannot provide a final or definitive judgment of the intrinsic merit or relevance of written materials for all types of purposes, but they can assist you in eliminating from consideration a large portion of useless materials.

The total process of evaluating literature is complex; this assignment deals only with a preliminary, though essential part of that process. This part of the process can only indicate the books and journals which are most generally quoted and used by a majority of the practitioners in various subject fields. Thus it can distinguish the better items from the more mediocre, but it cannot distinguish the best item for any given purpose from among the materials which meet its criteria. Also, there are always those few unique items which seemingly, violate nearly ever external criterion of value but which still possess intrinsic merit. No general framework, such as that indicated here, can substitute for expert guidance or for the exercise of your personal attention to the characteristics of scholarly literature as you progress toward becoming an independent student.

Framework for the Evaluation of Literature

The following framework is designed to focus your attention upon those parts of the evaluation process which can be accomplished by a brief examination of the book or journal as an artifact. What can we know from an inspection of the item? The various parts of a book or journal article constitute a series of signals which can provide you with important clues to the significance of an item if you know how to interpret them. Thus you can interpret the significance of:

1. The Form of the Publication. In a physical sense, we can readily determine whether the item is a book, journal or pamphlet, whether it is large or small in overall dimensions and whether or not it is long or short in length. In terms of its intellectual form and design, we can determine whether it is a monograph, a novel, a research report, an epic of the proceedings or some professional meeting or conference. Each of these forms, and many others we could have mentioned, exist to fulfill a recognized need and we must distinguish among them if we are to realize the

intention of their respective authors and publishers. All books and journal articles are not created equal and not every item that claims to be scholarly shall enter into the kingdom of knowledge.

The basic communication function of the journal is to provide the first reports of scholarly research and theoretical discussions. A second function is that of presenting reviews of current books, abstracts of articles, comments on material in current periodical literature and reviews of special areas. Thus journal articles provide the latest, up-to-date opinions and data upon developments within the various subject disciplines. Books in monographic form, on the other hand, are usually less current than journals, but generally are more reliable, authoritative and comprehensive. Pamphlet literature is a special class in itself providing a means for extended discussion of highly current topics, generally in a controversial manner which soon have only a historical value.

The choice, then, of the particular form of literature you select while browsing depends upon the needs of your specific topic or problem. It is rare that only journal articles or only books will meet all the informational needs for a Monteith assignment. Depending upon the characteristics of your topic, then, there is a form of literature which is more likely than others to convey the type of information you need. Within that form of literature, be it a book, journal article or a pamphlet, there are authors whose recognized competence entitles them to more respect than other writers, and likewise there are differences among publishers regarding the quality and integrity of their respective publications.

The first "principle" or rule of evaluation, consequently, states that we must know what kind of material we are reading and we should know this as early in the process as possible, preferably before we begin to read it extensively. But how can we be expected to know what sort of material we are reading before we begin to read? (In this discussion we are focusing upon the characteristics of books because they are the most mature and elaborate form of literature. Journal articles and pamphlets share many of the same features possessed by books, so our remarks may be applied with qualifications to all the forms of literature which you will commonly encounter).

We can know what kind of a book it is upon the basis of information obtained from what is conventionally called the "front matter" of a book. The front matter consists of the title page, table of contents, preface and introduction. These are signals which the author gives us to indicate what he intended his work to say and how he wanted to organize it. Thus, our second set of clues is:

2. The Title Page. The title page is to the book what the face is to the human being. It is the principal means by which we can quickly identify a given item of literature. Just as the human face is composed of parts, each of which contributes to the total

impression we have of a person, so the title page of a book has parts and each one contributes to the judgment we can make of the book. The main elements of a title page are the author, title of the book and the location and name of its publisher.

  a. The author. Within Western cultures, the author has traditionally been the predominant facet around which we have iden- tified and organized our intellectual systems and the literature which has documented these systems. Thus most books, especially those of a scholarly nature, generally try to give evidence of the qualifications of their respective authors by indicating: 1) academic degrees he holds, 2) institutional affiliations and position, viz. Jacques Barzun, Ph. D. Dean of the Graduate School, Columbia University, 3) previous books published and any other information that can be indicated briefly which lends credence to his implicit claim of competence.

  b. The title. The title serves various functions. In an elementary sense, it serves to distinguish one book from another. Substantively, however, it can provide us with many clues as to the purpose and intention of the author and assists us in the judgment of whether to stimulate the reader's curiosity or to convey a symbolic theme; others are built upon a word or an allusion in the book that, in itself, is likely to be misunderstood. In expository writing, however, authors generally take considerable effort to make their titles as accurate and descriptive of the contents of the work as possible. A well chosen title provides clues as to its manner of treatment by the author. In many cases, titles are complemented by sub-titles which provide further clarification of the purpose and contents of the work.

  c. The publisher. The publisher is an important clue to the quality of a book. As agents for placing books into the public domain, publishers have a legal responsibility for them as well as an economic stake in their success. Consequently publishers try to select manuscripts of high quality which will also find an adequate market. Within the world of knowledge, however, there are simply too many subject areas for each publisher to cover individually. There is, accordingly, a "division of labor" among publishers with each of them tending to specialize in certain subject areas. Within these areas, publishers try to establish their reputations for quality and completeness of coverage. Thus within each major subject field, there are certain publishers who issue a disproportionate number of the better works in that field. Judgment as to whom these publishers who comes with experience in using the literatures within respective fields, but even there the pattern changes as new publishers try to get a foothold in expanding their sales.

  The above remarks apply particularly to the commercial pub- lishers, i.e., those firms which use their own risk capital to pub- lish books on the open market for a profit. A sub-variety of commercial publishers is the vanity press. The vanity press is composed of firms who receive payment from authors for the publication of their respective books. If the sales of the book are sufficient, sometimes the author is able to get his money back, but few vanity presses have best sellers. Generally, the quality of books from vanity presses is inferior to that from other commercial houses or university presses but nevertheless the vanity press performs a valuable social function in keeping open a freedom of expression which can be limited to the economic considerations of commercial presses or by the academic conservatism of university presses.

Another type of publisher which is becoming increasingly more important for the dissemination of scholarly materials is the university press. University presses are supported and operated by universities as an integral part of their social responsibility to the scholarly community and to the general public. The function of the university press is to place in the public domain of knowledge the work of scholars or other significant literature which cannot be distributed profitably by commercial publishers. University press books and other materials, accordingly, are usually of high quality, but they occasionally have their "dogs" also.

The last general type of publisher is the government, especially the various agencies of the U. S. government. As an effect of the expanding role of government within our society, the various agencies at the local, state and federal levels are important sources of information on virtually every aspect of our culture. Like information from any other source, government documents must be carefully evaluated for bias, completeness of information, sources of data and by the general criteria we use for judging any other item. Merely because an item is a government document does not give it any special claims for adequacy unless it is supported by these general criteria; on the other hand, merely because it is a government document, we should not dismiss it as a piece of political propaganda, although some of them are.

d. Date of publication. Depending upon the form of literature involved, the publication date of a book is of varying importance. In standard and current inspirational and recreational literature date of publication is of minor importance, as the value of the book depends not so much on its timeliness as on its literary quality. In informational literature, however, date of publication is generally quite significant in indicating the present value of a book. A book written by a lady doctor on mental health in 1925 would be of little value in an analysis of current trends in mental health care today.

Knowledge of the date of publication of the individual works of a given author is frequently useful and often necessary for an adequate interpretation of their significance whithin the intellectual growth and sometimes radical change in the viewpoint of an author. Freud, for example, changed many of his viewpoints during the course of his career. In interpreting any of his works, it is useful

to know at what period of his career it was published; the same
thing, of course, can be said for the work of any serious scholar.

Determining the date of publication of a book, in a legal
sense, is not difficult because on all copyrighted material it must
be indicated on the back side of the title page. The copyright date,
however, is always later than the actual date or time during which
the book was written. A closer approximation of the time that a
book was actually written may often be indicated by the date on the
preface or introduction which is usually the last thing an author
writes before sending his manuscript off to the publisher. The copyright date and the date on the preface or introduction may both be
different from the date which publishers frequently put on the title
page itself. This "imprint date" simply indicates the date that the
publisher printed the book and it may legally be up-dated every time
a new printing is made, even though no changes were made in the
text itself.

e. Edition. The "edition" of a book is the whole number
of copies of a book printed any time or times from one setting-of
type. A given work may be reprinted many times, but unless there
are substantial changes in the text the edition does not change. However, unless the changes in a text are any but the most trivial, the
publisher will want to see that they are legally protected with a new
copyright and to be able to call the work a "revised and enlarged"
edition, second edition or some similar notice. Thus, a work that
has gone into two or more editions carries with it a certain presumption of intrinsic merit since it has obviously been accepted by
many people within its subject field. For example, Alfred Marshall's
Principles of Economics, a standard classic in the field, which was
originally published in 1890, is still being used in its eighth edition
which was issued in 1920. Even though it is obviously an "old"
book, the fact that it has gone through so many editions should be
a signal that here is a book that many people considered worthwhile.

3. The "Dedication" in a book. Following the title page
of a book, many books contain a dedication of the work to some
person or persons whom the author wishes to honor by his work.
Historically, this practice is a carry-over from the days when the
authors had patrons, either the local lord or later a wealthy member of the aristocracy, who supported their work. Today, while
most of them are fairly innocuous homages to wives, children or
mothers, a significant number of them still attempt to indicate some
sense of intellectual indebtedness to persons who have influenced
the author. For this reason they may be a signal indicating the
possible biases or value systems of the respective authors.

4. The Preface. The preface comes next. It is usually
written by the author; if not, it may be shifted to some other person. In modern times, it is usually a succinct statement of the
need which the book is intended to serve, a statement of the author's
purpose, possibly a detailed analysis of the way in which the book
should be employed. It may contain acknowledgements for help

received by the author in his work, or for professional courtesies extended to him. Prefaces are therefore not to be ignored, for the whole benefit you get from a book may depend upon principles for its use there set forth. The preface is usually more specific than the introduction, to be discussed later, but the two often exchange some functions. If the preface states the method of use or the circumstances for which the book is written, it is an essential guide to choice, suitability, and use.

5. Tables of Contents. Tables of contents are "maps" to the terrain of a book. They are just as useful in the first reading of a book as a road map is for touring in strange territory. There are many, many kinds of tables of contents. In novels, the table is useful chiefly to tell you at what page each chapter begins and its title, but in such works the chapter titles are likely to be imaginative rather than descriptive. Since novels are usually read wholly and straight through, there is little lost except the loving care which some novelists expend upon their chapter titles.

Other types of works, such as informational literature, furnish a table of contents by which the reader can find with greater assurance that part of the book which concerns him. It affords a conspectus, or mental survey, useful in orienting the reader in the larger field of which his interest is a part. He may thus save himself blunders of comprehension while picking up clues about the general drift of the book which enable him to understand more fully, remember more easily, and read more swiftly.

6. List of Illustrations. In an illustrated book, the list of illustrations usually follows the table of contents. The ordinary reader will find himself confronted with no real difficulties in using it unless the arrangement is unusually inept. In some few books, the list of illustrations may distinguish "illustrations" from "plates, " the reason being that special illustrations, particularly colored matter, require special processes, and appear as unnumbered inserts rather than as numbered pages. Be prepared to accept and use many similar variations of techniques in the list of illustrations, but consider the list when you are choosing a book so that you may know how well the work fits your needs.

7. Introductions. Introductions to books present a major problem when one is determining the usefulness of the book to prospective readers. In general, they should provide just what their name implies. They may, however, say little to guide the reader if such directions have already been committed to the preface. They may be (and usually are) written by someone other than the author. Sometimes the identity and value position of the author of the introduction is a better clue to the merit of a book than is the author of the text.

Specialists who prepare for publication the works of another man, which is to say "editors, " not uncommonly produce introductions which may of themselves become somewhat monumental

pieces of writing for their style or for their content.   The field of
foreign language studies often produces works in which the text is
merely a matter for practice reading, whereas the introduction
contains the essential treatise on grammar and syntax which makes
the text itself comprehensible.   The "introductory matter" of
Webster's Collegiate Dictionary (only twenty pages) is as necessary
to the full use of the work as any part of the volume which follows
it.

    8. The Body of the Text: Typographical Layout and other
Features.

    a. Heads. Within the body of the text, there will not be
found as much uniformity of practice as in the "front matter" of
title page, table of contents, etc., for the infinite variety of its
purposes calls for many different methods of presentation.   But
there are a number of devices commonly used to aid the reader
to more efficient use of the work.

    In a book of thoroughly conventional kind, divided into chap-
ters as it usually is, further subdivisions may be desirable.   One
common practice is to print at the top of every verso (left hand
page) the title or an abridgement of it, and at the top of every
recto (right hand page) the titles of the chapters.   Many books,
notably text books, employ other typographical devices to signalize
topics and their divisions, and thus offer two very important advantages.   Since they afford you the easiest and readiest means of
acquainting yourself with the scope and content of a chapter before
you read it through; the rate at which you read and the accuracy
with which you remember are both greatly improved.   Books which
are not read through but consulted only in part, such as handbooks
and other types of reference books, must, if they are not to absorb
too much or our time, provide a ready means for "finding the
place."   This need may be met by an analytical table of contents
or an index; if these are not well executed, the running heads and
similar devices become all-important.   Learn to recognize and use
them in your evaluation of the potential merits of a book.

    b. Notes, foot and otherwise. Within the body of the text
there arises a constant need in certain kinds of books for footnotes, which commonly serve any of three or four functions.   1)
In the first place, the writer may wish to provide necessary information for the reader without interrupting the flow of his remarks.
A brief explanation of a point which might remain obscure or cause
misunderstanding, particularly when definitions are needed, is a
common function of the footnote.   2)   A second is that of developing a footnote, the author can throw out a suggestion, indulge in a
reminiscence, or give some part of his work a completeness which
in the text would be only an annoyance.   3)   Footnotes are also
the readiest means of providing cross references within various
parts of the text without disrupting the progressive development of
the argument or series of propositions the author is attempting to
establish.   4)   A fourth and fundamentally important use of the

footnote is to cite the source of material taken from other books; and it is necessary at this point that we anticipate a later section dealing with book lists or bibliographies. If the author has provided at the end of his work a separate, formally alphabetized bibliography, he can refer to any book in it by means of a condensed footnote.

Not all books present bibliographies as separate entries. Many professional periodicals require that the writer give the author, full title, city and year of publication, and other pertinent information in a footnote appended to the first passage requiring such documentation. All subsequent footnotes referring to that book are likely to be much condensed, and they will commonly employ abbreviations which it is necessary that you should know.

An author's "style" of footnoting, i. e. the extent to which he uses them, his purposes in so doing, the kind of sources he depends upon--does he depend upon first hand, primary sources or does he cite secondary sources and what are their quality--provides us with a quick basis for judging the probable scholarly merit of a book. Since styles in footnoting vary with the personal predilection of authors, the mere absence of footnotes does not condemn a book as being unscholarly, but the presence of an inept style certainly can.

c. Appendixes. Many times authors find that several points in the text would profit by expansion or more detailed treatment, but that a footnote does not furnish adequate space. In such cases, they may grow to any desired length and appear as appendixes, the first major division following the text. There is no imaginable limit to the kinds of appendix which the reader may expect to encounter. He will find charts, diagrams, maps, brief treatises on methodology and other pertinent subjects, reproductions of original documents for comparisons, tables of statistics. The advantages offered by this means are very often ignored because, having finished the text, the unwary reader is likely to clap shut the book and stretch himself with the satisfaction of accomplishment. These parts of a book, self-effacing as they may seem, are not to be ignored because of their location, but sought out in their suburban retreats like skilled though remote advisers.

d. Glossaries. The reader in any field is likely to find himself faced with the need of developing familiarity with a new set of terms. To fit this need many books furnish an alphabetical listing of terms which should not only be consulted as the need arises, but learned so that the entries become a part of the reader's ordinary working speech. The glossary is an incomplete lexicon of words that fit a special need created by the subject matter of the book.

e. Bibliography. The discussion of footnotes anticipated the treatment of the bibliography, which conventionally follows the glossary. It has many purposes. It is, first of all, an indication of the fundamental soundness of the work you are reading if it is a list of works consulted by the author. No writer in any field will risk his professional standing by producing a book which presupposes the examination of source material and predecessors without detailing his materials. 2) In the second place, since bibliographies are also intended for the reader's convenience and to aid him in his own studies, some writers go beyond the "works consulted" kind of bibliography and try to present a list as complete as humanly possible of all the material which may be found anywhere dealing with a given subject, even though the author makes no claim to having examined all of it. Such bibliographies go far beyond the mere listing of books, accessible or rare. They list diaries, journals, letter, portraits, manuscripts, notebooks, public documents and records whether found in the private collections of enthusiasts, in libraries or museums, or merely among the personal effects of chance possessors.

The forms observed in most older bibliographies show very little variation from certain standard procedures. It is common to list "original" or "primary" sources separately from "secondary" sources. A primary source is any kind of document believed to furnish direct evidence or information based on personal knowledge. Secondary sources are the books and other materials derived from original sources; they must be taken into account, for they represent an accumulating body of data, interpretation, and correction. Some bibliographies will make further distinctions in form, listing manuscripts, diaries, and the like separately from printed material. Some, in giving the works consulted, separate conventionally bound books from periodicals, and these in turn from general reference works like encyclopedias, but this practice is not universal.

Increasingly today, as Sherman Kent indicates in Writing History, scholars are veering away from the old practice of uncritically listing all the books they consulted for a given project. More and more are they using the "note" as the proper vehicle for bibliographical information. The note, besides being infinitely more useful than the barren alphabetized book list, is more pleasant and informing both to write and to read.

In essence this bibliographical note is a short critical essay about the materials which the author has used in writing his study. Author's name, book title, publication dates, and so on are all incorporated into running sentences.

Arrangement of the material within a note, or any sort of bibliography for that matter, ought to follow one general pattern. Within this large scheme personal preferences, and the peculiar demands of the material will make the detail of every note different from the last. The general pattern is simple. Every note should be made up of at least two (and sometimes three) main sections. The first of these (when it is used) is apt to be the shortest, for it is the one which deals with bibliographical aids. That is, it starts with a discussion of bibliographies and bibliographical articles and essays which cover the literature of the topic.

The second section is the most important for it is here that the author discusses his sources. He should describe them in the order of their weight and their closeness to what he believes the truth. His description should consider the form of the materials-- whether printed or manuscript--where they are to be found, the state of their preservation, their completeness, how they are sorted, indexed, catalogued, or calendared. In the last analysis it is the topic of the essay which determines what is and what is not source material.

The third section comprises the so-called secondary litera- ture; it should contain all material which cannot be positively identi- fied as source items. It too should be subdivided into at least two subclasses: monographs and general works. If newspapers and journals of opinion, autobiographies, memoirs, and diaries have been used and if they are not classable as original sources, they should come in this section in their own subclass.

While an author may misuse the scholarly functions of both footnotes and bibliography, together they form an external index of some of the sources and influences which contributed to his work. The pattern they prescribe give us clues for judging the quality of workmanship and probable merit of the item. For example, if a book or journal article was published in 1961, but no footnotes or bibliographical references were later than, say, 1940 we have reason to suspect the item or, at the very least, it is a signal for us to investigate why the author did not use any later literature. It may be such an esoteric topic that no significantly relevant litera- ture has been published since that time, on the other hand, the author may have actually written it in 1940 and only now published it without bothering to revise it--stranger things have happened in scholarly publishing.

Another kind of clue is the relative dependence upon primary as compared to secondary sources and also upon monographic litera- ture as compared to journal articles. Given the demands of specific topics, the peculiarities of literature in various subject areas and the variations in the personal styles of authors, there is no general rule as to what proportions should pertain in these ratios; for the purpose of a quick evaluation of a book or journal article, we should simply be sensitive to the fact that some balance should be maintained among them. The more that we know about the substantive problems in a given subject field and about the generally recognized authorities who have published works in the area, the more significant will be our scanning of footnotes and bibliographies. Of course, practitioners may not share any con- sensus about a ranking of the major substantive problems or who the "generally recognized authorities" are within any given subject field but finding out those details is part of the fun in mastering a discipline.

f.   Indexes.   An index is the back door to a book.   Essentially, an index is the book reduced to its essential themes, places,
topics and persons mentioned therein.   The one purpose in making
an index to any book is to make all the information in that volume
fully available to any reader without delay.   This is a comparatively
simple matter as far as it concerns references to names of places
and of people--though even these can present difficulties--but some
skill and experience are required wherever it is desired to make
references to ideas and define and indicate the different aspects of
a subject.   Indexing, in fact, is no mechanical process; if it is to
be of use, it requires thought and consideration in every phase of
its construction.   Since all the uses to which a work may be put
cannot be predicted, the index must by its completeness attempt to
anticipate everyone's questions.   Obviously, this is an impossibility,
but a good index provides a sufficient range of entries for discovering whether the specific items of information we are seeking can be
located within a particular book.   The usefulness of many otherwise
valuable books has been seriously impaired by the lack of an index
or by a poorly designed one.

The above listed parts are the major elements of a book.
Obviously, not every book you will encounter will have all of them.
Taken together they make up a typographical "model" of the book
as an instrument of communication.   Until now, we have discussed
each of these parts separately, but our judgment of the probable
merit of a book will be based upon the total impression it makes
upon us.   In other words, it is the relationship between these parts
and their common consistency which provides us with the basis for
our judgment.   For example, if the author's qualifications on the
title page are set forth impressively and if the title promises us
something like an "Intellectual History of Western Civilization, " but
the table of contents indicates a vaguely defined scope covering only
the intellectual history of certain periods in England and the United
States, the footnotes only referring to generally known secondary
sources and the bibliography limited in its coverage, our obvious
conclusion would have to be that there was a gross inconsistency
between the promise of the author's qualifications and the title and
the actual accomplishment of the text.   Thus, even in our quick
evaluation of books and journal articles while we are browsing in the
library, if we are perceptive we can detect a certain proportion
between the various parts of a book, a certain fulfillment of expectations which the various parts of a book or journal article cause us
to develop.   How many times all of us have spotted a catchy title
on the shelf, a new cover on a book, only after examing the table
of contents, a quick flip through the footnotes and a glance at the
bibliography to decide that this item is or is not for us.   If we
have a little more time, perhaps we dip into the preface and introduction and look up a few key terms in the index.

In any event, we do go through a decision-making process in
selecting books and journal articles, bring to bear our prior knowledge and attitudes along with the new impressions we have gained
from our brief scanning of the item.   The more adequate our

background knowledge and the more sensitive we are to the bibliographical characteristics of written materials we have indicated in
these notes, the more efficient our use of the library will be.

Bibliographical Note

The problems we have considered in these Notes are covered
extensively in the literature on the art of reading and in some books
on research techniques. A "how-to-do-it" book which still retains
its value and "message" after many years is Mortimer J. Adler's
How to Read a Book: The Art of Getting a Liberal Education (New
York: Simon and Schuster, 1940; also available in a more recent
paperback edition). Another how-to-do-it book which was useful in
writing these Notes is E. Wayne Marjarum's How to Use a Book
(New Brunswick, Rutgers University Press, 1947). Of the books on
research techniques, the best brief, but admirably adequate treatment may be found in Sherman Kent's Writing History (New York:
Appleton-Century-Crofts, 1941). A more extended treatment of
essentially the same themes may be found in Jacques Barzun and
Henry F. Graff, The Modern Researcher (New York: Harcourt,
Brace and Co., 1957).

Author_____ Discussion Leader_____
Student_____ Time of Discussion Section_____

Book Evaluation

Hypothetical Background Situation:
Suppose that you are a university student who is writing a paper on one of the following five topics: (check the appropriate topic for your discussion section)

_____The American Social Conscience

_____The American Legal System

_____Civil Liberties

_____U. S. Immigration

_____Anarchism and Radicalism in the U. S.

Your Task:
You are to evaluate quickly each of the volumes in the set of books specified for your topic and decide whether or not it is useful for the writing of your paper. All of the books in the set deal with the topic indicated.

Evaluation Criteria:
The following are external characteristics which are helpful in making such a preliminary judgement, such as you must make in using an open shelf library. You may possibly thumb quickly through the work or scan it, too.

Remember!

You are using the criteria indicated to get started on a bibliography for a paper from this set of books. Use only those criteria you need to help you decide about a particular book. You may not need to use all criteria for each book.

As soon as you feel able to make up your mind, skip to Parts H and I of this check list.

Of course, whether a work is ultimately excellent or not can only be decided after much more careful scrutiny.

A.   Date of Publication (check):
       (Glance at Title Page, Reverse Side of Title Page and Forward or Preface).

       _____Out of Date   _____Up to Date   _____Timeless

B.   Publisher (check or question mark):
       (Glance at Title Page).

_____University Press   _____University Press specializing in this field

_____Commercial Press   _____Commercial Press specializing in this field

_____Vanity Press   _____Government Publication

C. Its form of publication (check):
    (Glance at the Title Page, Preface, Table of Contents and Typographical Layout).

_____Monograph   _____Anthology: Collected set of readings, etc.

_____Textbook

_____Research Report   _____Proceedings of Conference or Symposium

_____Volume of a scholarly journal

_____Other: (indicate)

_____

D. Author's qualifications (check each relevant term):
    (Glance at Title Page, Preface and Introduction).

_____Qualified: By first hand experience_____
                 By personal acquaintance with people who were there_____
                 By official position_____
                 By scholarship specifically in this area_____

_____Not qualified   _____No indication

E. Bibliography (Check as many as relevant):
    (Glance at Title Page and Bibliography Section).

_____Does not exist   _____Includes primary sources

_____Exists   _____Annotated Bibliography

_____Bibliographic Essay   _____Short, selective Bibliography

_____Extensive Bibliography   _____Includes only secondary sources

F. Index (Check as many as relevant):
    (Glance at the Index).

_____Does not exist

_____Exists

_____Seems well organized

_____Seems extensive

G.   Consistency (Check appropriate square if there seems to be consistency between parts indicated; mark "no" in appropriate square for inconsistency. (Glance at Title Page, Table of Contents, Bibliography, Index and footnoting).

	Form of publication						
	Title	Contents	Foreword	Introduction	Footnoting	Bibliography	Index
Title							
Contents							
Foreword							
Introduction							
Footnoting							
Bibliography							
Index							

H.   Judge the merit of each book according to the following (Check one of the last three judgments, and as many others as are relevant).
(Glance at Preface, Bibliography, Introduction and Index).

_____Has a seemingly full bibliography, or footnoting, would lead me to other possibly useful materials.

_____Gives background or contextual information

_____It is a primary document

_____It seems to be a scholarly work

_____It seems to be a work worthy of looking at more carefully

_____One of its articles seems worthy of looking at more carefully
(Indicate the article's author:_____)

_____It seems useless for my purpose

I.   State the positive and/or negative characteristics upon which you made your decision and underline the crucial one.

JOYCE ASSIGNMENT

For information and references on James Joyce examine each of the three sources* listed on the attached sheet.

Write a report, no more than a page or two, comparing and contrasting them as to:

1) Comprehensiveness. How thoroughly do they seem to cover materials available on Joyce?

2) Informativeness. How much direct information (i. e., not simply references) do they provide?

3) Selectivity. To what extent are the references selected or evaluated?

4) Usability. Is it easy (or hard) to find information and references? To understand them?

5) General value. How would each contribute:

a) If you were preparing an exhaustive bibliography on Joyce?

b) If you were preparing to do a study of some rather obscure aspect of his work?

c) If you were interested in acquiring a thorough but general acquaintance with his work and influence?

6) Value for this section of the Humanities course. How helpful are they in providing references which seem to deal with one or all of the four ways of looking at the Portrait considered in the course?

*All locations indicated on the attached sheet refer to the General Library, 2nd floor, Humanities Division unless otherwise specified.

Sources Used for Joyce Assignment

The following is a list briefly annotated of the sources examined for the Joyce Assignment. This list is neither selective nor exhaustive; it includes some major reference tools and critical studies; it excludes others.

The list is divided into three parts corresponding to the three levels of bibliographic function identified in discussion of the assignment.

Category I--Bibliographies and Indexes. Each of the sources listed is comprehensive and non-selective within its defined scope. None offers direct information about the references or about the subjects covered.

1) <u>Annual Bibliography of English Language and Literature</u>.
1920-to date.   Index to all kinds of publications, books,
pamphlets, articles, doctoral dissertations, etc. Language
section arranged according to subject; literature section
arranged chronologically.   Further subdivided--e.g.,
Twentieth Century
   a) General -- arranged by topic e.g., Anthologies, Drama,
       etc.
   b) Authors -- (about whom articles indexed have been
       written), alphabetically arranged.

2) <u>Bibliographic Index: A Cumulative Bibliography of Bibliog-
raphies</u>.   1937-to date.   Index of book. length bibliographies and of bibliographies printed in periodicals, books,
and pamphlets.   Arranged alphabetically by subject. Titles
are those of the bibliography or of the book, periodical,
or pamphlet in which the bibliography appears.

3) <u>Card Catalogue</u> - Index to whole books in the Wayne Library.

4) <u>Essay and General Literature Index</u>.   1900-to date. Index
to collections of essays and composite books on all subjects.   Each article indexed under author and subject-
heading alphabetically arranged.

5) <u>International Index</u>.   1907-to date.   Index to articles in
a large number of scholarly journals in the social sciences
and humanities.   Each article indexed under author and
subject-heading.   Alphabetically arranged.

6) <u>Publications of the Modern Language Association (PMLA)</u>.
Bibliography, 1921-to date.   Index to all kinds of publica-
tions, books, articles, pamphlets, etc.   Primary arrange-
ment, Six Sections -- General and Miscellaneous, English,
American, Romance, Germanic, and East European
Languages and Literature.   Each section subdivided.
English Literature arranged chronologically.

Category II.   Abstracts and surveys.   All but one of the sources
listed provides either a) brief information on Joyce plus selected
bibliography or b) brief information, sometimes evaluative, about
the references cited.   The exception, Parker's <u>Bibliography</u> might
as logically have been placed in Category I above, but it does include information about charateristics of editions, issue, etc.

1) <u>Abstracts of English Studies</u>.   1958-to date.   Abstracts of
articles from a large number of scholarly and literary
periodicals including the <u>James Joyce Review</u>.   Periodical
titles alphabetically arranged.   Abstracts arranged under
titles of periodicals from which they are taken.   Four
part annual index -- 1) of journals from which abstracted
articles are taken, 2) author - title list of abstracted
articles, 3) general index, 4) title index.

2) Dictionary of National Biography. 6th supplement. Brief scholarly biography. Bibliography of a few major critical and biographical studies.

3) Encyclopedia Britannica. (any edition after 1947) "Joyce, James." Brief discussion of Joyce's life, career, and writings. Bibliography of four major studies.

4) Howarth, Herbert. The Irish Writers, 1880-1940. London: C. Tunling and Co., Ltd., 1958. Eight essays on Irish writers and literature. One essay devoted to Joyce. Index.

5) Parker, Alan. James Joyce: a Bibliography of His Writings, Critical Material, and Miscellanea. Boston: The F. W. Faxon Co., 1948. Divided into three parts corresponding to title. Attempts to be inclusive. Occasional entries annotated. No index.

6) Daiches, David. The Present Age, After 1920. London: The Cresset Press, 1958.
A survey of recent literature. Divided into two parts. Part one - five essays on recent literature. Part two - bibliographies of poetry, fiction, drama, general prose. Bibliographies arranged by author. List author's works and selected critical studies.

7) The Year's Work in English Studies. 1919/20 - to date. Survey articles on all kinds of publications, books, pamphlets, articles, etc. Selective. Evaluative. Articles arranged chronologically. Two indexes - "Authors," "Authors and Subjects Treated."

Category III. Books on Joyce. The basic purpose of the sources listed is not bibliographical, but informative. The bibliographies provided may be extensive or brief. The references are selected in terms of the author's primary purpose.

1) Ellman, Richard. James Joyce. New York: Oxford University Press, 1959.
Definitive biography of Joyce. Carefully documented. Index.

2) Givens, Seon (ed.) James Joyce: Two Decades of Criticism. New York: Vanguard Press, Inc., 1948.
Collection of essays by various authors on various aspects of Joyce's life and writings. Seven page bibliography of Joyce's writings and critical studies. Index.

3) Hutchins, Patricia. James Joyce's Dublin. London: Grey Walls Press, Ltd., 1950.
Description of the Dublin Joyce knew. Illustrations. No Index.

4) Hutchins, Patricia. James Joyce's World. London: Methuen and Co., Ltd., 1957.
Describes places where Joyce lived, studied and wrote.

Points out where references to these places occur in his
writings.   Index.

5)   Sullivan, Kevin.   Joyce Among the Jesuits.   New York:
     Columbia University Press, 1958.
     A study of Joyce's "Jesuit schooling." Five page bibli-
     ography of manuscript material and critical studies.
     Index.

6)   Noon, William T.   Joyce and Aquinas.   New Haven: Yale
     University Press, 1957.
     Study of Joyce's "Thomism." Index.

7)   Magolaner, Marvin and Kain, Richard M.   Joyce: the
     Man, the Work, the Reputation.   New Haven: Yale Univer-
     sity Press, 1956.
     Three Parts -- 1) Discusses aspects of Joyce's life in
     which there has been biographical and critical confusion.
     2) Brings together "best criticism available on each of
     Joyce's major works." 3) History of Joyce's critical
     reputation.   Thirteen page bibliography.   Index.

8)   Magolaner, Marvin.   Time of Apprenticeship: the Fiction
     of Young James Joyce.   New York: Abelard Schuman, Ltd.,
     1959.
     Study of Joyce's craftsmanship during his younger days.
     Index and bibliography.

*Register for this Assignment   Science of Society 0131
  Today, October 1, 10:30-5:00   Fall, 1963
  in Room 20 (Basement) 631
  Merrick

Instructions for the Library Assignment

1. The article   "Independence in the Library," serves as a model for the assignment. A careful reading of it will save you time.

2. The assignment is to be done in the library. You will use the card catalog, two periodical indexes, the Oxford English Dictionary, and the Syntopicon to find answers pertaining to an idea like "independence."

   a. Use the main card catalog on the first floor. All the rest of the library tools you will use are on the second floor of the library.

   b. The indexes and the Oxford English Dictionary are located on tables in the area just to your left as you come up the stairs or get off the elevator.

   c. One copy of the Syntopicon will be on special reserve, behind the circulation desk on the second floor. You may sign for it there. Another copy will be kept at the reference desk on the same floor when it is not in use. You may ask for this one, if the other is out.

3. A member of the Science of Society staff will be on hand at one of the tables on the second floor of the library in case you need help with the assignment. (We will have a sign saying "Monteith" to identify him.)

4. The assignment should take you no more than one hour to do. If you find yourself spending a disproportionate amount of time on any one question, you are probably on a wild goose chase. Do not pursue wild geese. See the instructor who is there to help you.

*5. You must work on the assignment at the time you are scheduled to do it. (This limitation is necessary to avoid traffic jams in the library.) If it happens that you cannot come when you are scheduled, try to swap your ticket with another student. Or come to Room 13, 631 Merrick for another ticket.

6. ONE MORE THING!

   Hand in with your completed assignment a paragraph, no more than a page, in which you present a metaphor for your word-concept and explain how the metaphor illuminates the idea. Remember to hand in the original and a carbon copy of this part of the assignment.

Independence in the Library

For thousands of years men have thought about, talked about, written about the ideas discussed in this, the first section of the Science of Society course. For almost as long they have attempted to preserve the records of these ideas in libraries. However, changes in the technology of communication have increased the size and complexity of the record to such a degree that the library of today is concerned less with problems of preservation and more with making the heritage of ideas accessible to the reader.

Suppose you want to draw on this heritage which has been stored in the library. What will you find? How are the ideas organized? What kinds of aids are provided for your search? What difficulties will you encounter? Will there be unexpected treasures?

Here is a sample. Using the term "independence," it illustrates what happens when you try to use such a word as the key to unlock two or three reference books, an index or two, and the card catalog.

The idea of independence is ancient, but we might begin by finding out when and how the word "independence" was first used in the English Language. The source is the Oxford English Dictionary.1 First the definition:

(1) The condition or quality of being independent; the fact of not depending on another...; exemption from external control or support; freedom from subjection, or from the influence of others; individual liberty of thought or action. Rarely in bad sense: Want of subjection to rightful authority, insubordination.

The earliest recorded use in England is quoted:

1640 Bp. Hall Humble Remonstr. (R.) Some... can be content to admit of an orderly subordination of severall parishes to presbyteries, and those again to synods; others are all for parochiall absoluteness and independence.

Note that the term is used in connection with ecclesiastical, geographical organization and that the reference is not to independence of the individual but independence of an organized group. The connotation is one of local autonomy as contrasted to hierarchical control. The status of the author suggests that the word is used in a derogatory sense, but the tone of the quotation itself does not necessarily imply such an interpretation.

More than a hundred years later, we find the term quoted in the same context as it is used in our own Declaration of Independence:

1775 (28 Nov.) in W. H. Foote Sk. North Carol. (1846) 43 Resolved, That delegates. . . from this colony, in Continental Congress, be empowered to concur with the delegates of other colonies, in declaring independence, and in forming alliances.

Here the emphasis is on delegated <u>power</u> to declare independence and this power is coupled with that of forming alliances with
other independent colonies. Again the reference is to the independence of the organized group, but the connotation is one which stresses capacity and responsibility rather than insubordination.

A contrasting quotation from the same period:

> 1783 Burke <u>Rep. India</u> Wks. 1842 II. 50.   That general spirit
> of disobedience and independence which has. . .prevailed
> in the government of Bengal.

Again the context is political, but the tone is clearly derogatory, implying rebelliousness.

Turning from the etymology of the word in England to its use
in America, we find in the <u>Dictionary of American English,</u> [2] the
following definition:

> Freedom from political control of England; political separation
> from England.

Note that the meaning here is not really different from that implied
in the last two quotations above, but the context is specific. Independence of the colonies necessarily meant independence from England.

The earliest quotation is:

> 1768 <u>N. H. Prov. Papers</u> VII 250.   The House of Burgesses
> (of) Va. . . . have therefore thought proper to represent
> . . . That they do not affect independence of their parent
> kingdom.

For some notion of the venerable history of the idea of independence, we might turn next to a new reference book, one which
is known as the <u>Syntopicon</u>. [3]

This work is organized around a series of 102 articles, each
of which discusses one of the ideas about which western man has
concerned himself.   The editors point out that they have been
admittedly arbitrary both in their choice of ideas for discussion and
in the number they have designated as "great." Our word "independence" is not among the chosen few.   It does appear, however,
among the 1800 topics listed in the index.   There are references
to the articles on 1. Government, 2. Liberty, 3. Revolution, and
4. State.   A rapid scanning of the article on Liberty suggests the
almost infinite relationships in which the idea of freedom, liberty,
and independence have occurred.   To illustrate the point, Tolstoy
is quoted:

> What is sin, the conception of which arises from the conscious-
> ness of man's freedom?   That is a question for theology. . .
> What is man's responsibility to society, the conception of
> which results from the question of freedom?   That is a
> question for jurisprudence. . . What is conscience and the
> perception of right and wrong in actions that follow from
> consciousness of freedom?   That is a question for ethics. . .

How should the past life of nations and of humanity be re-
garded--as the result of the free, or as the result of the
constrained activity of man?   That is a question for history.

Two quotations from the article illustrate use of "independence"
as it is used in the Declaration of Independence:

> Negatively, independence is a freedom from limitation or
> from being subject to determination by another.   Positively,
> independence implies self-sufficiency and adequate power.

Note the echo here to the quotation from Bishop Hall.

> The historians report the age-old struggle on the part of men
> and of states for liberty or independence.

In the topical outline which follows the article on Liberty, the
rubric which seems most closely related again, to the Declaration
is:

> X6c.   The struggle for sovereign independence against the
>   yoke of imperialism or colonial subjugation.

This, in turn, leads to the outline-index to the "Great Idea" of
liberty as it appears in the "great books. "   Under X6c, we find a
long list of citations, beginning with the book of Exodus from the
Old Testament, including the Declaration of Independence, and end-
ing with Hegel's Philosophy of History.   As a gesture toward the
many books which have not been designated "great" the article con-
cludes with a bibliography of other works on the subject.   Among
them, for instance, are History As the Story of Liberty, by Croce,
and Whitehead's Adventures of Ideas.

The card catalog presents a somewhat different experience.
Suppose you would like to see Jefferson's classic statement of the
American definition of independence, the Declaration of Independence.
If you look under JEFFERSON, THOMAS, PRES. U. S. 1743-
1826, you will find a good many books by him and even more about
him, but the Declaration is not among them.   (Was he not the
author? Did he have collaborators?   Or must a state document
forego the human touch of being the work of a single man?)   In
any case, to judge from the works listed, this single man had a
broad range of interests.   Note the following titles, for example:

> An essay towards facilitating instuction in the Anglo-Saxon
> and modern dialects of the English language.   For the use
> of the University of Virginia.

> Thomas Jefferson's Farm Book, with commentary and relevant
> extracts from his other writings.

> Thomas Jefferson's Garden Book with relevant extracts from
> his other writings.

If you look under DECLARATION OF INDEPENDENCE, you
will find a card referring you to: U. S. - DECLARATION OF
INDEPENDENCE.   (Is this a reminder that other states have de-
clared independence, or is it, merely the library's device to file
the Declaration with other books about the United States?)

Under U. S. - DECLARATION OF INDEPENDENCE there are
a number of books about the Declaration, among them the following
items of historical interest:

Boyd, Julian Parks
The Declaration of Independence; the evolution of its text as
shown in facsimiles of various drafts by its author.   Issued
in conjunction with an exhibit of these drafts at the Library
of Congress on the two hundredth anniversary of the birth
of Thomas Jefferson.   Washington, Library of Congress, 1943.

Clearly the famous author of the document which has come to
be considered well-nigh sacred had to revise and rewrite, just as
you must revise and rewrite one of your papers.

Suppose you decided next that it would be interesting to find
out what the men who fought in the War of Independence thought
about the idea of independence.   If you happen to look under WAR
OF INDEPENDENCE or REVOLUTIONARY WAR, you would find
nothing.   Under AMERICAN REVOLUTION there is a card which
refers to U. S. - HISTORY - REVOLUTIONARY WAR.   (Other states
have revolted and libraries try to bring together some of the materials relevant to a country.)   In the drawer labeled U. S. -
HISTORY (BY PERIOD) are listed hundreds of books on the Revolution.   A guide card among them is labeled PERSONAL NARRATIVES.
The following is an example of the cards filed behind it:

973. 308   Commager, Henry Steele, 1902-   ed.
C735s   The spirit of 'seventy-six; the story of
              the American Revolution as told by participants,
              ed. by Henry Steele Commager and Richard
              B. Morris.   Indianapolis, Bobbs-Merrill,
              1958.

Exploration of the card catalog, beginning with just the word
"independence, " leads one into something of a labyrinth.   Under
INDEPENDENCE there is a "see" reference to AUTONOMY.   Under
AUTONOMY only one book is listed:

325. 31   Plamenatz, John P.
P691o   On alien rule and self-government.   London,
              Longmans, 1960.

This is a recent book; its title suggests that it is a theoretical
treatment.   But why is there only one book listed under this subject
heading?   A "see also" reference card provides a clue: it refers
the reader to SELF-DETERMINATION, NATIONAL.   Under this
heading there are six books listed, most of them dealing with

political settlements of national determination following World War I. But another "see also" card refers to:

ALLEGIANCE
AUTONOMY
MINORITIES
PLEBISCITES
SOVEREIGNTY

Following up the lead to just one of these headings, SOVEREIGNTY, we find some thirty titles most of which provide a more general and philosophical emphasis. And again there is a "see also" card, this time referring to:

ACT OF STATE
GOVERNMENT LIABILITY (INTERNATIONAL LAW)
SELF-DETERMINATION, NATIONAL
SOCIAL CONTRACT
STATE, THE
STATE RIGHTS
STATE SUCCESSION
SERVITUDES (INTERNATIONAL LAW)
JURISDICTION (INTERNATIONAL LAW)

If you were faced with the task of compiling a list of all the books in the library with something to say about independence, independence in the political sense only, you would be obliged to consult all of the headings listed above and all those to which they in turn might lead. Even if the topic were strictly limited to the precise connotation with which the word is used in the Declaration, the task would be formidable.

It is commonly assumed that the card catalog is the best, if not the only, key to the resources of the library. This description of an exploration of the catalog for materials on the idea of independence illustrates exceptionally well its limitations, the difficulties it presents to the user, something of the inherent structure which must be understood if it is to be used competently, and, most important, the fact that its efficiency is relative, depending upon the purpose for which it is used and the amount of information you bring to it.

At one end of the scale it is a highly efficient instrument for locating any given single book, when that book is precisely identified. To the degree that the identification is less precise, the catalog becomes less efficient. (Suppose you started out not knowing the title of the Declaration of Independence and tried to find the document stating the colonies' renunciation of allegiance to England. A search through the materials on the colonial and revolutionary periods of our history would undoubtedly bring to light a reference to the exact title, but the process would be cumbersome.)

The catalog is reasonably efficient for the purpose of indicating all the books the library has which are written by one person. (But note that the Declaration was not listed among the works of Jefferson.) Furthermore, the catalog does not list by individual author or title, works which are parts of larger collections. An essay or a letter written by Jefferson and published as part of a collection of several authors would not be likely to be revealed as an individual entity in the card catalog.

Even more relative is the efficiency of the catalog as an instrument for locating materials on subjects. In general, the more concrete the subject the more efficient it is; the more abstract the subject, the less efficient it is. (Following the cross-references to U.S. - HISTORY was an easy task; the organization of this section into non-chronological and chronological subsections was readily apparent; and a rapid scanning of the guide cards on the Revolutionary War brought quickly to light the pertinent sub-heading -- PERSONAL NARRATIVES.) The search for materials on the idea of independence, however, led into a real labyrinth. Part of the difficulty arises from the fact that the catalog is organized alphabetically. The only way in which it can express logical relationships is by using sub-headings and cross-references. The reader must spend a tremendous amount of time following up leads, and essentially he must supply his own logic. In this respect, the catalog is very different from the Syntopicon, which is a selective instrument, and which sets up and uses a logical pattern of relationship.

An index such as the Syntopicon, therefore, it clearly emerges, is a more efficient instrument than the catalog for locating materials on such ancient and abstract concepts as independence. But it presents a danger which cannot be overemphasized. However valiantly it attempts to include all possible contexts and relationships in which such abstract ideas may be considered, it inevitably must reflect the philosophical assumptions and limitations of its authors. The seductive neatness of its logic must be resisted, for the ideas with which it deals merit something better than pre-packaged thinking.

These ideas are still much in the news. To see what is being said about them today we turn next to the Readers' Guide[4] and the International Index to Periodicals.[5] In the former, the volume which covers March, 1959-February, 1960, there is a reference from INDEPENDENCE, DECLARATION OF to DECLARATION OF INDEPENDENCE. Interestingly enough, under the latter there is listed an article titled "Liberty and 1776" in Hobbies Magazine. (Do people collect momentos of the occasion?)

INDEPENDENCE, POLITICAL refers the reader to AUTONOMY and under the latter there is an article from Reporter Magazine, "Talking Back to Africa." Here we see evidence of the relevance of the idea to current affairs.

In the International Index to Periodicals there is nothing listed under INDEPENDENCE. A reference from INDEPENDENCE, DECLARATION OF to DECLARATION OF INDEPENDENCE leads to articles such as "Congressional Debate on Slavery and the Declaration of Independence, 1819-1821," from the American Historical Review. Clearly the journals indexed in International Index, and consequently the articles listed, are scholarly rather than popular. It is reasonable to assume that for college level work the

International Index is more useful than the familiar Readers' Guide.[6]

Although there are no articles listed in the International Index
under the word INDEPENDENCE, it is unlikely that the scholarly
journals have ceased discussing the concept. If you take a clue
from the card catalog and try AUTONOMY, you will still find
nothing. Under SOVEREIGNTY, however, there are a number of
articles on national sovereignty and there is also a "see also" reference to:

>   AIRSPACE (INTERNATIONAL LAW)
>   EQUALITY OF STATES (INTERNATIONAL LAW)
>   INTERNATIONAL ORGANIZATION
>   MONARCHY
>   NATIONALISM
>   SELF-DETERMINATION, NATIONAL
>   THE STATE
>   STATES RIGHTS

Obviously, this index, like the card catalog, leads one into a
labyrinth of relationships among ideas. From the point of view of
efficiency, the index suffers from its lack of selectivity and from
the exigencies of its alphabetical framework. There is comfort,
on the other hand, in the knowledge that the index is inclusive (for
the large number of scholarly journals it covers), that it is kept up
to date through regular supplements, and that its- labyrinthine
organization of sub-headings and cross-references is unlikely to
pre-set the reader's approach to the abstract idea.

In general, this search for "independence" provides a fairly
apt illustration of the fact that the library is no longer merely the
storehouse in which the recorded heritage of ideas is preserved
but also has become more and more an organized system for making these ideas accessible. The systematic nature of the library
is demonstrated, for example, in the two general types of reference books we used, the direct and the indirect. The dictionaries
are direct in the sense that the information they provide is complete as far as it goes. The OED provided direct information
about the first recorded use of the word "independence." The card
catalog and the indexes are indirect in the sense that they merely
tell what books and articles may contain the information sought.
One might say that the direct tool provides data, the raw material
for your work; the indirect tool helps you find data. [7]

Another distinction can be drawn between the card catalog and
the indexes, on the one hand, and the Syntopicon on the other. The
former are inclusive; the latter is selective. Furthermore, as
indicated earlier, the former follows an alphabetical organization,
the latter a logical organization. The selective, organized tool may
offer efficiency, the non-selective tool offers comprehensiveness
and flexibility.

The two indexes demonstrated another systematic characteristic. In many instances, the choice of tool for a search for

information depends upon the _form_ in which such information is recorded. Journal articles are not listed in the card catalog; they are indexed in periodical indexes. (Specialized indexes are also available for government documents, films, music, etc.) Similarly, tools may be distinguished one from another on the basis of the subject or level of information they cover. Both the Readers' Guide and the International Index cover fairly general areas, the one on the level of popular writing, the other on the level of scholarship. But neither would be satisfactory in the search for highly specialized information.

Anyone who uses the library is helped immeasurably by an awareness of distinctions such as these. The better he understands what function each kind of tool is best able to perform, the more likely he is to select carefully among the various tools the library offers. The card catalog is a pretty poor instrument for dealing with general concepts; it is almost the only sure instrument for locating a particular book in a particular library. The Readers' Guide is almost useless as an instrument for locating articles of a scholarly nature, but the International Index is one of the most important tools for this purpose.

The student who recognizes these factors understands that the library offers not only buried treasure but a fairly efficient kit of tools for digging. Such a student is well on his way toward achieving "independence in the library."

Notes

1. Sir James A. H. Murray, Oxford English Dictionary, being a corrected re-issue, with an introduction, supplement and bibliography, of A New English Dictionary on Historical Principles, founded mainly on the materials collected by the philological Society (Oxford: Clarendon Press, 1933) 12 vols. and supplement.

   This monumental work serves a different function from any other standard English Dictionary. It traces the history of every word now in use or known to have been in use since 1150. (There are a few minor classes of words omitted.) Changes in spelling, usage, and meaning are given and illustrated with quotations, exactly cited. It includes a total of 414,825 words and 1,827,306 quotations, probably the largest single collection of quotations in the English language.

2. Sir William Alexander Craigie and James R. Hulbert, Dictionary of American English on Historical Principles. (Chicago: University of Chicago Press, 1936-44). 4 vols.

   Using the same method as that used by the OED, this is designed to show "those features by which the English of the American colonies and the United States is distinguished from that of England and the rest of the English-speaking world." It includes words originated in America, words in greater currency here, and words connected with the history of the country. Cf. Pref., p.v.

3. The Great Ideas. A Syntopicon of Great Books of the Western
    World, Mortimer J. Adler, editor in chief. (Chicago: Encyclo-
    pedia Britannica, 1952.)
        Essentially designed as an index to the set of the "great
    books" sponsored by the Great Books Foundation, these two
    volumes attempt to map out major concepts of Western civiliza-
    tion.   Included are articles on 102 "great ideas," each of which
    is followed by a "topical outline," an outlined index to refer-
    ences to these ideas in the "great books," and a list of refer-
    ences to others works of interest in connection with these ideas.
    Eighteen hundred topics are listed in the index with references
    to the articles in which they are discussed.

4. Readers' Guide to Periodical Literature, 1900-date. (New
    York: H. W. Wilson, 1905-   ).
        An author, title, subject index to articles in general and
    popular magazines.   Published semi-monthly, cumulated at
    intervals through the year, annually, and finally into biennial
    permanent volumes.

5. International Index to Periodicals, devoted chiefly to the human-
    ities and the social sciences, 1907-date. (New York: H. W.
    Wilson, 1916-   ).
        An author and subject index to about 200 scholarly journals,
    mostly in English.   Published quarterly, cumulated annually,
    and finally into triennial permanent volumes.

6. Similar indexing and abstracting services such as the Public
    Affairs Information Service Bulletin, Psychological Abstracts,
    the Bibliographical Index, and the Art Index are of particular
    importance for specialized fields of study.

7. It is also true, of course, that there is direct information to
    be gathered from the catalog cards (the fact that there were
    several drafts of the Declaration, for example).   There is also
    indirect information in the OED. (You might be moved to pur-
    sue further a lead given in the OED to find out, for example,
    about Burke's attitudes toward American independence.)

Bibliographic Essays Used in
Science of Society 132 Library Assignment
Spring, 1962

Communication

Festinger, Leon. "Informal Social
Communication," Psychological
Review, LVII, (September,
1950), p. 271-282.

Communication - Language

Hoijer, Harry. "The Relation of
Language to Culture," in
Anthropology Today. Edited by
A. L. Kroeber. Chicago: Uni-
versity of Chicago Press, 1953.
p. 554-573.

Culture (1)

Hallowell, A. Irving. "Culture,
Personality and Society," in
Anthropology Today. Edited by
A. L. Kroeber. Chicago: Uni-
versity of Chicago Press, 1953.
p. 597-620.

Culture (2)

Kelly, Gail. "Anthropology," in A
Reader's Guide to the Social
Science. Edited by Bert F.
Hoselitz. Glencoe: Free Press,
1959. p. 188-210.

Institution

Lee, Leon. "Institutions and Ideas
in Social Change." American
Journal of Economics and
Sociology, XVIII, (January,
1959), p. 127-128.

Pattern (1)

"Pattern in Biology, Linguistics,
and Culture," in An Appraisal
of Anthropology Today. Edited
by Sol Tax, Loren C. Eiseley,
Irving Rouse, Carl F. Voegelin.
Chicago: The University of
Chicago Press, 1953. p. 299-
321.

Pattern (2)

Kroeber, A. L. (ed.) Anthropology
Today. Chicago: The University of Chicago Press, 1953.
Refer to "Pattern" in the
index.

Perception (1)   Lindzey, Gardner. (ed.) Handbook
                                  of Social Psychology. Vol. I
                                  and II.   Cambridge, Mass.:
                                  Addison-Wesley Publishing Co.,
                                  Inc., 1954.
                                        Refer to "Perception" in the
                                  index, volume II.

Perception (2)   Reitman, Walter. "Psychology," in
                                  A Reader's Guide to the Social
                                  Sciences.   Edited by Bert F.
                                  Hoselitz.   Glencoe: Free Press,
                                  1959. p. 210-241.

Personality (1)   Lindzey, Gardner. (ed.) Handbook
                                  of Social Psychology. Vol. I
                                  and II.   Cambridge, Mass.:
                                  Addison-Wesley Publiching Co.,
                                  Inc., 1954.
                                        Refer to "Personality" in the
                                  index of volume II.

Personality (2)   Reitman, WalterR. "Psychology," in
                                  A Reader's Guide to the Social Sci-
                                  ences. Edited by Bert F. Hoselitz.
                                  Glencoe: Free Press, 1959. p. 210-
                                  241.

Primary Groups   Shils, Edward A. "The Study of the
                                  Primary Groups," in The Policy
                                  Sciences, Recent Developments
                                  in Scope and Method.   Edited
                                  by Daniel Lerner, Harold D.
                                  Lasswell et. al. 2nd ed.
                                  Stanford: Stanford University
                                  Press, 1959.   p. 44-69.

Role (1)   Sarbin, Theodore R. "Role Theory,"
                                  in Handbook of Social Psychol-
                                  ogy.   Edited by Gardner
                                  Lindzey, Vol I. Cambridge:
                                  Addison-Wesley Publishing Co.,
                                  1954.   p. 223-258.

Role (2)   Neiman, Lionel J. and Hughes,
                                  James W.   "The Problem of
                                  the Concept of Role - a Re-
                                  survey of the Literature,"
                                  Social Forces, XXX (1951), p.
                                  141-9.

Small Groups (1)

Blau, Peter M. and Moore, Joan W. "Sociology, " in A Reader's Guide to the Social Sciences. Edited by Bert F. Hoselitz. Glencoe: Free Press, 1959. p. 158-187,

Small Groups (2)

Hare, Paul A. "Areas for Research in Small Groups, " Sociology and Social Research XLII, (July, 1958), p. 430-5.

Socialization

Child, Irwin L. "Socialization, " in Handbook of Social Psychology. Edited by Gardner Lindzey, Vol II. Cambridge, Mass.: Addison-Wesley, 1954. p. 655-692.

Appendix IV
Independent Study and the Academic Library*

This paper discusses the library implications of independent study defined in two ways. The first part accepts the most literal definition and points to the rather obvious facilities and services the library might be expected to provide in accordance with the degree to which the student is "independent," that is, responsible for his own study. The second part discusses the library implications of "acquiry" and "inquiry," [1] referring particularly to our experiences with inquiry at Monteith College.

"Independent" vs. "Individual" Study

When an independent study program is designed to accommodate a burgeoning student population, it may simply inundate the library. More students need more chairs and tables, more books, more librarians to charge out the books. But this impact stems from the increasing enrollment not from the independent study as such. Let us begin this discussion, therefore, by limiting ourselves to the kind of program which is likely to have more than a merely quantitative impact on the library.

From the start we can rule out the kind of independent study which involves programmed textbooks or teaching machines and the kind which calls upon the student to read the purchased books he would have read in a traditional course, merely providing him with less direct assistance in mastering them. If the students use the library as a study hall, such a program will call for space, but otherwise it will have no effect.

Similarly, let us rule out the kind of independent study which is organized around a long list of required readings. Such a course makes the same demands on the library whether the evidence of student reading is expected to appear in class recitation, group discussion (be the instructor authoritarian, permissive, or not present

*This paper was first published in "Approach to Independent Study," comp. by Winslow R. Hatch, "New Dimensions in Higher Education No. 13"; U. S. Office of Education, (Washington: Government Printing Office, 1966.)

at all), quizzes, papers, or merely in a final examination.   Thus
the number of students rather than the style of presentation makes
a difference to the library, if the library is expected to provide
the books on the reading list.   (The ever-increasing availability of
paperback editions makes it less and less necessary or economically
efficient for the library to provide such readings.)

The independent study program which would seem to have more
than just such a purely quantitative impact on the library is the
kind which calls for individualized work.   It is the sort in which
the student is not merely expected to study alone and at his own
pace but is also given considerable freedom to determine what and
how he shall study.   In honors seminars, tutorials, directed reading courses, and undergraduate research projects, the student is
usually expected to develop his own line of inquiry and to pursue
it in his own way.   If more students are enrolled in programs of
this kind, the multiplication of individual choices will clearly require greatly expanded library collections and larger and more
specialized reference collections and services.   Indeed, if such
programs are offered to large numbers of students, many college
libraries will find it impossible to provide adequate resources for
them.

But are we not still talking about a quantitative impact on the
library?   Does the tremendous growth of independent study programs
really mean only that libraries need better support so that they can
provide more of the same, or does it mean also that a different
order of library service is required?   To find the answer to this
question, let us begin by considering the library requirements of
individualized work in certain typical "conventional, " i.e., non-
independent courses.

No independent study program opens up a wider range of
potential subjects on which the library might be expected to provide
materials than the library paper traditionally assigned in freshman
English.   Here the student is obliged to locate library sources and
he is expected to follow prescribed procedures in using them, but
he is, at least theoretically, utterly free to write on any topic he
chooses.

Similarly, for the term paper assigned in most conventional courses the student is often expected to use sources other than his textbook or the books listed as collateral or "optional" readings for the course. Here the range of topics is not so broad, because it falls within the limits set by the scope of the course. But the student will be expected to delve more deeply into his chosen topic. The typical term paper, then, not only allows the student considerable leeway in his choice of topic but also encourages him to explore that topic in some depth.

At a more advanced level, the librarian is accustomed to dealing with the intellectual elite of the student body, those students who enroll in small, advanced seminars, those who sometimes become the proteges, the research assistants, almost the junior colleagues of certain members of the faculty. Such students are encouraged to develop their own specialized interests and to pursue them intensively. In the process, they often tax the resources of an undergraduate library.

Each of these situations in conventional courses calls for individualized study. But in each case there are limits which keep the demands on the library within manageable bounds. The freshman English professor is never so concerned with the student's freedom in choosing a topic for his paper as he is with the student's experience in locating, organizing, and presenting information. The student is encouraged, if not required, to choose a topic on which materials are readily available.

Similarly, the prudent term-paper writer is likely to select a topic on which the library has adequate holdings. Such a topic may gain an extra advantage from the fact that the library collection usually reflects the particular interests of the faculty.

When we move to the work of the academic elite in the advanced seminar, the tutorial, or the independent reading course, there is no longer an assumption that the student is expected to fit his pattern to the available cloth. There is, usually, nevertheless, a certain self-limitation which arises from the close association such students have with the faculty; the interests of these students usually stem from the enthusiasms of the faculty. Inquiry at this

level, moreover, while not precisely limited, is at least shaped by
the student's previously acquired familiarity with his field.   The
direction of his inquiry is inevitably influenced by his knowledge of
the field's major concepts, its classic authors, its accepted
methodology, even its journals and societies.   The library requirements of individualized work at this level are, in short, not very
different from those of the faculty.   The library provides for them
as well, or as poorly, as it serves the needs of the faculty.

   In short, the reason why individualized work in such conventional situations does not seriously overtax the resources of the
library is that the independence of the student is never as complete
as it seems.   His work is pre-structured in one way or another.
The professor recommends topics, he suggests readings, he guides
procedures, he serves as a model-in one way or another he
directs the inquiry.   Only in the case of the academic elite, does
the pre-structuring derive at least partly from the student's own
knowledge and background in his field.   Does this mean, then, that
the opportunity for all-out independent study can and should be offered only to those students who have acquired a solid background
in a subject field, and even then, perhaps, only to the more gifted
among them?   I think not.   But it does mean that we must find
some substitute for faculty pre-structuring, not only to keep the
work within the range of the library's capacity to support, but also
to make it a fruitful learning experience for the student.

   We may be able to arrive at some conception of what such a
substitute might be as we consider the library implications of the
acquiry-inquiry dichotomy.

          An Inquiry into "Acquiry vs. Inquiry"

   In his pamphlet, What Standards Do We Raise, Hatch indicates
that:

> A distinction should be made between "instructing" and "teach-
> ing."   The necessity of making this distinction is the demon-
> stration that in the act of acquiring information the actual
> presence of a teacher is not necessary and may not be desir-
> able; that individual students can "instruct" themselves (inde-
> pendent study) and apparently do this quite effectively.   If

"informers" or "instructors" have to be drafted to manage acquiry, such as a librarian or a technician in a learning resources center, they can be drawn from the ranks of those who are most adept at purveying information. Teachers may need to assemble and prepare such materials as books, films, and tapes; they may occasionally make televised and other presentations, transcribe their lectures and "program" some of their materials. But they should not curtail - or be permitted to curtail - the amount of time they have for "teaching. "[2]

This statement, examined in the light of the distinction made above between independent and individualized study, suggests that where students are independent in the sense of being free to work alone and at their own pace, "teachers may need to assemble.... materials. " Let us put this type of independent acquisition of information in the category with independent study through teaching machines, textbooks, or prescribed readings and rule it out of the present discussion as having no impact other than quantitative on the library. But where students are also given some measure of independence in deciding what and how they will study, the librarian may be called upon to "manage acquiry, " to "instruct, " to "purvey information. "

These three terms are used almost as if they were synonyms. It seems to me that they are not. Perhaps a discussion of the flavor of difference among them may shed light upon the new role, or rather different emphasis in role, for the librarian which is indicated in the quoted statement.

Librarians would probably express the function of "purveying information" as "assisting the student in his search for information." This is not a new function at all; this is what they do all the time. But neither is it a substitute for the "pre-structuring" which, as we have seen above, makes it possible for libraries to cope with the individualized work in conventional courses.

Such pre-structuring is much more clearly suggested in the phrase "to manage acquiry. " Managing the acquisition of information suggests planned learning experiences. The idea of the planned learning experience is one which deserves much closer examination than we can give it here, but, for the moment, let us say that it

implies at least that appropriate resources should be available,
that they should be organized for retrieval, and that the student's
experience in retrieving information should be neither the passive
acceptance of "spoon-feeding" nor the active but time-consuming
process of trial-and-error.   It should be a genuine learning experience in itself; it should contribute to the student's sense of
satisfaction in the kind of discovery which results not from the
lucky accident but from constructive effort.

Concern that the student's acquisition of information in the
library or in the "learning resources center" be a true learning
experience is also implied in the suggestion that the librarian (or
technician) serve as an "instructor."   But where "management of
acquiry" suggests planned learning experiences, "instruction" suggests accommodation to students' individual difference in capacity,
interest, need, cognitive style.

Up to now college and university librarians have rarely been
given the opportunity, let alone the responsibility, to manage acquiry
(except in the sense of acquiring and organizing the library collection) or to instruct (except in the sense of helping students locate
information).   If they are to do so now, in connection with independent study programs, they must be drawn into active collaboration
with the teaching faculty.

If they are to have appropriate resources available and managed
in such fashion as to enhance the student's learning, they must
work closely with the faculty in deciding what materials are to be
assembled and how they are to be organized.   They should strive
to become - and be accepted as - learning materials experts.

If they are to instruct students in the acquisition of information, they must be privy to the teaching aims of the faculty.   They
need to know the answer to the question: information for what?
They should be able not merely to assist the student in his search
for information, but also to help him discover what information he
needs, to help him develop a strategy for the acquisition of information.

If they are to instruct effectively, moreover, they must know

something about theories of learning, about educational philosophy
and psychology, about principles of curriculum construction, about
teaching methods and procedures, about the social forces which
affect education.   They must see themselves, and must be seen by
faculty and students alike, not as clerks, not as information
specialists, not as purveyors of information, but as educators.

In summary, the case presented thus far argues that independent study defined as "independent acquiry" has implications for the
library which are not merely quantitative but which indicate a significantly different role for the academic librarian.   It follows that
any college which embarks on a program of independent study so
conceived must be concerned not only that the library have adequate
space and adequate resources but also that it have enough librarians,
librarians who are qualified to take on this new and extremely de-
manding role, and that these librarians are given more than formal
opportunity to collaborate with the teaching faculty.

Let us now consider the possible library implications of
"independent inquiry. "   Hatch defines inquiry as "that process of
learning and of teaching in which information is examined.   It is
that which is done after information has been provided or learned;
it is the reason for acquiry.   Inquiry is the essence of honors, of
independent study - properly understood and practiced - and of prob-
lem-oriented instruction."3

In discussing the library implications of independent inquiry
so defined, I should like to draw upon certain of our experiences
at Monteith College, particularly one which demonstrates the relationship between "inquiry" and "acquiry. "   The first major undertaking students encounter at Monteith is a freshman research project
assigned in the social sciences course in the third quarter of the
freshman year.   The assignment is highly valued by the faculty -
and they communicate this view to the students - as an experience
which can convey a fundamental understanding of the nature of
social science, the kinds of problems it deals with, its basic
assumptions, the various approaches, theories, methods and techniques it employs.   Each student must select a research question
which interests him, develop a plan for studying the question, carry

out the plan, and report on his results. (Since this is freshman
work, it is, of course, elementary and limited in scope. But it
is "real" and "original" work all the same.)

Here the inquiry is likely to begin with a problem stated in
very general terms; the student acquires information, perhaps about
how others have tackled similar problems, and he attempts to
refine his own statement. He may arrive at a general hypothesis.
The inquiry now moves toward speculation as to potential indicators to be used in formulating an operational statement of the
hypothesis; the student acquires information which helps him decide
which indicators promise to be valid. The inquiry next turns to
methods of gathering data pertaining to the selected indicators; the
student acquires information about research techniques and instruments. And so on and on. Inquiry leads to acquiry, acquiry to
further inquiry.

The first time this project was assigned we attempted to make
the student's acquisition of information as independent as possible.
Every student was required to use the library to orient himself to
his own problem. (Some students selected problems for which the
library became also a source of data, e.g., in historical or content
analysis studies.) He was expected to find sources which would
help him define his problem and place it in the context of published
social science research, sources which would suggest appropriate
data-gathering methods and instruments, and sources of background
information. In preparation for this library work we offered a
one-hour briefing on some of the major bibliographical tools in the
social sciences and we distributed copies of the Wayne State University Library handbook.[4] The results of this sink-or-swim approach
were almost disastrous to the cause of independent inquiry. The
students were lost and baffled and angry, and the faculty were
dismayed at the quality of the references which appeared in the
final papers. Many students reported that this university library
of a million volumes had "nothing" pertaining to their problems.
Most found "something" but what they found the faculty judged inappropriate for college level work. As a result, many of the instructors were ready to conclude that freshman students simply could

not be trusted to find their own sources in the library, that they
had to be told what to read.

Hatch states that:

> Quality may be indicated by a college's disposition to make
> a distinction between the acquisition (acquiry) and the examina-
> tion (inquiry) of information.   It is manifested in its success
> in getting students to accept a larger role in "acquiry" and
> in getting its faculty to make their teaching a joint "inquiry." 5

Having examined our first unhappy experience with the library
component of the freshman research project we have concluded that
our difficulties arose neither from unwillingness of our students
"to accept a larger role in 'acquiry' " nor from the faculty's unwillingness "to make their teaching a joint 'inquiry.' " It resulted,
rather from the interplay between inquiry and acquiry, from the
students' lack of adeptness in the intellectual process of using the
question (inquiry) to shape the course of the search for information
(acquiry) and then of using the information to direct further inquiry.
From our work with the Monteith program, we have found, in
general, that average freshman students suffer from the following
handicaps:

1. They have a basic misconception of the function of information in inquiry, that is, they look for and expect to
   find "the answer to the question" instead of evidence to
   be examined.

2. They are unsophisticated in evaluating books.   In the
   necessarily rapid process of using the open shelves, they
   select books without taking into account such clues to
   their probable worth as date of publication, qualifications
   of author or sponsor, quality of references cited, etc.
   They select, instead, on the basis of relevance, (as close
   as possible to "answering the question"), readability ("not
   too technical"), and persuasiveness ("I agree with it").

3. They think that the card catalog, the classification system
   (i. e., the arrangement of books on the open shelves), and
   the Readers' Guide are the keys to the contents of the
   library, without really understanding the organization, the
   limitations and the advantages of these tools.

4. They are not aware of the organization of scholarly literature, i. e.,

   a. They do not appreciate the subtle difference between
      organization in terms of theory, concept, approach,

method, school, style, etc., characteristic of the
organization of the disciplines, and organization in
terms of subject, form, period, and place, characteristic of the organization of the library.

b. They are not acquainted with the bibliographical tools
which provide access to scholarly literature, i.e., the
"guides to the literature," the surveys of research,
the annual reviews, the abstracts, the special indexes,
etc.

In the conventional, non-independent program, the constant
guidance of the faculty obviates these difficulties.   It is possible
that an independent study program which provided for intensive
collaboration between librarians and faculty and which then gave
librarians responsibility for "managing acquiry" or instructing
could make similar guidance available.   But it is also possible
that students can be taught how to identify, locate, and use information in the quest for understanding, that capacity for independent
inquiry need not be merely a concomitant of mastery of a field of
specialization, as it is now for the elite student, but an instrument
for learning for all students.

This is the possibility we are exploring at Monteith.   Since
our first experience with the freshman research project, we have
made considerable progress toward diagnosing the problem we encountered and devising methods of dealing with them.   We hope that
the results of our efforts in this direction, to be presented in the
final report of the Monteith Library Project, will contribute significantly to the achievement of a more precise view of the implications of independent study for the academic library.

> Patricia B. Knapp
> Monteith College
> Wayne State University
> December, 1963

Notes

1.   For a discussion of this useful distinction, see Winslow R.
     Hatch, What Standards Do We Raise? (New Dimensions in
     Higher Education, No. 12; Washington: U. S. Government
     Printing Office, 1963.)

2. Ibid., p. 22.

3. Ibid., p. 21.

4. Monteith has no library of its own; our students use the University Libraries.   It should be noted that the library's capacity to provide resources for independent inquiry is less of a problem here than it would be in a smaller institution.   The question of what the student derives from the experience, however, is still to the point.

5. Ibid., p. 5.